CANADIANS: DO YOU HAVE A FINANCIAL PLAN

A banker's guide to a secure financial future for you and your family

EMMA SHAOYI LI, CFP, CIM

ISBN: 9798339978411

DISCLAIMER

The information in this book is intended as a general reference tool for understanding the principles and practices of personal finance and does not constitute financial advice. Each individual's financial situation is unique, and it is recommended to consult with a qualified financial professional before making any financial decisions.

The field of finance and taxation is subject to frequent changes. While efforts are made to ensure the information is up-to-date, some content may become outdated. This is particularly relevant for residents of regions with specific rules, such as Quebec. Readers are encouraged to stay informed about policy changes and seek professional advice tailored to their circumstances.

The author and publisher disclaim any liability for any direct or indirect loss or damage arising from the use or reliance on the information contained in this book. Professional guidance is recommended to ensure that financial strategies or decisions are appropriate for your specific situation.

ABOUT THE AUTHOR

Emma's journey in the world of finance is as dynamic as the places she's called home. Born in Northern China, she began her academic journey in the fast-paced city of Shanghai. Her curiosity and love for learning led her to England, where she earned her Master's degree from the University of Liverpool. Now, she lives in Vancouver with her partner, Grant, and their energetic Border Collie, Pistachio, finding joy in the city's natural beauty despite the famous rain.

Professionally, Emma is a Chartered Investment Manager (CIM®) and a Certified Financial Planner (CFP®), bringing a wealth of expertise in wealth management and financial planning. But it's not just her credentials that set her apart; it's her genuine passion for helping people understand and take control of their finances. Over the years, Emma has honed the ability to break down complex financial concepts into simple, actionable steps, empowering her clients and readers to make informed decisions.

Wish you and your family good health and prosperity.

Emma

CONTENTS

PROLOGUE

Welcome Aboard: Your Journey to Financial Security Starts Here

I cannot emphasize enough the peace of mind that comes from getting your financial affairs in order and building up some savings. When I first started my career in personal finance as a bank teller, I was earning just over $17 an hour. Unfortunately, I was living in one of the most expensive cities in Canada — Vancouver. The cost of living, especially housing, has been sky-high for the past two decades. Although I was working full-time, I couldn't afford to live on my own, and I wasn't able to save much either.

One incident stands out clearly in my memory: I accidentally scratched the car next to mine while backing out of a parking garage (my driving skills were clearly not at their best). I was left with two options - pay for the repair out of pocket or face higher auto insurance premiums. Do you know how much it costs to repair a scratch on a car? I know. It's $1,800. At the time, I didn't have that much in my bank account. The stress and anxiety this caused me was overwhelming. Looking back now, it seems trivial, but at the time, it felt like the biggest problem in the world. The $50 increase in my monthly insurance premium certainly didn't help me build up my savings either.

Had I been able to save that money beforehand, the situation wouldn't have impacted my mental health as much. This experience taught me that your financial situation has a profound impact on your stress levels and overall well-being. Reflecting on it now, I realize that beyond the high cost of living, I was also living beyond my means, which led to my poor financial situation. Why did I insist on having a car when I could have taken the bus to work? You'd be surprised how much owning a car truly costs - not just the monthly payments, but also insurance, fuel, maintenance, and wear and tear. There's always something to fix: filters, fluids, and brake parts I never knew existed until they needed to be replaced.

I'm not saying you shouldn't have a car, but it's essential to consider the full cost. Perhaps you can share a car instead of having two in your household. That could be how you fund your child's RESP. Just something to think about.

My motivation to write this book comes from a deep desire to share my knowledge with those who need it most. Over the years, I've witnessed how a lack of information and resources can cause people to struggle with financial decisions. The personal finance system in Canada is notoriously complex, leaving many Canadians in need of practical guidance and clear advice on how to navigate their financial journeys.

While there are countless books on investment strategies and economic theories, there's a noticeable shortage of books offering practical, actionable advice on personal finance that people can use right away. People in academic fields often don't take the time to simplify financial matters for the general public, while practitioners in personal finance rarely write books. I aim to bridge this gap. I've personally benefited from extensive study and work experience, and I'm passionate about sharing what I've learned in the practical field of personal finance with people in need.

When it comes to personal finance, it's easy to encounter conflicting opinions. There's so much noise in this field that it can be hard for people to sort through all the information and find a clear path. In this book, I aim to provide Canadians with the essential knowledge and facts they need to make informed and confident financial decisions. I genuinely believe that everyone can benefit from reading this book. My hope is that readers will walk away with actionable advice to improve their personal financial situations and formulate a financial plan.

SETTING THE STAGE FOR SUCCESS

Laying the Groundwork for Your Financial Masterpiece

Part 1 of the book sets the foundation for your financial journey by focusing on the importance of having a solid financial plan. It begins with understanding why a financial plan is essential and guides you through the different financial needs that arise at various life stages. You'll learn how to choose the right financial services to match your needs and decide whether to manage your finances yourself or seek professional help. This section also introduces you to Canada's financial institutions and the role bank accounts play in your overall financial strategy. By the end of this part, you'll be well-equipped to start building a financial plan tailored to your unique circumstances.

THE FINANCIAL BLUEPRINT

Why You Need a Plan Before Building Your Financial House

Introduction: Are You Moving Forward or Simply Moving?

Have you ever felt like you're constantly busy but not really getting anywhere financially? Do you find yourself working hard every day yet still worrying about your financial future? If so, you're not alone. Many Canadians share these feelings, and the difference between simply working hard and making meaningful progress often comes down to one crucial element: a well-crafted financial plan.

In this chapter, we'll explore why having a financial plan is essential for achieving your life goals. We'll delve into what a financial plan entails, how it can transform your financial journey, and why now is the perfect time to start charting your path toward financial security and prosperity.

The Tale of the Horse and the Donkey: A Lesson in Purposeful Planning

Let me share a story from ancient China that beautifully illustrates the power of having clear goals and a solid plan.

Long ago during the Tang dynasty, a horse and a donkey were the best of friends. One day, the horse was chosen to accompany the monk Xuanzang on an epic journey to India to seek sacred Buddhist scriptures. The donkey, meanwhile, continued his routine work, tirelessly circling the millstone in the village.

Seventeen years later, the horse returned to Chang'an, the capital city, carrying the precious scriptures. Eager to reunite, the horse visited his old friend and began sharing tales of incredible adventures: crossing endless deserts, climbing towering mountains, facing scorching heat, and witnessing breathtaking landscapes. The donkey listened in awe and exclaimed, "You've experienced so much! I can't even imagine traveling such distances."

The horse replied thoughtfully, "In truth, we've walked similar distances over these years. The difference is, I had a clear goal and moved steadily toward it, experiencing the vast world along the way. You, however, kept moving in circles around the millstone, confined by your surroundings and never advancing beyond them."

The Moral of the Story

This simple story highlights a profound truth: having clear goals and a purposeful plan can lead you to extraordinary places, while aimless effort can leave you stuck in the same spot despite all your hard work.

Just like the horse and the donkey, many of us spend years working diligently but without a clear financial direction, ending up no closer to our dreams than when we started. The key to breaking free from this cycle is to define what you want to achieve and create a roadmap to get there - a financial plan.

Understanding the Importance of a Financial Plan

What Is a Financial Plan?

A financial plan is much more than just a budget or an investment strategy. It's a comprehensive roadmap that outlines your current financial situation, defines your short-term and long-term financial goals, and details the strategies and steps needed to achieve them. A good financial plan takes into account various aspects of your financial life, including income, expenses, savings, investments, insurance, taxes, and estate planning.

Why Do You Need a Financial Plan?

Having a goal is only the beginning. To turn your aspirations into reality, you need a solid plan and the discipline to implement it. Think about saving money: merely thinking about it won't increase your account balance. You need to actively save and manage your finances to see real growth. According to Statistics Canada, nearly 100,000 personal bankruptcies are filed annually, and within the next decade, approximately one in every five Canadians could face financial collapse. These alarming statistics highlight the urgent need for effective personal financial planning. Having a financial plan provides numerous benefits that can profoundly impact your life:

- **Clarity and Direction:** It helps you clearly define what you want to achieve financially and lays out a path to get there.
- **Informed Decision-Making:** With a plan in place, you can make smarter choices about spending, saving, and investing.
- **Financial Security:** Planning helps you prepare for unexpected events and ensures that you're on track to meet your future needs.
- **Peace of Mind:** Knowing that you have a structured plan reduces financial stress and allows you to focus on enjoying life.
- **Goal Achievement:** Whether it's buying a home, sending your children to university, or retiring comfortably, a financial plan increases the likelihood of reaching your goals.

Without a financial plan, it's easy to drift aimlessly, much like the donkey circling the millstone, expending energy without making real progress. A plan empowers you to take control of your financial destiny and move confidently toward the future you desire.

Many Canadians share similar aspirations when it comes to their finances and lifestyle: Owning a home, enjoying a comfortable lifestyle, having time for family and hobbies, saving for a prosperous retirement, and helping children with their education. Some also aspire to leave a financial legacy for their children. But what do all these goals have in common? They all require money.

Whether we like it or not, our ability to achieve our life goals is largely influenced by our financial situation. A financial plan helps you make sure that your dreams don't remain just that—dreams. It turns those dreams into achievable goals by providing a clear path to follow.

The Elements of a Financial Plan

So, what exactly does a financial plan involve? Here's a quick overview:

- **Budgeting:** Understanding where your money is coming from and where it's going is the first step. A budget helps you manage your income and expenses, ensuring you have enough left over to save and invest for your future.
- **Saving and Investing:** A good financial plan outlines how much you should be saving and where you should be investing your money to grow your wealth over time.
- **Debt Management:** It's important to have a strategy for paying off debt, whether it's a mortgage, student loans, or credit card debt. Managing debt effectively frees up more money for saving and investing.
- **Insurance and Risk Management:** Life is unpredictable, so having the right insurance is crucial to protect your assets and your family from unforeseen events.
- **Retirement Planning:** How much will you need to retire

comfortably? A financial plan helps you figure that out and outlines the steps you need to take to get there.

- **Estate Planning:** What will happen to your assets when you're gone? Estate planning ensures that your wishes are honoured, and your loved ones are taken care of.

What This Book Will Cover

If you've ever found yourself lying awake at night with questions like these, this book is for you:

- Am I truly financially secure?
- Do I know who to turn to when I have financial related questions?
- How much money will I really need to retire comfortably?
- What should I do if I don't have enough retirement income?
- Would my family be financially stable if something were to happen to me?
- Is my investment strategy truly aligned with my financial goals?
- How can I protect myself from fraud and financial exploitation?
- What will happen to my money, my home, and my belongings when I pass away?
- How can I minimize the impact of taxes on my estate?
- Do I have the right insurance to protect myself and my family?
- What can I do today to secure a better financial future for myself and my loved ones?

This book is designed to address these critical financial questions, providing clear, actionable answers and pointing you toward the resources and tools you need to take control of your financial future. The best way to overcome anxiety about your financial situation is by having a solid plan and taking action. When you know where you're headed and have a clear strategy in place, it brings a sense of control and calm. Instead of worrying about the unknown, you can focus on the steps you need to take to secure your financial future. The book is divided into six comprehensive sections, each focusing on a key aspect of financial planning:

PART 1: SETTING THE STAGE FOR SUCCESS

Part 1 of the book sets the foundation for your financial journey by focusing on the importance of having a solid financial plan. It begins with understanding why a financial plan is essential and guides you through the different financial needs that arise at various life stages. You'll learn how to choose the right financial services to match your needs and decide whether to manage your finances yourself or seek professional help. This section also introduces you to Canada's financial institutions and the role bank accounts play in your overall financial strategy. By the end of this part, you'll be well-equipped to start building a financial plan tailored to your unique circumstances.

PART 2: TAXES – TURNING A NECESSITY INTO A STRATEGY

Taxes are a part of life, but in Part 2, we explore how to manage them strategically. This section provides an overview of the Canadian tax system, including how to file your income taxes and the key tax considerations for business owners. We also delve into the Alternative Minimum Tax (AMT) and present smart tax strategies that can help you minimize your tax burden. The purpose of this part is to help you navigate the tax landscape effectively, ensuring you keep more of what you earn and avoid common tax pitfalls.

PART 3: GROWING YOUR FINANCIAL GARDEN

Part 3 focuses on growing your wealth through smart budgeting, investing, and saving strategies. It covers everything from the basics of budgeting and building an emergency fund to more advanced investment options like mutual funds, ETFs, and segregated funds. You'll also explore lesser-known investment vehicles, learn about registered accounts like RRSPs and TFSAs, and understand how to assess and manage market risk. This part serves as a comprehensive guide to growing and protecting your wealth, helping you make informed decisions that align with your financial goals.

PART 4: RETIREMENT – THE FINAL FRONTIER

Retirement planning is the focus of Part 4, where we discuss how much you need to retire comfortably and what to do if you find yourself short on retirement income. This section provides a cheat sheet for understanding government pensions like CPP and OAS and demystifies work pensions, including defined benefit and defined contribution plans. We also explore additional retirement savings options, such as group RRSPs and individual pension plans. The goal of this part is to ensure you're prepared for retirement, no matter where you are in your financial journey.

PART 5: PROTECTING YOUR FORTUNE

In Part 5, we shift focus to protecting the wealth you've worked hard to build. This section covers the essential role of insurance in your financial plan, including health, disability, and life insurance. You'll learn about creative strategies for using whole life insurance and understand the importance of creditor insurance and trusts in protecting your assets. We also discuss how to protect yourself from fraud and financial exploitation. The purpose of this part is to provide you with the tools and knowledge to safeguard your financial future against life's uncertainties.

PART 6: LEAVING A LEGACY

The final part of the book, Part 6, focuses on estate planning and ensuring your legacy is preserved. We guide you through what happens when someone passes away, the steps you can take to prepare, and the intricacies of estate and succession planning, particularly for business owners. This section concludes with a call to action, encouraging you to take the necessary steps today to secure your financial future and protect your loved ones. The goal of this part is to help you plan for the inevitable, ensuring your wishes are respected and your legacy endures.

My Commitment to You:

As part of my commitment to making financial education accessible, I'm dedicating 100 hours each year to offer Question and Answer sessions to readers like you. It's my small way of giving back and helping you take charge of your financial future.

If you're interested, feel free to email me to schedule a one-hour session:

<u>canadianfinancialplan@outlook.com</u>

Since appointments are on a first-come, first-served basis, I'd suggest getting in touch sooner rather than later.

Why I'm Offering This: I understand that navigating personal finance can be challenging. My goal with these sessions is to provide you with relevant information that helps you feel more confident and in control of your financial decisions.

To make the most of our time together, please include in your email the topics you'd like to discuss. This will allow me to prepare tailored information. I look forward to the opportunity to assist you and help you achieve your financial goals.

Reading Guide:

This book is designed to be a comprehensive guide covering every aspect of personal finance and financial planning. However, I understand that it's a lot of content to go through, and some chapters may be more relevant to your situation than others. To ease the journey, know that you don't need to read every chapter to gain the benefits of this book. You can skip certain chapters that don't align with your current interests or needs.

I have included reminders at the beginning of those chapters to let you know if it's okay to skip ahead without missing out on key concepts or affecting your understanding of the overall content. This way, you can focus on the topics that matter most to you and revisit other sections when they become more relevant. Relax, take your time, and dive into the parts that resonate with your financial goals and situation.

Conclusion: Begin Your Journey to Financial Empowerment

This books offers a comprehensive guide to personal finance, tailored to help Canadians make informed and confident financial decisions at every stage of life. By blending foundational knowledge with practical advice, this book is an essential resource for anyone looking to achieve a secure financial future for themselves and their family.

If you find all these tasks daunting, don't worry. This book will highlight professional services available and discuss potential fees, enabling you to manage your finances effectively, even if you prefer a hands-off approach. By the end of this book, you will feel empowered and inspired to take control of your personal finances. Remember, having a compelling goal and a clear plan to achieve it can make all the difference. Let's embark on this journey together and create a financial future you can be proud of.

(2)

LIFE'S FINANCIAL MILESTONES

From First Job to Golden Years: What You Need at Every Stage

Introduction

Life is a journey full of changes and milestones, each bringing its own set of financial challenges and opportunities. As we discussed in the last chapter, setting clear financial goals is crucial. But what happens when life throws you a curveball or presents you with a significant life event?

I met Carol (an alias) on a trip to Toronto. Carol, a gracious woman with silver streaks in her hair and a determined spark in her eyes, had been visiting her daughter in Vancouver for a few days. Her journey wasn't merely for leisure; it was also a much-needed break from the relentless responsibilities she faced back home. Carol's husband, Mark, had been very ill. Mark is unable to get up or move around by himself. Despite having a Personal Support Worker to assist during the day, the weight of care fell heavily on Carol's shoulders. As strong and brave as Carol is, the stress of managing his care was immense, and the emotional toll was even greater.

It was a disturbing and heartbreaking moment when Carol discovered Mark was ill. It was an afternoon, and Mark had been alone for a while. When Carol joined him in the room, Mark was agitated, asking why she hadn't responded to him. He claimed to

12

have been talking to her for the last half hour. Confused, Carol reassured him that she had just arrived. Then, Mark mentioned the people he had seen in their home, accusing Carol of inviting them over without asking him. But there was no one else there — just Carol and Mark. She realized that something was terribly wrong and then decided to get Mark to the hospital. Her heart pounded with anxiety on the way over. The weeks that followed were a blur of hospital visits, medical consultations, and tough decisions. Thankfully, Mark's condition has been slowly improving, allowing him to return home. Luckily, two of their children live close by and visit every now and then to help out. It is good that Mark has Carol and his children to care for him. However, I couldn't help but think about what Carol would do when she needs care in the future. She told me that she hopes to stay home and remain independent as long as possible. She also does not want to burden her children. She might eventually move to a senior home down the road. Fortunately, she has always made responsible financial decisions, giving her the financial safety net for her future care needs.

In the face of health changes and the reality that people are living longer than ever, the need for long-term care becomes inevitable. With the aging population in Canada, the cost of long-term care is estimated to double in the next decade. Therefore, making arrangements for aging and long-term care is of paramount importance. Whether you want to remain in your own home with assistance or move to a senior care facility, having a plan and the financial means to support it is crucial.

Carol's story is a poignant reminder that life can change in an instant. Life is unpredictable, and the best way to face its challenges is through preparation and foresight. Just as Carol had to navigate the difficult journey with her husband, so too must we all think ahead, ensuring that we. and those we love, are cared for, no matter what the future holds. Whether it's starting your first job, getting married, buying a home, or facing health challenges, each stage of life requires thoughtful financial planning to ensure stability and peace of mind.

In this chapter, we'll explore how various life changes can impact your finances and what steps you can take to stay ahead of the game.

Remember, being prepared isn't just about having a plan — it's about adapting that plan as life evolves.

Finding Your First Full-Time Job

Landing your first full-time job is a pivotal moment in your financial journey. It's the beginning of your career and the foundation upon which you'll build your financial future:

- **Budgeting and Saving:** Now that you're earning an income, it's time to establish a budget and set savings goals. Focus on increasing your net worth by paying down debts like student loans and regularly contributing to savings accounts like your TFSA, FHSA, and RRSP. These early steps will set the stage for long-term financial security.

- **Emergency Fund:** If you haven't already, start building an emergency fund. Aim for three to six months' worth of living expenses to cover unexpected costs or financial setbacks. This fund will act as your safety net, providing financial security during challenging times.

- **Review Your Work Benefits:** Take the time to understand the benefits offered by your employer, such as extended health insurance, disability and life insurance, and pension or RRSP matching plans. These benefits are valuable components of your long-term financial plan.

- **Investing:** Begin educating yourself about investing. Start with low-cost index funds or ETFs and gradually increase your investment knowledge. Investing early allows you to benefit from compound growth over time.

- **Professional Development:** Invest in your future by pursuing further education or certifications in your field. Enhancing your skills and qualifications can increase your earning potential, giving you more financial flexibility as your career progresses.

Taking these actions early in your career will help you establish a strong financial foundation, setting you up for long-term success.

Getting Married

Marriage is a significant life event that can have a profound impact on your finances. As you join lives with your partner, it's important to take proactive steps to manage your finances together:

- **Communication and Planning:** Sit down with your partner to discuss your financial goals, priorities, and expectations. Create a joint budget that reflects your combined income, expenses, and savings objectives. Open and honest communication about money is essential for a successful marriage.
- **Update Legal Documents:** Review and update your legal documents, including your wills, power of attorney, and beneficiaries on insurance policies and retirement accounts. Marriage often changes your beneficiaries and decision-making preferences.
- **Joint Finances:** Decide how you will manage your finances as a couple. Will you merge accounts, keep them separate, or use a combination of both? Determine who will be responsible for paying bills, managing investments, and tracking expenses.
- **Insurance Coverage:** Evaluate your insurance needs and update or combine policies to reflect your new marital status. Bundling coverage, such as health, auto, and home insurance, can potentially lower your premiums.
- **Tax Considerations:** Understand the tax implications of your new marital status. As a married couple, you may be eligible for certain tax benefits or credits, such as the spousal amount credit or pension income splitting if you are retired.

By taking these steps, you can navigate the financial aspects of marriage more smoothly and build a strong financial future together.

Having Children

Welcoming a new addition to your family is an exciting and joyous occasion, but it also brings important financial considerations.

- **Budgeting for Baby:** Prepare a comprehensive budget that accounts for the additional expenses associated with a new baby, including diapers, formula, clothing, childcare, and medical costs. Factor in both one-time and ongoing costs to ensure you're financially prepared.
- **Review Insurance Coverage:** Evaluate your extended health insurance plan to understand coverage for dependants. Consider increasing life insurance coverage to protect your family financially in the event of an unexpected tragedy.
- **Savings and Investments:** Start or boost your savings efforts to prepare for future expenses, such as education and extracurricular activities. Open a Registered Education Savings Plan (RESP) to save for your child's post-secondary education and take advantage of government grants.
- **Estate Planning:** Update your estate plan to reflect your growing family. Ensure that you have a will in place to designate guardians for your child and specify how your assets should be distributed.
- **Maximize Benefits:** Take advantage of government benefits or programs for families, such as the Canada Child Benefit (CCB) or provincial childcare subsidies. Look into parental leave policies in your province and workplace benefits like parental leave top-up.

By planning ahead and managing your finances wisely, you can provide a secure future for your family and enjoy the journey of parenthood with confidence.

Buying a Home

Buying a home is a major milestone, often accompanied by significant financial implications. It's important to be well-prepared for the responsibilities that come with homeownership.

- **Budget Assessment:** Evaluate your current financial situation and determine how much you can afford to spend on a home. Consider factors such as your income, existing debts, and monthly expenses.
- **Down Payment Savings:** Start saving for a down payment well in advance. Aim to save at least 20% of the home's purchase price to avoid mortgage insurance and secure more favourable loan terms.
- **Mortgage Pre-Approval:** Obtain pre-approval for a mortgage to understand how much you can borrow. Pre-approval gives you a competitive edge in a competitive housing market.
- **Understanding Mortgage Options:** Research different types of mortgages, such as fixed-rate mortgages, adjustable-rate mortgages (ARMs), and government-insured loans, to determine which option best fits your financial goals and risk tolerance.
- **Additional Costs:** Beyond the purchase price, homeownership comes with additional costs such as property taxes, legal fees, maintenance, and insurance. Be prepared for these expenses and understand the true cost of homeownership to avoid financial strain after buying your home.

By taking these steps and educating yourself about the financial aspects of homeownership, you can make informed decisions and enjoy your homeownership journey with confidence.

Job Changes or Layoffs

Job changes, whether voluntary or involuntary, can have significant financial implications. With careful planning, you can navigate this transition smoothly.

- **Evaluate Your Finances:** Assess your current financial situation, including your savings, debts, and monthly expenses. Determine how long you can sustain yourself financially without a steady income and plan accordingly.
- **Severance Package:** Review any severance package or benefits if you're leaving your job. Understand the terms and conditions, such as severance pay, health insurance coverage, and retirement benefits.
- **Transfer Your Pension:** Decide what to do with your employer-sponsored pension plan. You may have the option to leave the funds in the existing plan, roll them over into a new employer's plan, or transfer them to a Locked-in Retirement Account (LIRA).
- **Unemployment Benefits:** If eligible, apply for unemployment benefits to provide temporary financial support while you search for a new job.
- **Negotiate Salary and Benefits:** When considering job offers, evaluate the compensation package, including salary, bonuses, health benefits, and retirement plans. Negotiate for the best possible terms to maximize your financial well-being.

By managing your finances strategically during a job transition, you can mitigate financial stress and position yourself for success in your career journey.

Retirement

Approaching retirement is both exciting and crucial. It's a time to ensure your financial security for the years ahead.

- **Evaluate Retirement Readiness:** Assess your current financial situation, retirement savings, and anticipated retirement expenses. Use retirement calculators or consult a financial advisor to determine if you're on track to meet your goals.

- **Pension Plan Consideration:** Depending on your employer's pension plan, you may need to transfer your pension plan to your own financial institution upon retirement. Consider seeking professional advice for making these decisions.
- **Create a Retirement Budget:** Develop a budget that outlines your expected income sources and projected expenses. This will help you manage your finances effectively during retirement.
- **Maximize Retirement Savings:** If you're 50 or older, take advantage of catch-up contributions if there were any to retirement accounts like RRSPs and TFSAs. These additional contributions can boost your retirement savings.
- **Healthcare Planning:** Understand the costs and coverage options for healthcare in retirement. Consider purchasing supplemental health insurance or long-term care insurance to protect against unexpected medical expenses.

By planning carefully and staying informed, you can approach retirement with confidence and enjoy a financially secure lifestyle.

Divorce

Divorce can be both emotionally and financially challenging. Taking proactive steps can help protect your financial well-being during this difficult time.

- **Consult with Professionals:** Seek guidance from financial advisors, divorce attorneys, and other professionals who specialize in divorce planning. They can provide valuable insights and help you understand your rights and options.
- **Negotiate Fairly:** Work collaboratively with your spouse to negotiate a fair settlement. Consider options like mediation or collaborative divorce to resolve disputes amicably and avoid costly litigation.

- **Assess Your Finances:** Take stock of your current financial situation, including assets, debts, income, and expenses. Understanding your financial standing will help you make informed decisions during the divorce process.
- **Gather Financial Documents:** Collect important financial documents, such as bank statements, tax returns, investment accounts, and insurance policies. Having these documents on hand will facilitate the division of assets and liabilities.
- **Protect Your Credit:** Monitor your credit report regularly and take steps to protect your credit score during the divorce process. Close joint accounts and credit cards if necessary and establish individual accounts to maintain financial independence.

By taking these proactive steps and seeking professional guidance, you can protect your financial interests and lay the foundation for a secure financial future as you navigate the divorce process.

Inheritance

Receiving an inheritance can be both a blessing and a responsibility. It's important to approach it with careful consideration and strategic planning.

- **Assess Your Financial Situation:** Start by evaluating your current financial situation, including your income, assets, debts, and financial goals. Understanding your financial landscape will help you make informed decisions about managing your inheritance.
- **Seek Professional Guidance:** Consider consulting with a financial advisor, accountant, or estate planning attorney to help you navigate the complexities of managing an inheritance, such as holding the inheritance in a sole account under your own name can potentially protect it from divorce claims.

- **Develop a Financial Plan:** Create a comprehensive financial plan that incorporates your inheritance into your overall strategy. Prioritize paying off debts, saving for retirement, or funding education baed on your goals.
- **Avoid Impulse Spending:** While it may be tempting to splurge with your inheritance, take a thoughtful and disciplined approach to spending. Focus on your long-term financial goals.

By taking proactive steps and seeking professional guidance, you can maximize the benefits of your inheritance and use it to achieve your financial goals.

Health Challenges

Facing health challenges can be emotionally and financially overwhelming. Taking proactive steps can help alleviate some of the financial burdens during difficult times.

- **Review Your Health Insurance Coverage:** Thoroughly review your health insurance coverage, including deductibles, copayments, and coverage limits. Understand what medical services are covered and what expenses you may be responsible for out-of-pocket.
- **Review your Disability Insurance:** If you're unable to work due to your health condition, disability insurance can provide income replacement. Review the disability insurance you may have through your employer or your individual policy if you have set up one in place.
- **Seek Financial Assistance Programs:** Investigate financial assistance programs offered by hospitals, clinics, and government agencies to help offset medical costs.
- **Arrange for Long-Term Care:** If you have long-term care insurance, review your policy to understand what services are covered, such as in-home care, assisted living, or nursing home care. Determine when you can start using these benefits and any limitations on coverage.

- **Have Conversations with Family:** Openly communicate with your family about your health challenges, the prognosis, and how it may impact your day-to-day life and finances. If you require caregiving, discuss the potential role of family members in your care. Determine who might be available to help with daily activities, medical appointments, or decision-making, and whether you'll need to hire professional caregivers.
- **Create or Update Legal Documents:** If you haven't already, consider appointing a power of attorney (POA) for both financial and healthcare decisions. Ensure your will is up-to-date, reflecting your current wishes regarding the distribution of your assets, guardianship of dependents, and any specific bequests.
- **Mental and Emotional Well-being:** Managing a health challenge can be emotionally taxing. Engage in self-care activities that promote your mental and emotional well-being, such as mindfulness, meditation, or simply spending time with loved ones.

By taking these proactive steps and staying informed about your financial options, you can better navigate the financial impacts of major health challenges and focus on prioritizing your health and well-being.

Spouse's Passing

The loss of a spouse is one of life's most difficult challenges. Amid the emotional turmoil, it's crucial to address the financial impacts and take necessary actions to ensure stability.

- **Assess Financial Situation:** Take stock of your spouse's financial affairs, including bank accounts, investments, debts, and insurance policies. Understanding the complete financial picture will help you make informed decisions.
- **Notify Relevant Parties:** Notify financial institutions, employers, insurers, and government agencies of your

spouse's passing. This includes canceling subscriptions, memberships, and notifying creditors.

- **Review Estate Plan:** Review your spouse's estate plan, including their will or trust. Seek guidance from legal and financial professionals to ensure compliance with legal requirements.
- **Accessing Benefits and Insurance:** Determine your eligibility for survivor benefits, such as CPP, life insurance proceeds, and retirement accounts.

By addressing the financial impacts of losing your spouse with care and attention, you can safeguard your financial well-being and move forward with confidence.

Conclusion

Life is unpredictable, and each stage of life presents unique financial challenges. By taking proactive steps, staying informed, and seeking professional guidance when necessary, you can navigate these changes with confidence. Remember, financial planning is a lifelong journey that requires flexibility and foresight.

As you continue on this journey, the next chapter will explore the various financial services available to help you meet your goals. We'll discuss what services fit your needs, how to choose the right ones, and how to make the most of the resources at your disposal.

3

MATCHING SERVICES TO NEEDS

Finding the Right Tools for Your Financial Toolbox

Introduction

Do you know who to turn to when you have financial questions? Navigating your financial journey can sometimes feel overwhelming, especially with the multitude of options and decisions to make. Whether you're just starting out, building your wealth, or planning for retirement, having the right financial support can make all the difference. But how do you know who to turn to for advice that suits your specific needs?

In this chapter, we'll take a closer look at the various financial services available to help you . Think of it as selecting your seat on a financial flight—whether you need the basics, more personalized support, or top-tier wealth management, there's an option that fits your needs and comfort level. We'll explore the different services, their costs, and who they're best suited for, so you can make informed choices as you chart your financial course.

Economy Cabin: Regular Personal Banking

Regular personal banking is like flying in the economy cabin of an airplane—basic, no-frills, and reliable. It covers everyday financial needs such as savings and checking accounts, mortgages, personal loans, debit and credit cards, and basic investing options like mutual funds and GICs. You can access these services at your local bank branch or online. The individuals who assist you often hold titles like personal banker, banking advisor, or financial services representative. They can provide information and guidance on your basic banking and investment needs.

Credit unions, online banks, and traditional banks offer these services with a focus on accessibility and functionality. The advantage here is that you can handle your finances comfortably and securely. However, you won't have a dedicated advisor working with you, so you might need to repeat your story each time you need assistance. This is the perfect option for those who are just starting their financial journey or those with straightforward needs.

Fee Structure: The primary investment vehicle available in personal banking is mutual funds, with fees known as Managed Expense Ratios (MER). These typically range from 2% to 2.5% for actively managed funds, and 0.3% to 0.7% for passive index funds.

Business Class: Financial Planner Services

Stepping up to business class brings you into the realm of financial planners — dedicated professionals who know your financial story and work with you to create a long-term plan. Financial planners typically hold designations like Personal Financial Planner (PFP) or Certified Financial Planner (CFP), which equips them with knowledge in areas such as investment, retirement planning, taxes, insurance, and estate planning.

Financial planners are ideal for those with more complex financial needs or those who prefer a more personalized approach to managing their money. With assets typically over $100,000, you gain access to a range of services tailored to help you achieve your financial goals. Most banks and credit unions have financial planners in branch offering financial planning services.

Fee Structure: Financial planners often recommend mutual funds, with fees structured as MERs similar to personal banking: 2%

to 2.5% for actively managed funds, and 0.3% to 0.7% for passive index funds.

First Class: Investment Counsel

For those with significant assets and more complex needs, first class offers the services of investment counsellors. These professionals, often holding a Chartered Financial Analyst (CFA) designation, provide bespoke investment strategies and have access to in-house specialists such as insurance, tax, and estate planning experts. It's like having a private suite with a dedicated attendant, ensuring all your financial needs are met.

Investment counsellors typically serve clients with investable assets over $1,000,000, offering a more hands-on approach to wealth management with the added benefit of lower fees on mutual funds. Each of the big banks has its own Private Investment Counsel channel. There are also other non-bank affiliated independent Investment Counsel firms such as Burgundy Asset Management, Leith Wheeler, Mawer Investment Management, and Connor, Clark & Lunn Financial Group etc.

Fee Structure: The investment vehicles used are firm-managed mutual funds with very low MERs, typically ranging from 0.03% to 0.2%. The investment counsellor then charges a management fee on top, typically ranging from 1% to 1.5%, resulting in a total fee of 1.03% to 1.7%.

First Class with Star Alliance: Full-Service Brokerage (Wealth Management)

When you want the full range of investment options (not limited to mutual funds managed by one specific firm) and a comprehensive service, full-service brokerage is the way to go. It's like flying first class with access to all the perks of an entire airline alliance. You have a personal advisor who can guide you through the vast market of investment options, including mutual funds, ETFs, individual stocks, bonds, and alternative investments.

This service is perfect for those with investable assets over $750,000 who want a long-term, in-depth relationship with a financial advisor. Advisors here often hold designations such as Chartered Investment Manager (CIM) or Chartered Financial Analyst (CFA). Just like investment counsellors, advisors in Full-Service Brokerage work with high-net-worth individuals and organizations to formulate and implement long term financial and wealth transfer plans, having access to in house specialists such as insurance specialist, tax specialist and will and estate specialists. The Full-Service Brokerages within the banks are BMO Nesbitt Burns, ScotiaMcLeod, RBC Dominion Securities, TD Wealth Private Investment Advice, CIBC Wood Gundy, National Bank Financial Wealth Management. There are also other Full-Service Brokerages such as Aviso Wealth, Canaccord Genuity, Raymond James Ltd., Leede Jones Gable, PI Financial, and Richardson Wealth etc.

Fee Structure: there are mainly two types of accounts, each with its own fee structure in full-service brokerage:

- **Commission-based:** For each trade that occurs in the account, a commission is charged. This commission is usually a percentage of the trade's proceeds, typically ranging from 0.1% to 0.5%, with a minimum charge applied per trade. Certain investments occur more commissions than others.
- **Fee-based:** A flat management fee, usually ranging from 1% to 2%, with no commissions charged on trades. Note, if the advisor uses mutual funds as the investment vehicle, the advisor fee is on top of the mutual fund MER. For example, if your advisor charges a 1.5% management fee for the services they provide, and they use a mutual fund with a 1.0% MER (Managed Expense Ration), the total fee you pay would be 2.5%.

Being Your Own Pilot: Self-Directed Trading Platforms

For those who prefer to take control of their own investment portfolios, self-directed trading platforms offer the tools you need to manage your investments independently. It's like being your own pilot — thrilling and empowering, but requiring knowledge and skill to avoid turbulence.

These platforms give you full access to most publicly traded securities, including stocks, certain bonds, mutual funds, and ETFs. This option is ideal for those who are confident in their investment knowledge and want to take full control of their investment decisions. The bank owned self-directed trading platforms are BMO InvestorLine, Scotia iTRADE, RBC Direct Investing, TD Direct Investing, CIBC Investor's Edge and National Bank Direct Brokerage. There are also some other self-directed trading platforms like Questrade, Qtrade, Wealthsimple Self-Directed Investing etc.

Fee Structure: Commission-based, typically charging $7 to $10 per trade. Some platforms, like Wealthsimple, offer commission-free trading.

Using a Co-Pilot: Robo-Advisor Investing Platforms

If managing your own investments feels overwhelming, a Robo-Advisor can act as your co-pilot, guiding you through the financial skies with automated investment management. These platforms use algorithms to manage your investments based on your risk tolerance and financial goals, providing a balance between control and support.

Robo-Advisors are perfect for those who want to invest without the need for in-depth financial knowledge or constant management. They offer a helping hand while keeping you on course. You guessed it; some of the big banks also have Robo-Advisor Investing Platforms. They are BMO Smartfolio, Scotia Smart Investor, RBC InvestEase, TD Automated Investing. Other Robo-Advisor Investing Platforms include Justwealth, Questwealth Portfolios, Nest Wealth Direct, Wealthsimple Managed Investing, CI Direct Investing (formerly WealthBar), ModernAdvisor, Qtrade Guided Portfolios etc.

Fee Structure: Typically, a flat management fee ranging from 0.3% to 0.6%, plus the MER of the products used, resulting in a total fee of 0.4% to 1.1%.

Conclusion

Whether you prefer to sit back and enjoy the ride, fly in style, or take control of the cockpit, there's a financial service out there to suit your style and needs. As you continue your financial journey, remember that the right service can make all the difference in reaching your goals.

In the next chapter, we'll explore the question of whether you should manage your own finances or work with a professional advisor. We'll also discuss the qualities to look for in a financial advisor to ensure you have the right co-pilot on your journey to financial success.

4

WHO'S IN THE DRIVER'S SEAT?

Deciding Whether to Steer Your Financial Ship or Hire a Captain

Introduction

Are you better off managing your own finances, or should you seek the guidance of a professional advisor? Now that we've explored the various financial services available, this question might be on your mind. Deciding whether to take control of your financial journey or enlist the help of a professional boils down to three key elements: your interest in financial management, the time and energy you can dedicate, and the complexity of your financial needs.

In this chapter, we'll guide you through these considerations, helping you determine whether to be your own financial pilot or rely on a seasoned advisor to help you navigate. We'll also discuss what qualities to look for if you choose to work with a professional, ensuring you find the right partner for your financial journey.

Should You Manage Your Own Finances?

Interest:

Do you enjoy learning about and managing your finances? If you're passionate about investing and financial planning, the DIY approach might be for you. It can be rewarding to take charge and directly influence your financial outcomes. However, if the thought of navigating financial markets or tax strategies feels overwhelming, you might prefer the peace of mind that comes from working with an advisor.

Time and Energy:
Managing your finances requires a significant investment of time and energy. Ask yourself if you have the time to monitor markets, adjust your portfolio, and stay updated on financial trends. If your schedule is already full, taking on this additional responsibility might cause unnecessary stress. It might be more beneficial to focus on what you do best — whether that's growing your business or advancing your career — and leave financial management to the professionals. Even Albert Einstein might have struggled to develop the theory of general relativity if he had spent all his time managing his investments!

Complexity of Your Needs:
The complexity of your financial situation is another crucial factor. Simple financial needs might be manageable on your own, but if you're juggling multiple income streams, managing significant investments, planning for retirement, or efficiently transferring wealth to the next generation, professional guidance can be invaluable. Experts can help you navigate these challenges effectively, ensuring you make informed decisions that align with your goals.

1. Manage Your Own Finances

If you decide to take control, there are abundant resources available to help you succeed. Books, online courses, and financial news outlets offer a wealth of information on investment strategies, tax planning, and wealth management.

One-time Consulting:
If you're comfortable managing most aspects of your personal finances but need occasional professional advice, independent regis-

tered financial advisors can fill this gap. They typically charge by the hour, ensuring unbiased advice tailored to your specific situation. For example, you might pay $250 per hour for consulting services, with a total fee of $2,500 for a comprehensive financial plan.

2. Working with a Professional Advisor

If you decide that working with a professional advisor is the best option and like the idea of having someone to turn to for all your financial questions, the next step is finding the right person to help you. But where should you start?

Where to Find a Professional Advisor:

- **Visit Your Local Branch:** Many banks and financial institutions have financial planners on-site, ready to assist with your needs.
- **Company Websites:** For more specialized services like investment counselling or full service brokerage advisors, visit the company's website to find advisor profiles. You can cross-reference these profiles with LinkedIn for additional insights into their experience and qualifications.
- **FP Canada Website:** Use the "Find a Financial Planner" tool on the FP Canada website to locate Certified Financial Planners (CFPs) in your area.
- **Ask Trusted Sources:** Recommendations from family, friends, or other trusted professionals can be invaluable in finding a reliable advisor.

Qualities to Look for in an Advisor

Finding the right advisor is about more than just credentials. It's about finding someone who aligns with your goals and values — someone you can trust with your financial future.

When I initially moved to Canada, I needed to open a bank account and apply for a credit card. I had a tenured Senior Financial Advisor helping me at my local bank branch. While applying for the credit card, the advisor told me that because I was new to Canada, I did not have a strong credit history here. To get approved for the credit card application, she suggested adding Credit Card Balance Protector insurance. She explained that with this insurance, there would be less chance of me defaulting on the credit card balance, increasing the likelihood of my application being approved. After approval, she assured me I could easily cancel the insurance with a phone call—easy peasy. I remember thinking how lucky I was to have this experienced advisor helping me; otherwise, I might have been declined for the credit card application without this insurance trick. How inconvenient that would have been! I trusted her and her experience completely.

Do you want to know what the truth was? After working in banking myself, I learned that having Credit Card Balance Protector insurance does not impact your chances of getting approved or not. What it does do is that it slightly boosts the advisor's bonus and make them look good in front of their manager. What is more, in Canada, it is illegal to induce a customer with misleading information to buy a second product, which is often known as tied selling. Condolences to my misplaced trust! Were the consequences of the advisor's misconduct significant? Not really. I just needed to make that extra phone call. Would I use her services again in the future? Never! Who knows if she would recommend me some ill-fitted investments just to earn some sales commission? This experience taught me an invaluable lesson: not every person has the integrity to do the right thing, especially under sales pressure. While the majority of people do, there are always a few bad apples in every field. The consequences of working with those bad apples are too significant to neglect.

It's crucial to find the right person to ensure your financial well-being is not at risk. Below are some qualities you should look for in a good advisor:

- **Knowledge and Experience:** Your advisor should have a deep understanding of financial principles and strategies. While professional designations like CFP or CFA are important, practical experience in navigating various financial landscapes is equally crucial.
- **Listening to You:** An advisor should take the time to understand your unique goals, values, and concerns. If they're more focused on pushing their own agenda, it's like dancing with a partner who keeps stepping on your toes. You need someone who listens and tailors their advice to your unique situation.
- **Organized Approach with Effective Execution:** A dedicated advisor is organized and committed to helping you achieve your financial goals. They should have a clear process for meetings and planning, ensuring they stay on top of your financial needs. In addition, even the best plan is useless if not executed properly. Your advisor should be able to implement strategies effectively, ensuring your financial plan translates into real-world results.
- **Coordinator (The Financial Quarterback):** A great advisor acts as the quarterback for your financial team, coordinating various experts like tax professionals, lawyers, estate planners, and insurance specialists to ensure all aspects of your financial life are in sync.
- **Educational Approach (Heart of a Teacher):** An advisor should be able to explain complex financial concepts in a way that makes sense to you. They should help you understand your options so you can make informed decisions, rather than just making choices on your behalf.
- **Reasonable and Transparent with Fees:** Fees matter because they directly impact your long-term returns. Your advisor should be upfront about what you'll pay, and their fees should be reasonable — generally, total fees should not exceed 2% unless they have a stellar track record of adding value elsewhere.

Conclusion

Deciding whether to manage your own finances or work with a professional advisor is a personal choice, influenced by your interest, time, and the complexity of your financial needs. If you decide to go it alone, there are ample resources to guide you. However, if you prefer the expertise and support of a professional, choosing the right advisor is crucial.

In the next chapter, we'll take a closer look at the financial institutions in Canada, exploring who exactly is handling your money and the landscape of financial services in the country.

5

MEET YOUR MONEY'S BFFS

Understanding Canada's Financial Institutions: Who's handling your money?

Reading Guide Reminder: This chapter is more about fun facts than must-know information. If banking history or the financial institutions' landscape isn't your thing, feel free to skip ahead — it won't impact your ability to set goals and make plans. But if you're curious, dive in and enjoy!

Introduction

Have you ever wondered how Canada's financial institutions evolved from simple banks to the complex financial powerhouses they are today? In this chapter, we'll explore the landscape of Canada's financial institutions, uncovering their transformation over the years and what it means for you as a consumer. Whether you're looking for traditional banking services or advanced wealth management, understanding the players in this space can help you make informed decisions. Let's dive in!

The Evolution of Canada's Financial Landscape

Before the 1980s, Canada's financial industry was neatly divided into four pillars: banking, investment, trust, and insurance. Each of these sectors operated independently, focusing on specific financial services:

- **Banking:** The foundation of financial services, banking involved accepting deposits, lending money, and offering basic financial services like checking and savings accounts, loans, and mortgages.
- **Investment:** Investment services were focused on helping individuals and institutions grow wealth through various investment vehicles like stocks, bonds, and mutual funds.
- **Trust:** Trust companies managed and safeguarded assets on behalf of clients, ensuring they were distributed according to the clients' wishes.
- **Insurance:** Insurance companies provided financial protection against unexpected events, offering policies that covered life, health, property, and casualty risks.

The Integration of Financial Services

Over the last few decades, Canada's financial landscape has seen a significant shift. The big banks began integrating these four pillars, merging their operations to provide a comprehensive suite of services under one roof. By the 1980s and 1990s, the major banks had acquired nearly all trust and brokerage companies, and they launched their own insurance and mutual fund businesses.

This integration means that today, you can access almost all your financial needs — banking, investments, insurance, and trust services — from a single institution. This shift towards offering a one-stop shop for financial services aims to make managing your finances more convenient, efficient, and tailored to your needs.

Meet the Big Six: Canada's Major Financial Institutions

Canada's financial landscape is dominated by six major banks, often referred to as the "Big Six." Each of these banks offers a comprehensive range of services, integrating the traditional pillars of finance into their operations.

1. Royal Bank of Canada (RBC):

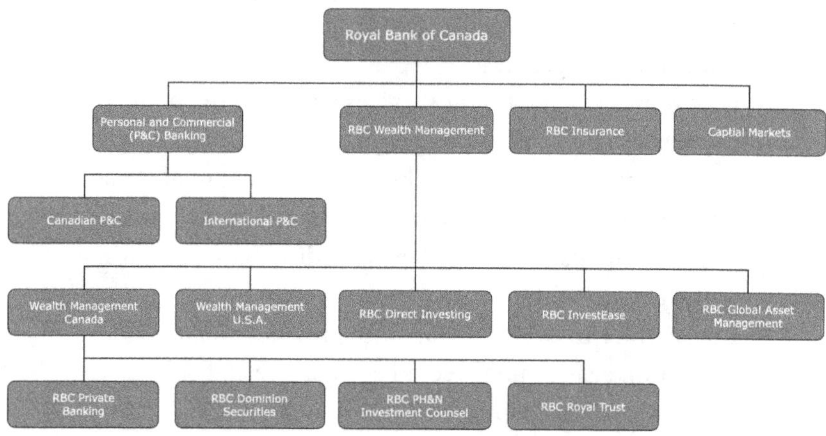

The largest bank in Canada by market capitalization, RBC offers personal and commercial banking, wealth management, insurance, and capital markets services.

2. Toronto-Dominion Bank (TD):

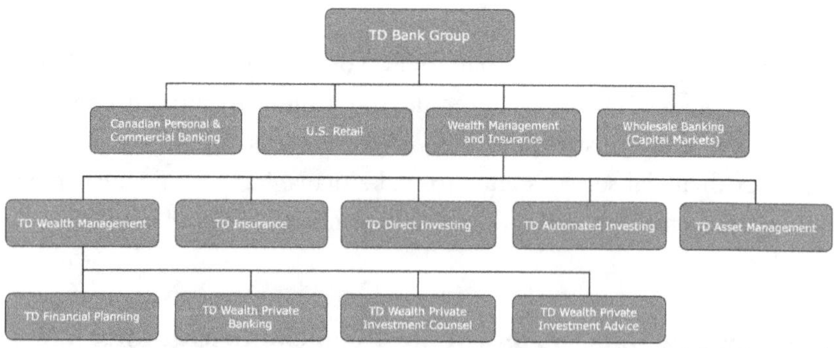

Known for its significant presence in both Canada and the U.S.,

TD offers a wide range of services, including personal and commercial banking, wealth management, and capital markets.

3. Scotiabank:

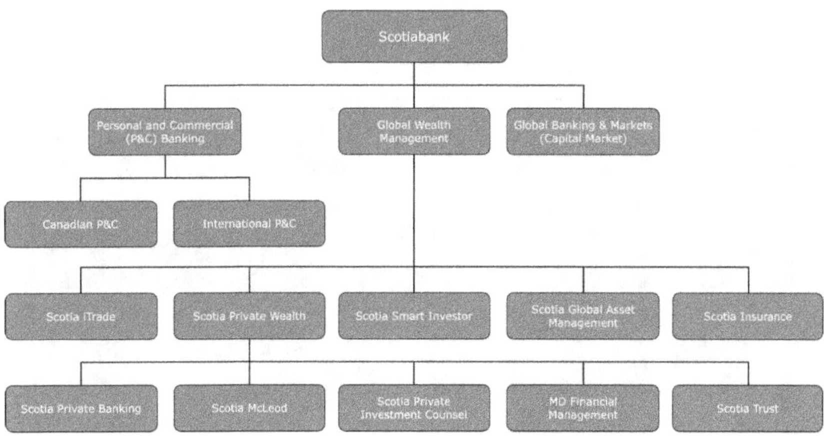

With a strong international presence, Scotiabank provides personal and commercial banking, wealth management, and global banking services.

4. Bank of Montreal (BMO):

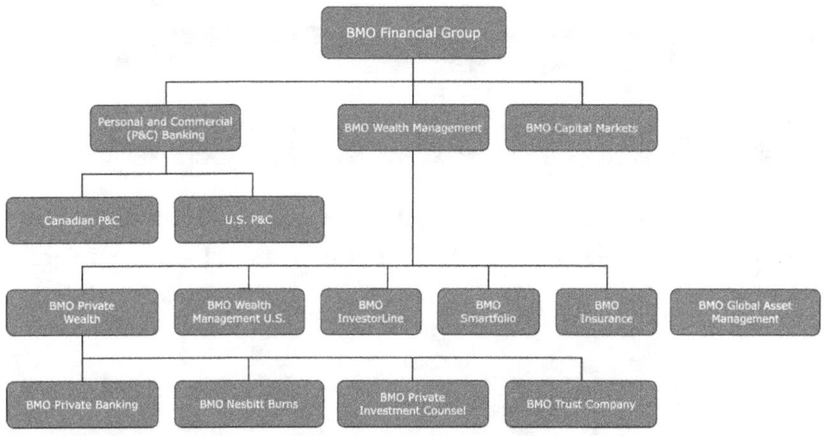

The oldest bank in Canada, BMO offers personal and commercial banking, wealth management, and capital markets services.

5. Canadian Imperial Bank of Commerce (CIBC):

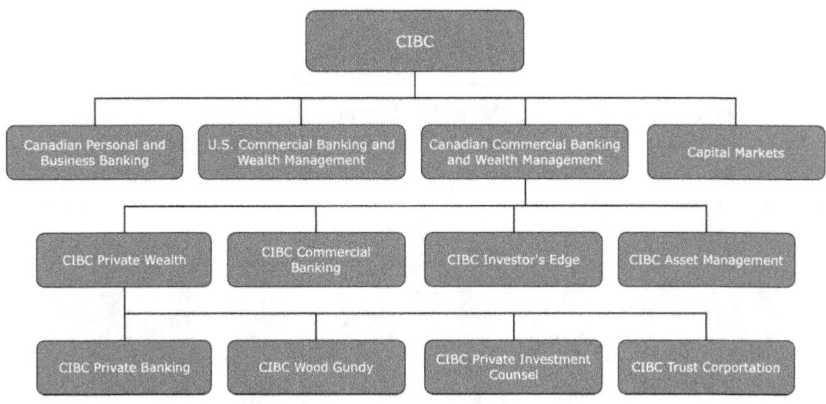

CIBC offers personal and commercial banking, wealth management, and capital markets.

6. National Bank of Canada:

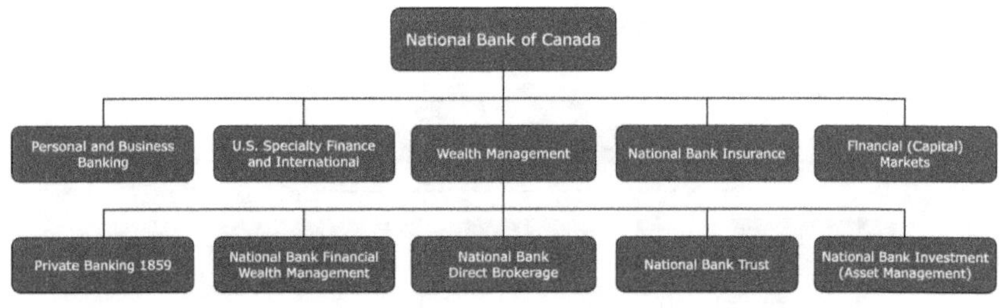

While smaller in scale compared to the others, National Bank is a key player, particularly in Quebec, offering personal and commercial banking, wealth management, and financial markets services.

Did you know? Canada's big banks are primarily owned by individual and institutional investors. For instance, as of May 2024, less than 1% of TD Bank's stocks were owned by its senior executives. The rest are held by mutual funds, public companies, institutional investors, and individual investors. This means that the $10.8 billion profit TD made in 2023 largely benefits its vast majority of shareholders.

Understanding Financial Services: A Quick Overview

Now that we know the major financial institutions in Canada, let's explore some of the services they offer beyond basic personal banking:

What does Commercial Banking involve?

Commercial banking offers a variety of financial services to businesses, from small local shops to massive corporations. Think of it as a one-stop shop for business loans, lines of credit, commercial mortgages, and cash flow & treasury management. For example, your local grocery store might use the commercial banking service to get a loan for opening a new location in the neighbouring city.

What is Wealth Management really?

Wealth management combines financial planning, investment management, and other services to help high-net-worth individuals manage, preserve, and grow their wealth. This includes things like retirement planning, estate planning, and tax strategies. One thing we need to know is that wealth management won't make you rich, at least not within a short period of time, but it will help you and your family stay rich! You might have heard of the Three-Generation Curse of Wealth:

1. The first generation, the builder, accumulates wealth through hard work and determination.

2. The second generation, the maintainer, preserves the wealth.
3. But the third generation, the squanderer, often wastes it all away.

Wealth management aims to break that curse. It's about using tools and strategies to protect your hard-earned money from those spendthrift offspring so your wealth can go further down the line.

What is Private Banking? How is it different from regular banking?

You might have heard that billionaires like Elon Musk have a clever trick up their sleeves when it comes to accessing cash without selling their stocks. Instead of selling and getting hit with capital gains taxes, they borrow against the shares they own.

Here's how it works:

Billionaires have excellent credit, so banks are more than happy to lend them money with very favourable interest rates. It's like taking a loan out on your house, but instead of a house, they use their Tesla or SpaceX shares as collateral. This way, they avoid selling their stocks and triggering capital gains taxes, all while keeping their cash flow fluid.

Think of it as a secret menu at an exclusive restaurant – only high-networth individuals get to enjoy these perks. It's a classic private banking service designed to keep the wealthy, well, wealthy. Private banking services include:

- **Personalized Service**: Private banking provides a dedicated private banker who understands your unique financial goals and needs. They can take care of most of your banking needs though phone calls or email requests, including making payments from accounts, issuing bank drafts, loan and mortgage applications, investment transactions. You barely need to step into a physical branch.
- **Customized lending**: Private banking often provides tailored credit solutions, such as high limit mortgage, loans

and lines of credit against investment portfolios and whole life insurance, often with lower interest rates and higher limits compared to regular banking, for people with more complicated borrowing needs.

In essence, private banking offers enhanced attention, expertise, and personalized financial management and lending. However, this customized service comes at a cost, typically ranging from $100 to $200 per month currently, varying among financial institutions. There are also usually loan origination fees involved with the customized lending. There may be fee rebates available based on factors like investable assets and specific profession, such as certain medical professionals can access private banking services for a lower fee. Like everything else, the actual delivery of claimed services hinges on the capabilities and professionalism of the individual private banker you work with. Referrals from trusted friends or professional networks can come in handy in finding the right person if you need this service.

What is Full-Service Brokerage

As opposed to Discount Brokerage (self-directed online trading), where no human advisor involved and you are mostly managing investment on your own, a full-service brokerage offers a wide range of financial services, including investment advice, portfolio management, financial and estate planning, and insurance advice. If you think it sounds eerily similar to wealth management, you are not crazy. It is part of the wealth management puzzle, just without the Banking service piece.

What is Investment Counsel?

Investment counsel refers to professionals or firms providing personalized long-term investment advice and management. Usually with proprietary managed products, meaning if you use RBC PH&N Investment counsel service, then the investment products in your portfolio are mostly RBC managed mutuals funds.

What is Asset Management?

You can think of asset management firms as manufactories of mutual funds and ETFs. Asset management involves managing investments to maximize returns while mitigating risks. Asset management firms like BlackRock and Vanguard manage mutual funds, ETFs, along other investment products.

What is Capital Market?

Capital markets are venues where savings and investments are channeled between suppliers who have capital and those who need capital. In simple terms, it helps those who have the money find the people who need the money. This can involve issuing stocks and bonds, buying and selling businesses, and exchanging foreign currencies, among other financial activities.

Conclusion

Canada's big banks have evolved into comprehensive financial service providers, integrating everything from basic banking to complex wealth management under one roof. This integration offers you convenience and expertise, making it easier to manage your financial needs efficiently.

As we transition to the next chapter, we'll dive into the basics of banking and bank accounts, breaking down what's important to know about them.

6

BANK ACCOUNTS UNPLUGGED

The Unsung Heroes of Your Financial Orchestra

Introduction

Have you ever thought about how your choice of bank accounts impacts your financial well-being? While most of us use bank accounts every day, the nuances of managing them effectively often go unnoticed. In this chapter, we'll explore the basic bank account types in Canada, weigh the pros and cons of sole versus joint accounts, and point out common banking pitfalls that can lead to unnecessary fees or complications. By the end, you'll have the knowledge you need to make smarter decisions about your bank accounts and manage your money more effectively.

Basic Bank Account Types

In Canada, banks offer several types of accounts to cater to different financial needs:

- **Checking Accounts:** These are your go-to accounts for everyday transactions. They allow you to deposit money, write checks, and pay bills. Most checking accounts come with a debit card, making it easy to access your funds.

45

- **Savings Accounts:** Designed to help you grow your money, savings accounts typically offer interest on the balance. These are ideal for setting aside funds for future needs or emergencies.
- **Specialized Accounts:** These include business accounts, which are tailored for entrepreneurs, and foreign currency accounts, which are useful if you frequently deal with non-Canadian currencies.

When choosing a bank account, it's important to compare interest rates, fees, and account perks to find the best fit for your needs.

Sole Accounts vs. Joint Accounts

When I worked in banking, I often encountered clients requesting to change their account ownership from sole-owned to joint. The reasons for these requests were usually:

- **Ease of Managing Joint Expenses:** Sharing an account can simplify managing household or joint expenses, making it easier to track and pay bills.
- **Estate Planning:** Account ownership rolls over to surviving account holders upon one owner's passing. Some elderly parents add their adult children as joint account owners so the ownership will transfer directly to the children, simplifying estate distribution and saving on probate fees.

However, there might be unintended consequences with changing account ownership you need to know :

- **Loss of Control**: Adding another person means they have equal access to the funds. If relationships sour or misunderstandings occur, it could lead to disputes or unauthorized withdrawals.

- **Exposure to Creditors**: If the joint account holder has debt or faces legal judgments, creditors including children's divorced spouses could claim the funds in the joint account, putting your money at risk.
- **Impact on Eligibility for Benefits**: Adding a joint owner might affect eligibility for certain benefits or assistance programs if the account balance is considered part of the joint owner's assets.
- **Ownership change cannot be revered:** Once the account ownership changed from sole to joint, it cannot be reversed. You cannot remove a joint owner from an account unless the joint owner passes away. However, you do have the option to close the account and transfer all balance out.

While joint accounts can simplify managing shared expenses or estate planning, they come with potential risks. We will look at an example to understand the impacts:

Consider Jane, who added her daughter Emily as a joint owner of her savings account to simplify estate planning. Unfortunately, Emily was going through a divorce, and during the asset division, her husband claimed a portion of the balance in the joint account. Since the account was jointly owned, part of the balance was considered Emily's assets, putting Jane's hard-earned savings at risk.

This example highlights the potential dangers of joint accounts. In some cases, it may be wiser to keep sole accounts and only open joint accounts for specific purposes, transferring money into the joint account as needed.

Common Pitfalls in Banking

Maintaining a healthy relationship with your bank is crucial for managing your finances smoothly. Here are some common pitfalls to avoid:

1. Overdraft Fees and NSF Charges:

- **Avoid Overdrafts:** Always ensure there is enough balance in your account to cover checks, preauthorized transactions, and automatic payments. Overdrafts can result in fees of $5-$10 per transaction.
- **Non-Sufficient Funds (NSF) Fees:** If a check or payment is returned due to insufficient funds, you could be charged an Non-Sufficient Funds (NSF) fee, typically ranging from $30 to $50. This can also harm your banking reputation, making it harder to get access to funds or credit in the future.

2. Depositing Checks from Unreliable Sources:

- **Bounced Checks:** If you deposit a check from someone who doesn't have enough money in their bank accounts, the check will bounce, and you could be charged a check return fee of $5-$10. Repeated incidents can tarnish your trustworthiness with the bank.
- **Alternative Payment Methods:** Whenever possible, opt for Interac e-Transfers or wire transfers instead of checks. These methods are safer and more reliable, as these payments can only be initiated when there are enough balance in their bank accounts.

Conclusion

As we've explored, choosing and managing the right bank account is fundamental to your financial success. Whether it's a checking account for daily transactions or a savings account to help grow your wealth, understanding the types of accounts available and the potential pitfalls can make a big difference. Whether you opt for a sole or joint account, being aware of the benefits and risks will help you make informed decisions that align with your financial goals.

Now that you have a grasp of bank accounts, it's time to dive into another crucial aspect of personal finance: navigating credit. In the next chapter, we'll explore how credit works in Canada, the types of credit facilities available, and, most importantly, how to use credit wisely to avoid falling into the debt trap. By understanding the do's and don'ts of credit, you can maintain a healthy financial future while leveraging credit as a tool for growth rather than a burden.

7

DEBT DODGEBALL

How to Navigate Credit and Avoid the Debt Trap

Reading Guide Reminder: This chapter is especially relevant for those who use credit as part of their financial strategy. If you don't regularly carry debt, such as credit card balances or loans, feel free to skip ahead — you can always come back to this chapter if it becomes more relevant to your situation later on.

Introduction

Are you ready to navigate the complex world of credit and debt in Canada? Welcome to the intricate world of credit and debt in Canada, where your financial dreams can be realized — or dashed — depending on how wisely you manage your borrowing. Credit can be an incredibly powerful tool, unlocking opportunities like home ownership, education, or business ventures. However, if not handled responsibly, it can lead to financial stress and long-term debt that feels inescapable. In this chapter, we will explore the various forms of credit available, discuss how to use them responsibly, and delve into strategies for managing debt effectively.

Over-leveraged Household Debt: The Balancing Act

Canadians are known for their politeness, but when it comes to household debt, our situation is anything but courteous. The average household debt-to-income ratio in Canada is alarmingly high, resembling a tightrope walk without a safety net. Over-leveraging happens when you borrow more than you can comfortably repay, leading to financial stress and potential bankruptcy. The key to avoiding this pitfall is understanding your limits and exercising discipline in your borrowing habits.

Tips to Avoid the Debt Trap:

- **Know Your Limits:** Understand how much you can realistically afford to borrow and repay without compromising your financial stability.
- **Exercise Discipline:** Avoid borrowing more than necessary, and prioritize paying off your debt as quickly as possible.
- **Read the Fine Print:** Always read and understand the terms and conditions of any credit agreement before signing.

Now, let's dive into the various forms of credit available in Canada and the sneaky features you need to watch out for.

1. Credit Cards: The Financial Candy Store

Credit cards are like candy stores in the financial world. They offer instant gratification with a swipe, allowing you to buy now and pay later. But beware, those sweet deals often come with a bitter aftertaste — high-interest rates. Miss a payment, and you'll find yourself in the "never-ending lollipop" of debt. Always read the fine print about interest rates and fees to avoid unpleasant surprises.

Basic Facts About Credit Cards:
a. Credit Limit: The maximum amount of money a cardholder can borrow, determined by the credit card company based on factors like credit history and income.
b. Interest Rates: Typically range from 19% to 24% annual rate.

c. Statement Date vs. Due Date:

- **Statement Date:** The day the credit card issuer generates your credit card monthly statement.
- **Payment Due Date:** Typically three weeks after the statement date. It's important to make your credit card payments before the due date to avoid interest charges.

Sneaky Features to Watch Out For:

Minimum Payments Trap: Credit card companies only require card holders to make the minimum payment every month. Paying only the minimum amount due each month may keep your credit score intact, but it ensures that you remain in debt longer, incurring high-interest charges on the remaining balance. You should always aim to pay off the full balance whenever possible.

Over-the-Limit Fees: Exceeding your credit limit can result in fees (around $30). Keep an eye on your spending to avoid these unexpected charges.

Foreign Transaction Fees: Making purchases in foreign currencies can lead to additional fees. Check these fees before using your credit card abroad.

Grace Period: Interest is not charged on purchases if the full balance is paid by the due date. However, missing the due date eliminates the grace period, and interest is charged from the day of purchase, not from the due date.

Example:
Statement Cycle: January 1st to January 31st

Due Date: February 20th
Purchase: $5,000 on January 15th
Interest Rate: 22%

Scenario 1: Payment Made Before Due Date

If you pay the full $5,000 on or before February 20th, no interest is charged.

Scenario 2: Payment Made After Due Date

If payment is made on March 1st instead of February 20th, interest is charged from January 15th (the date of purchase), resulting in approximately $135 in interest. A costly mistake!

The example above highlights the consequences of missing a payment before the due date and how the grace period can work against you leading to high interest charges.

2. Line of Credit: The Financial Swiss Army Knife

A line of credit is like a Swiss Army knife for your finances—versatile, handy, and useful for a variety of purposes. The credit limit is revolving, so as soon as you pay off any balance, the full limit becomes available again. Whether you're planning a home renovation, facing an emergency, or making a major purchase, a line of credit can be a valuable tool. However, just like with a Swiss Army knife, if you're not careful, you could end up hurting yourself financially.

Key Differences from Credit Cards:

- **No Physical Card:** It works almost like a checking account. You can access the credit through online transfers, checks, or direct cash withdrawals.
- **No Grace Period:** Interest starts accruing immediately after funds are withdrawn.
- **Lower Interest Rates:** Generally lower than credit cards (Prime rate + 3% - 6%).
- **Repayment Flexibility:** The only payment required is the monthly interest payment.

- **Purposes:** Typically used for large purchases, home renovations, major appliances, or emergency funds.

Word of Caution: Because you are not required to make principal repayments, only interest payments, many people end up never paying the line of credit balance off, incurring indefinite interest payments every month. It's like throwing money into a fire! Try to pay off your line of credit balance whenever possible.

3. Personal Loans: The Reliable Friend

Personal loans are like that reliable friend who lends you money with a clear repayment plan. These loans usually come with lower interest rates compared to credit cards. However, don't get too comfortable — missing payments can damage your credit score and your relationship with the bank.

Example of How a Personal Loan Works:

- **Loan Amount:** $10,000 loan is issued to your personal checking account.
- **Interest Rate:** The bank charges you an annual interest rate of 5%.
- **Loan Term:** You agree to repay the loan over a fixed period, say three years (36 months).
- **Monthly Payments:** Based on the loan amount, interest rate, and loan term, the bank calculates your monthly payment to be $304.21.
- **Total Repayment:** By the end of the loan term, you will have repaid the original loan amount ($10,000) plus the total interest charges accrued over the term ($951.56).

Compared to a line of credit, a personal loan is not revolving, meaning once the loan is repaid, you lose access to the credit amount — you cannot borrow that $10,000 out again.

4. Payday Loans: The Financial Piranhas

Payday loans are the piranhas of the credit world — small, quick, and extremely dangerous. They offer immediate cash but at exorbitant interest rates and fees. Falling into the payday loan trap can quickly escalate, making it hard to swim out of debt. If possible, avoid payday loans at all costs.

Debt Management: Strategies for Staying Afloat

Debt management involves making informed and strategic decisions about how to handle your existing debts. Here are some practical strategies:

1. Prioritize High-Interest Debts

Focus on paying off high-interest debts first, as they accumulate interest more quickly. Make minimum payments on all debts, but direct any extra funds toward the debt with the highest interest rate.

2. Cut Back on Expenses

Look for areas where you can cut back on spending to free up more money for debt repayment. This might involve downsizing your living arrangements, reducing discretionary spending, or negotiating lower bills. These sacrifices may be painful in the short term, but they will benefit you greatly in the long run, both financially and mentally.

3. Increase Your Income

Explore ways to boost your income, such as taking on a part-time job, freelancing, or selling unused items. Use the extra income to accelerate debt repayment.

4. Consider Debt Consolidation

Consolidating high-interest debts into a single, lower-interest loan can make repayment more manageable. Here's how it works:

- **First Step:** The credit manager will sum up all your current debts, such as credit card balances, line of credit balances, and other personal loans, and consolidate them into a single loan.
- **Second Step:** They will work out a repayment plan. For example, for an annual interest of 7%, you will pay off this $50,000 consolidated loan over five years with a $990 monthly payment. If $990 per month is too high for you, they can extend the repayment period to lower the monthly payment.
- **Last Step:** They will cancel your other credit cards and lines of credit, leaving you with only one credit card with a significantly reduced credit limit. This way, you won't risk racking up high balances again.

How Does Debt Consolidation Help You?

With lower interest rates, more of your repayment goes toward reducing your debt principle, helping you pay off debts faster. Additionally, the forced repayment plan ensures that you make principal repayments on top of interest, which is crucial for getting out of debt.

Why Do Banks Agree to Loan Consolidations?

Banks agree to loan consolidations to reduce the risk of bad debt. When someone is drowning in debt and on the brink of default, banks get nervous about the possibility of not getting their money back. To avoid this, they may offer a break on the interest rate and help create a manageable repayment plan.

5. Seek Professional Help

If your debt feels like a mountain you can't climb, it's time to call in the pros. Consider reaching out to a non-profit credit counselling agency or a financial advisor. These professionals can offer personalized advice and help you craft a debt management plan that works for you. Think of them as your financial sherpas, guiding you up the mountain of debt and back down to financial stability.

Commonly asked Questions about credit

1. Prime Rate and Policy Rate – What are they, and Who Decides the Rates?

Prime rate: The prime rate is the interest rate that banks charge their most creditworthy customers for short-term loans. As of August 2024, the Canadian prime rate is 6.7%. It sets the baseline for other borrowing rates, such as credit card rates and variable-rate mortgages. In Canada, the prime rate is determined by individual banks and is influenced by factors like the Bank of Canada's Policy Rate, economic conditions, and the bank's own lending policies.

Policy Rate: The Bank of Canada decides what the policy rate is (4.5% as of August 2024). This is the interest rate that other banks are charged if they borrow money from the Bank of Canada. The Bank of Canada acts as the Lender of Last Resort for all banks, responsible for managing Canada's monetary policy, controlling inflation, and ensuring financial system stability.

When the Bank of Canada wants to stimulate the economy, it may lower the policy rate to encourage borrowing and spending. Conversely, when it wants to control inflation, it may raise the policy rate to make borrowing more expensive. The rate hikes in 2022 and 2023 were the Bank of Canada's attempt to bring down inflation.

2. What Factors Determine the Interest Rate You Could Be Charged?

Several factors influence the interest rate you receive:

- **Debt-to-Income Ratio:** The higher your debts compared to your income, the more likely the bank will slap you with a higher interest rate. This is because there's a greater chance you might not be able to repay the loan.
- **Credit History:** A stellar credit history can earn you a lower interest rate. It's like the bank rewarding you for your good financial behaviour.

- **Secured vs. Unsecured Loans:** If your loan is secured by an asset (like your car, house, or investment portfolio), you'll likely get a lower interest rate. This is because the bank can seize the assets if you fail to repay the loan. Mortgages are a classic example of secured loans.

In short, the riskier you seem to the bank, the higher the interest rates they'll charge to offset that risk they take on. So, manage your debts, keep a good credit history, and consider securing your loan with an asset to get the best rates possible.

3. What Impacts Your Credit Score?

Your credit score can open doors or slam them shut. Here's how to maintain a good credit history:

- **Payment History – Make Payments on Time:** Always pay on time. Set up automatic payments to make this easier.
- **Amounts Owed Relative to the Maximum Credit Limit – Maintain a Low Balance:** Keep your credit card balance within 10%-25% of your maximum limit. If your limit is $10,000, aim to keep your balance between $1,000 and $2,500.
- **Length of Credit History:** The longer your credit history, the better.
- **New Credit Inquiries and Applications – Keep Low Frequency:** Too many credit inquiries make you look desperate. Apply for new credit sparingly.
- **Variety of Credit:** Having different types of credit (credit cards, phone plans, lines of credit, mortgages) shows you're a versatile credit manager.

4. What Information Is Needed for Credit Applications?

When applying for credit, be prepared to provide:

Documents:

- Employment Paystubs (within the last 60-90 days)
- T4 Slips (for employees) or Income Tax and Benefit Return (for self-employed individuals)
- Notice of Assessments (NOA) from the CRA
- Statements of Your Investments

Credit Inquiry: The credit manager will ask for your consent to check your credit report and review the details with you.

5. Who Collects and Maintains Your Credit Report?

In Canada, two credit bureaus compile and maintain credit information: Equifax and TransUnion. When you open a credit account or apply for new credit, your activity is reported to these bureaus. They compile this information into your credit report, which includes details of all your credit accounts, inquiries, and payment history.

6. Common Reasons People Might Be Declined for Credit Applications

- **Thin Credit History:** This can happen to people who recently moved to Canada or have never used credit products before.
- **Poor Credit Repayment Record:** If you've missed payments in the past, it could affect your ability to obtain credit.
- **High Debt-to-Income Ratio:** If your overall debt level is too high, you may struggle to obtain more credit.

7. What to Do If Your Application Is Declined

If your application is declined, the credit manager will explain why and might suggest the following solutions:

- **Post Security:** Provide cash or an asset as security, and the bank may issue a credit card or loan with the same limit or lower. This helps build your credit record.
- **Having a Co-signer:** If someone with good credit record co-signs your loan, the lender may approve your application.
- **Improve Your Financial Situation and Try Again in 6 Months or a Year:** Reduce existing debts, make timely payments, maintain stable employment, and build up savings.

8. What are the risks to Co-Sign a Loan for Someone Else

Thinking of co-signing a loan for someone? It's a big decision, so here's what you need to know:

You're on the Hook: When you co-sign, you're agreeing to take responsibility if the primary borrower can't pay. You're legally obligated to repay the loan if the borrower defaults.

Potential Strain on Relationships: Money matters can strain relationships. If the borrower doesn't pay, it could lead to awkward interactions.

Credit Impact: The loan will appear on your credit report too. If payments are missed, your credit score will take a hit.

Debt-to-Income Ratio: Co-signing can affect your ability to borrow. Lenders will see this as your debt too, potentially lowering your borrowing power.

Examples:

Good Scenario: You co-sign a loan for your reliable niece. She makes all the payments on time, builds her credit, and after a few years, the loan is paid off. You're the family hero.

Bad Scenario: You co-sign a loan for a friend who promises to pay but then loses their job. They miss several payments, and you're left with the debt and a damaged credit score. Now they are avoiding your calls.

Conclusion

Navigating the world of credit and debt can feel like walking through a financial minefield, but with the right knowledge and careful planning, you can avoid the debt trap and use credit to your advantage. Credit, when used wisely, can be a powerful tool to help you achieve your goals, but it requires a clear strategy and a commitment to responsible borrowing.

Now that we've explored the various types of credit facilities and how to manage them effectively, it's time to take the next step in your financial journey — understanding mortgages. Mortgages are one of the most significant forms of debt many people will ever take on. In the next chapter, we will delve into the ins and outs of mortgages, including mortgage types, interest rates, and the critical factors you need to consider before committing to a mortgage. By mastering this knowledge, you can approach your home financing with confidence and ensure that your decisions support a stable and prosperous financial future.

8

MORTGAGE MAZE

Decoding Mortgages: Unraveling the Lingo and Finding Your Fit

Reading Guide Reminder: This chapter dives into the details of mortgages, which may not be immediately relevant if you're not in the market for a mortgage or if your mortgage is already paid off. Feel free to skip ahead—it won't affect your ability to grasp the other financial concepts in the book. But if you're curious or anticipate needing a mortgage in the future, you can always come back and revisit this chapter when the time comes. Enjoy!

Introduction

Are you ready to unlock the door to homeownership, but feeling overwhelmed by the world of mortgages? Welcome to the world of mortgages in Canada, where buying a home becomes possible even if you don't have all the cash up front. In this chapter, we'll break down the different types of mortgages, key terms, and the decision-making process to help you navigate the mortgage landscape with confidence. Whether you're a first-time homebuyer or looking to refinance, understanding these concepts is crucial to finding the right fit for your financial goals.

What Is a Mortgage?

A mortgage is essentially a loan that helps you buy a home. The key players in this process are you (the borrower), the lender (usually a bank or financial institution), and the house you want to buy. Here's a simple story to illustrate how a mortgage works:

Sean had his eye on Eric's house, which was listed for a million dollars. Sean had saved up $300,000, but that was just a fraction of the asking price. He turns to Eric and says, "Hey, how about I give you the $300k upfront, and for the remaining $700k, I'll pay you off over 25 years with some interest sprinkled on top."

But Eric wasn't sold on the idea. He wanted the full payment then and there. He wasn't keen on waiting for Sean to slowly chip away at the remaining balance. Instead, he suggests they head over to the bank. See, Eric had a smart plan up his sleeve. He figured if the bank could lend Sean the $700k, he'd get his full million, and Sean could sort out the repayment plan with the bank directly.

Sean liked the sound of that. So off he went to the bank, laid out his credit record and income, and wouldn't you know it, they agreed to loan him the $700k. They helped him set up a plan to pay it back in monthly instalments over the next 25 years. Because Sean wanted to have the same amount monthly payment for the next 5 years, so they set him up with a 5-year fixed rate mortgage term, at fixed interest rate, 5.14%, and a monthly payment of $4,127. Once the 5-year term is up, Sean will need to come back and re-negotiate a new interest rate with the bank.

In the end, Eric walked away with his cash, Sean got his dream house, and the bank? Well, they were happy to earn some interest on their loan. Everyone wins!

Key Mortgage Terminologies

Down Payment: The $300,000 Sean put down is called the down payment, the initial amount you pay when purchasing a home. In Canada, the minimum down payment usually starts at 5% of the home's purchase price. Your down payment size influences the type of mortgage you can get.

Mortgage Principal: The $700,000 Sean borrowed is the principal —the amount of money you need to borrow to buy your home.

Amortization: This is the period over which you'll pay off your mortgage, typically 25 or 30 years. Longer amortization means lower monthly payments but more interest paid over time, while shorter amortization means higher payments and less interest overall.

Home Equity: Home equity is the portion of your home that you truly own. It's the difference between your home's market value and the remaining balance on your mortgage. For example, if Sean's home is worth $1,000,000 and he has $700,000 left to pay on his mortgage, his home equity is $300,000.

Types of Mortgages: High-Ratio vs. Conventional

Based on the down payment size, mortgages generally fall into two categories in Canada: high-ratio and conventional.

High-Ratio Mortgage:

If your down payment is less than 20% of the home's purchase price, you're dealing with what's known as a high-ratio mortgage. The "high-ratio" refers to the fact that the mortgage amount is a large percentage of the home's value, making it a bit riskier for the lender. Because of this, the lender requires you to get mortgage loan insurance, which protects them in case you default on the loan. This insurance adds an extra cost to your mortgage payments, and it's typically provided by companies like CMHC, Sagen, or Canada Guaranty.

Conventional Mortgage:

On the other hand, if you can put down 20% or more of the home's purchase price, you're looking at a conventional mortgage. With a larger down payment, the lender views the loan as less risky, so you won't need to worry about paying for mortgage insurance. This can save you some money and make the whole mortgage process a bit simpler.

Understanding Mortgage Repayment Terms and Structures

Understanding mortgage repayment terms and structures can feel a bit overwhelming at first, but once you break them down, it starts to make more sense. Let's dive into the basics:

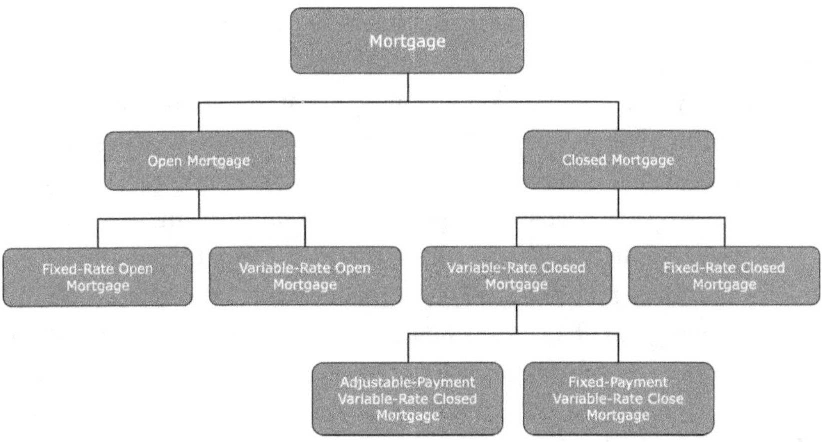

Open Mortgages vs. Closed Mortgages

Open mortgages are the most flexible option. They allow you to pay off your mortgage in full or make extra payments whenever you want, without any penalties. This kind of mortgage is perfect if you're expecting a big sum of money soon — like an inheritance or a bonus — or if you're planning to sell your home in the near future. The downside? Open mortgages typically come with much higher interest rates because of the flexibility they offer.

On the other hand, closed mortgages are much more structured. They have fixed terms and conditions, including penalties if you try to pay off the mortgage early. This type of mortgage is great if you prefer a predictable payment plan and don't expect any major changes in your financial situation. Closed mortgages usually come with lower interest rates compared to open mortgages, which is why most Canadians choose them.

Fixed-Rate vs. Variable-Rate Mortgages

When it comes to interest rates, you have two main options: fixed-rate and variable-rate mortgages.

A fixed-rate mortgage means exactly what it sounds like—the interest rate and your payment amount stay the same throughout the term, which usually ranges from 1 to 5 years. This option is ideal if you like stability and want to know exactly what your payments will be each month. The predictability is great, especially in a rising interest rate environment, but keep in mind that if you need to break your mortgage early, the prepayment penalties can be quite high.

If you're comfortable with a bit more risk, a variable-rate mortgage might be a better fit for you. With this option, the interest rate can fluctuate based on changes in the prime rate. One of the main advantages is that you often start with a lower interest rate compared to fixed-rate mortgages, which can save you money if rates decrease. However, the downside is that your payments could increase if interest rates rise. Another advantage of a variable-rate mortgage is that if you need to pay off your entire mortgage before the term ends, the penalty is typically just three months' interest, which can be significantly lower than the penalty for breaking a fixed-rate mortgage.

Adjustable-Payment Variable-Rate Mortgage vs. Fixed-Payment Variable-Rate Mortgage:

Now, to make things more confusing, within variable-rate mortgages, there are two subtypes: adjustable-payment and fixed-payment. With an adjustable-payment variable-rate mortgage, your payments change as the interest rate changes. This means your payment amount can go up or down, keeping your mortgage on track to be paid off as planned. While this helps you stay in sync with current interest rates, the downside is that fluctuating payments can make budgeting a bit tricky.

In contrast, a fixed-payment variable-rate mortgage keeps your payment amount steady, even if the interest rate fluctuates. If rates go up, more of your payment will go towards interest rather than the principal, which could mean you're not paying off your mortgage as quickly as you planned. However, this setup makes budgeting easier since your payment amount doesn't change — at least until you hit what's known as the "trigger point." If interest rates keep rising, you may eventually reach a point where you'll need to either increase your payments, make a lump sum payment, or switch to a fixed-rate mortgage with a higher payment.

Each lender has their own different trigger points. Below is a comparison of mortgage trigger points for variable-rate mortgages across major banks:

Bank	Mortgage Structure	Trigger Point
Bank of Montreal	Fixed-Payment Variable-Rate Mortgage	When the outstanding balance exceeds original mortgage balance
Bank of Nova Scotia	Adjustable-Payment Variable-Rate Mortgage	No Trigger Point
RBC	Fixed-Payment Variable-Rate Mortgage	When monthly payment is insufficient to cover interest
TD Bank	Fixed-Payment Variable-Rate Mortgage	When balance exceeds a specific property value threshold
CIBC	Fixed-Payment Variable-Rate Mortgage	When outstanding balance exceeds the original principal
National Bank of Canada	Adjustable-Payment Variable-Rate Mortgage	No Trigger Point

This table highlights the impact of the 2022-2023 interest rate increases on homeowners with variable-rate mortgages. For those with mortgages at Scotiabank and National Bank, monthly payments rose in tandem with the rate hikes. Meanwhile, RBC mortgage holders saw their payments increase, but only after their payments no longer covered the interest costs. On the other hand, customers with variable-rate mortgages at BMO, TD, and CIBC experienced minimal to no payment increases, thanks to these banks' higher thresholds for triggering payment adjustments. However, it will take longer for them to pay off their mortgages.

When choosing your mortgage provider, it's crucial to consider how each handles variable-rate mortgages, especially during periods of rising interest rates. The differences can significantly affect your monthly payments and overall financial planning.

Mortgage Structures: Traditional vs. Home Line

When it comes to structuring a mortgage, there are two common options: the traditional mortgage and the Home Line structure. Each has its own benefits and drawbacks, so it's important to understand how they work to choose the best fit for your needs.

How does a traditional mortgage work?

The traditional mortgage is what most people think of when they hear the word "mortgage." You borrow a lump sum of money from the bank, agree on a term for paying it off, and make regular payments until the loan is fully repaid. During this time, the bank holds a claim (or lien) on your property. Once you've paid off the mortgage, the bank discharges the lien, and you own your home outright with clear title. The simplicity of this structure is its biggest advantage—you have a clear path to full ownership. However, once the mortgage is paid off, you can't borrow against the equity in your home unless you take out another loan. In other words, it's not a revolving credit option.

How does a Home Line structure work?

Under a Home Line structure, you could have different components under the mortgage. Let's look at a diagram below as an example:

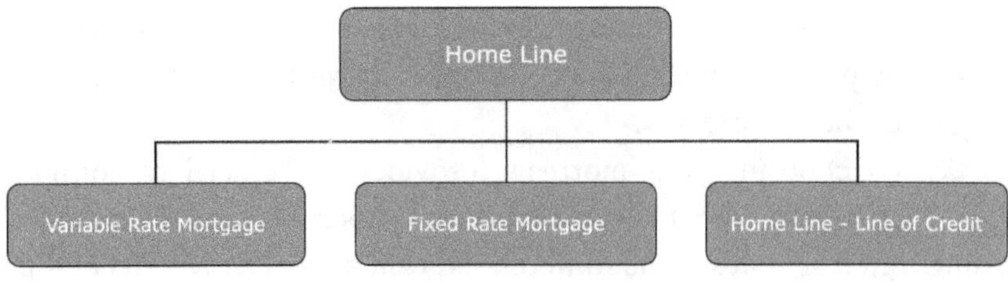

With the Home Line structure, you can have different components under it.

For example, you borrowed $500,000 to purchase your home. You choose to have 3 components:

- **Variable Rate Mortgage** for $250,000: you have the flexibility to prepay some of this principle off without severe penalty.
- **Fixed rate mortgage** for $250,000: you are able to keep part of the mortgage payment stable.
- **Home Line - Line of credit**: the credit limit for this component generally starts from $0, and then it will increase as you pay down the principle. This is a revolving line of credit secured against your home equity. There is no requirement for principal repayment, but interest payment is mandatory.

As you can see, the Home Line structure is a bit more flexible and versatile. It combines a traditional mortgage with a revolving line of credit that you can borrow against as needed. As you pay down your mortgage, you gain access to more of your home's equity, which you can borrow against when needed—for renovations, emergencies, or even investments. The main advantage of the Home Line is its flexibility, allowing you to tap into your home's equity without needing a separate loan application each time. One of the most common loan applications I worked on related to homes is bridge loan. A bridge loan is used when someone buys a new home before selling their current one. It provides the funds needed for the new home's down payment while they wait for the sale of their existing home to close. However, bridge loans come with fees, interest costs, and a more cumbersome application process, requiring both the buy and sell contracts to be submitted to the bank. With a home line of credit, you could avoid the hassle of a bridge loan altogether. Instead of going through an additional loan process, you could simply borrow from your available home equity to cover the new down payment. This convenience can make the home buying and selling process smoother.

However, the flexibility of the Home Line also comes with risks, including the potential to over-borrow, fluctuating interest rates, and stricter qualification requirements compared to a traditional mortgage.

In short, a traditional mortgage offers stability and a straightforward path to building equity, while the Home Line structure provides flexibility and ongoing access to your home's equity to borrow against. Your choice between the two should depend on your financial goals, borrowing needs, and personal tendencies — if you're prone to impulsive spending, the Home Line structure might not be the best fit for you. On the other hand, if you need access to funds for ongoing projects or potential emergencies, the Home Line structure could be a valuable option.

Ways to Save on Interest Costs and Pay Off Your Mortgage Early

If you're aiming to pay off your mortgage early and cut down on interest costs, there are several strategies you can consider to help you reach that goal:

Choose a Shorter Amortization

First, consider opting for a shorter amortization period. While this will result in higher monthly payments, you'll pay less in interest overall and own your home sooner. It's like ripping off a Band-Aid — initially uncomfortable, but you'll save money in the long run. If your budget allows, aim for a 15-year or shorter amortization period. This choice can significantly reduce your interest costs compared to a 25- or 30-year amortization.

Double Up Payments

Another effective approach is to double up your payments whenever possible. By making extra payments directly towards the principal, you reduce the amount of interest you'll pay over time. Even small additional payments can make a big difference.

Switch to Weekly or Accelerated Biweekly Payments

You might also want to switch to weekly or accelerated biweekly payments instead of sticking with a traditional monthly payment schedule. This adjustment can lead to significant interest savings over the life of your mortgage because you're essentially making an extra payment each year without feeling much of a pinch.

Make Anniversary Lump Sum Payments

And don't forget about making lump-sum payments on your mortgage anniversary. If you receive a bonus at work or a tax refund, consider putting that money directly towards your principal. These lump-sum payments can make a huge impact on reducing your mortgage balance and, in turn, the total interest you'll pay.

While these strategies can help you achieve mortgage freedom sooner, it's important to note that not all lenders offer the same flexibility with payments. So, when you're choosing a mortgage, be sure to ask about these options to make sure you can implement the strategies that work best for you.

Mortgage Lenders: Prime vs. Alternative

In Canada, mortgage lenders generally fall into two main categories: prime mortgage lenders and alternative mortgage lenders. Understanding the differences between them can help you choose the right mortgage based on your financial situation.

Prime mortgage lenders include major banks and financial institutions, like the Big Six banks, that you're likely familiar with. They offer some of the most competitive interest rates, but to qualify, you'll need a strong credit history and a stable income. The advantages of choosing a prime lender include lower interest rates, a wide variety of mortgage products, and the option for longer terms, which can provide more stability in your payments. However, the downside is that the qualification criteria are quite strict, making this option best suited for borrowers with solid credit and a steady income. As a general rule, prime lenders typically approve mortgage amounts of about 3 to 5 times your (and your spouse's, if applying together) annual income based on the current interest rate environment. If you require a mortgage larger than this, you may need to explore options with alternative mortgage lenders.

On the other hand, **alternative mortgage lenders** cater to those who might not meet the strict criteria of prime lenders. These lenders, such as Home Trust and Equitable Bank, are more flexible with their qualifications, making them a good option for borrowers with less-than-perfect credit records, irregular income, or other challenges. The pros of working with an alternative lender include tailored solutions that fit your specific situation and often a quicker approval process. However, the trade-off is that you will likely face higher interest rates and shorter mortgage terms.

So, if you have good credit and a stable income, a prime lender is probably your best bet for getting a lower interest rate and more favourable terms. But if your financial situation is a bit more complicated — whether you're self-employed, a new immigrant, or dealing with credit issues — an alternative lender might be the right choice for you, offering more flexibility in exchange for higher costs.

It's worth noting that working with a mortgage broker, as opposed to going directly to a bank, can give you access to a wider range of lender options without the hassle of shopping around for the best rates or approval terms yourself. However, keep in mind that some banks, like RBC and CIBC, don't work with mortgage brokers and instead have their own mortgage advisor channels. By understanding this and considering your unique financial situation, you'll be better equipped to make informed decisions about who to work with for your mortgage application and what terms to look for.

Did you know? The reason why prime lenders can offer mortgages at lower interest rates is they have access to a large pool of customer deposits with their extensive retail client base. When they lend out these deposits, they only need to add a modest markup to make a profit. In contrast, subprime lenders typically don't have access to such large deposits. Instead, they often need to borrow money or raise it from investors (such as Capital Direct or Gentai Capital), which incurs costs. To cover these expenses and still make a profit, alternative (subprime) lenders have to charge higher interest rates.

Conclusion: Finding Your Mortgage Match

Your mortgage is a key financial decision that can significantly impact your journey to homeownership. Understanding the various types of mortgages available in Canada and how they align with your financial goals, risk tolerance, and lifestyle is crucial. Whether you prefer the stability of a fixed-rate mortgage, the flexibility of a Home Line structure, or the accessibility of a alternative mortgage lender, the right choice will depend on your unique situation.

As you continue your financial journey, the next section of this book will explore another essential aspect of financial management: taxes in Canada. Understanding taxes will empower you to make informed decisions and optimize your financial well-being.

Part Two

TAXES – TURNING A NECESSITY INTO A STRATEGY

Strategies to Manage and Minimize Your Tax Burden

Reading Guide Reminder: This section of the book, chapter 9 to 13, dives into the world of taxes, a topic that can admittedly make some people's eyes glaze over. If the thought of taxes puts you to sleep, feel free to skip this part. While doing so might slightly impact your understanding of some tax-related planning strategies, you can always rely on a professional to handle those details for you. However, if you're curious and want to gain insight into the key tax components in Canada, stick with it and read on!

Taxes are a part of life, but in Part 2, we explore how to manage them strategically. This section provides an overview of the Canadian tax system, including how to file your income taxes and the key tax considerations for business owners. We also delve into the Alternative Minimum Tax (AMT) and present smart tax strategies that can help you minimize your tax burden. The purpose of this part is to help you navigate the tax landscape effectively, ensuring you keep more of what you earn and avoid common tax pitfalls.

9

THE TAX LANDSCAPE

Mapping Out the Canadian Tax System: Your Financial Terrain

Introduction

Jerry Seinfeld once said, "Pain is knowledge rushing in to fill a gap with great speed. When you stub your toe on the foot of the bed, that was a gap in knowledge. And you learned the bed was there real quick." Taxes might not be as physically painful as stubbing your toe, but they can certainly feel like it. Don't worry — take it slow, and this knowledge won't hurt as much.

Why should you care about taxes? Well, taxes are likely the single most expensive item on your paycheque. Over your working years, you will pay hundreds of thousands, even millions of dollars sometimes in taxes. Understanding how taxes work is crucial if you want to keep more of your hard-earned money. Knowing the basics of taxes will help you make informed decisions and ensure that you're not overpaying. Plus, a solid financial plan should always include tax planning. Offsetting some of the 30%, 40%, or even 50% income tax you're paying could yield the best investment returns you could ever have with the right strategy in place. So, gather your courage, and let's dive into some basic tax rules. "An investment in knowledge pays the best interest." – Benjamin Franklin. Ok, I think that's enough quotes to convince you to keep on reading.

The Canadian tax system is designed to fund government operations and public services, much like how we budget to cover our own needs and wants. Just like you need income to cover your expenses, the government collects taxes to fund things like healthcare, education, and infrastructure such as water pipes and roads. The Canada Revenue Agency (CRA) is the body that manages tax collection, ensuring that the funds are available to keep the country running. Our tax system is progressive, which means that the more you earn, the more you pay — a bit like a video game where the difficulty increases as you level up, except this game takes more of your coins as you progress.

There's the chatter about capital gains. Some people make it sound like the holy grail, while others treat it like the plague and tell you to avoid it at all cost. So, what exactly are capital gains, and how should you approach them?

Some people say setting up a corporation and paying yourself dividends instead of a salary will save you big tax money. Is it really that simple?

With these questions in mind, let's dive deeper into the Canadian tax system.

The Tax Sandwich

In Canada, there are multiple levels of tax. First, when money comes in, you face Federal and Provincial income tax. Second, when money goes out, you encounter consumer taxes like GST (Goods and Services Tax) and PST (Provincial Sales Tax) or HST (Harmonized Sales Tax). If you own property, you will also need to deal with annual property taxes paid to your municipal government. It's like a tax sandwich, with you in the middle.

Income tax is the main component of the Canadian tax system, and it comes in two layers: federal and provincial. Individuals are taxed based on their total income, which includes employment income, rental income, and investment income, among others. The tax rates increase as income rises.

For example, in 2023, the federal tax brackets range from 15% on the first $49,020 of income to 33% on income over $216,511. In British Columbia, provincial tax rates start at 5.06% for income up to $45,654 and rise to 20.5% for income over $240,716. The province with the highest combined income tax rate is Quebec, where it reaches 58.75% on income over $119,910, while Nunavut has the lowest combined rate at 44.50% on income over $165,429.

Understanding Marginal and Average Tax Rates

When discussing taxes, two terms often come up: marginal tax rate and average tax rate.

Your marginal tax rate is the percentage of tax you pay on each additional dollar you earn. For instance, if your income is $100,000, your marginal tax rate could be 36.5%, combining federal and provincial taxes. This means that if you earn an extra $1,000, you'll pay $365 in taxes on that amount.

On the other hand, your average tax rate is the total tax you pay divided by your total income. For example, if you earn $100,000 and pay $20,219 in taxes, your average tax rate is 20.22%. It's important to understand both rates, but keep in mind that your marginal tax rate determines how much additional tax you'll pay on any extra income. This is particularly crucial when considering tax savings on RRSP contributions, as we will explore later.

Tax-Free Basic Personal Amount (BPA)

The Basic Personal Amount (BPA) is essentially a "tax-free gift" from the government, allowing you to earn a certain amount of income without paying any federal income tax on it. For 2024, the Federal BPA is set at $15,705 for individuals earning $173,205 or less. For example, in British Columbia, the provincial BPA is $12,580 for those earning $165,430 or less. These amounts are adjusted annually, providing a cushion to ensure that not all of your income is subject to tax.

This means that if you or your children work part-time during the year and earn up to $12,580, you won't have to pay much, if any, tax on that income. This concept also applies to investment income from Registered Education Savings Plans (RESPs), which are generally not taxed, making them an effective way to save for education. We will talk about that in more details in chapter 20.

Investment Income: Interest, Dividends, and Capital Gains

Investment income can come in various types, but the three main types are interest income, dividend income, and capital gains. Each of these is taxed differently.

Interest Income:

Interest income from investments is treated like regular employment income and taxed accordingly. For example, if you earn $1,000 in interest, and your marginal tax rate is 30%, you'll pay $300 in taxes.

Dividend Income:

When you receive dividend income from Canadian corporations, you may benefit from a tax credit, which makes Canadian dividends more tax-efficient than regular income or interest. Here's a simplified calculation for federal level tax:

- If you receive $1,000 in dividends, you must gross it up by 38%, making it $1,380.
- You then pay tax on this amount at your marginal rate, the same 30%, which equals $414.
- However, you also get a tax credit of 15% on the grossed-up amount, reducing your tax by $207, so you owe only $207 in taxes on the $1,000 dividend.

Compare $207 in taxes on $1,000 of Canadian dividend income to $300 in taxes on the same amount of interest income, and you can clearly see the tax advantage of dividends.

It's important to note that only Canadian dividend income benefits from the preferred tax credit treatment. If your dividend income comes from a foreign country, like the U.S., it will be taxed the same as interest income, without any tax credit applied.

Capital Gains:

Capital gains are profits from the sale of assets like stocks, companies or real estate. The tax you pay on capital gains has recently changed, and here's the new rule:

For individuals, the first $250,000 in capital gains is taxed at an inclusion rate of 50%, meaning only 50% of that capital gains is taxable, but any amount above $250,000 is now taxed at a new inclusion rate of 66.67%. We will see an example to show how inclusion rate works:

> Grace sold her investment property and had a capital gain of $500,000. Her marginal tax rate is 53.5%. The tax owing on this capital gain is calculated as following:
> For the first $250,000:
> $250,000 x 50% x 53.5% = $66,875
> For the remaining $250,000:
> $250,000 x 66.67% x 53.5% = $89,171
> Total capital gain is $156,046.

Corporations and trusts now face a 66.67% inclusion rate from the first dollar. This change is intended to increase tax revenue for the government to fund housing initiatives.

Let's use the same example from previously:
If you sold your investment at a $1,000 gain. Only **50%** of that is taxable. Your marginal tax rate is the same 30%, the tax payable on this gain is:
$1,000 x 50% x 30% = **$150**

To sum it up, as we've seen above, even with the same $1,000 investment income and a consistent marginal tax rate of 30%, the amount of tax you owe can vary depending on the type of income:

- Interest income: **$300**
- Canadian eligible Dividend income: **$207**
- Capital Gain: **$150**

The tax savings from Dividend Income and Capital Gains are clear. Of course, it would be even better if there were no capital gains tax at all, like in places such as Hong Kong, Monaco, or the Cayman Islands. However, here in Canada, capital gains remain one of the most tax-efficient types of income, especially if you're in a high marginal tax bracket. You can strategically plan your investment portfolio to take full advantage of this benefit.

Understanding these components of the Canadian tax system can help you navigate your tax obligations more effectively. Whether it's choosing investments that offer better tax efficiency or knowing when to sell assets to minimize tax liability, being informed is key. Tax planning should be an integral part of your overall financial strategy because it directly impacts how much of your income you keep.

Conclusion

Taxes can seem overwhelming, but they're just another part of managing your finances. By learning the basics and staying informed about changes in tax laws, you can make smarter decisions that will benefit you in the long run.

In the next chapter, we'll dive deeper into Income Tax Returns and Filing, where we'll discuss the timing, general process, and tips for maximizing your refund. It's all about ensuring you don't leave any money on the table when it comes to your taxes.

THE ANNUAL TAX DANCE

Filing Your Income Tax: The Art of Staying on the CRA's Good Side

Introduction

My parents are nearing their 60s. Lived their whole life in China. Guess how many times they have filed personal tax returns? None. They never had to — any taxes they owed were automatically deducted from their paycheques (they do have a lot of other things to deal with though). But in Canada, most of us don't have that luxury. With all the tax forms we must file every year, it sometimes feels like we're training to become accountants.

When to File Your Tax

In Canada, individuals generally need to file their taxes annually by April 30th. If you miss this deadline, the taxman starts charging interest on any amount you owe. As of March 2024, the prescribed interest rate is a hefty 10%. On top of that, there's a late-filing penalty of 5% of the balance owing, plus 1% for each month you're late, up to 12 months. That means if you delay filing for a year, you could be hit with penalties of up to 17% plus interest. The lesson here is simple: file on time or face the music.

For most people with a single full-time job, there's usually no additional tax to pay at the end of the year because their employer deducts taxes from each paycheque. So, even if you file your taxes after the deadline, you're unlikely to face any penalties as long as you don't owe any extra tax. However, if you have multiple jobs, rental properties, investments, or are self-employed, you might owe taxes at the end of the year. In that case, it's crucial to file on time.

For corporations, the tax filing deadline is within six months of their fiscal year-end. For example, if the fiscal year ends on January 31st, taxes must be filed by July 30th. However, corporate taxes are typically due within two or three months after the fiscal year-end, depending on the business type. Many businesses opt to pay quarterly tax instalments to avoid penalties.

Understanding Personal Income Tax Calculation

Fortunately, you don't have to calculate your taxes manually. Online software can do the math for you as long as you input your tax slips correctly. If you prefer, you can hire an accountant to handle everything for you. But understanding how income tax is calculated can help you better grasp the strategies to reduce your tax bill — strategies we'll discuss in later chapters. Knowledge is power, especially when it can save you money!

Here's a simplified guide to how personal income tax is calculated:

1. Calculate Employment Income:

Start by adding up all sources of employment income, including salary, bonuses, and other taxable benefits. Think of this as gathering all the pieces of your income puzzle.

2. Calculate Investment Income:

Next, include income from investments, such as interest, dividends, and capital gains.

3. Determine Total Income:

Combine your employment income with your investment income to find your total earnings.

4. Calculate Taxable Income: From your total income, deduct eligible expenses and contributions, such as medical expenses, RRSP contributions, tuition credits and child care expenses etc. This gives you your taxable income—a bit like applying a discount to your total income.

5. Apply Federal and Provincial Tax Rates: Both the federal and provincial governments have their own tax brackets and rates. Apply these rates to your taxable income to determine how much tax you owe. It's a bit like navigating through a tax obstacle course.

6. Combine Federal and Provincial Taxes: Add up the federal and provincial taxes to get your total income tax.

7. Subtract Any Available Tax Credits: After determining your total income tax, you can reduce this amount by applying any tax credits you're eligible for. Tax credits directly reduce the amount of tax you owe, making them very valuable. These credits can include charitable donations, Canada caregiver credit, disability tax credit etc.

Example of Personal Income Tax Calculation

Let's break this down with a simple example. Suppose you live in British Columbia, your employment income is $50,000, and you have $10,000 in investment income, which includes $7,000 in capital gains, $2,000 in interest, and $1,000 in eligible dividends. You also made $2,000 in RRSP contributions. Here's how it all adds up:

Step 1-3:

Total Income:

- Employment income: $50,000
- Capital gain (50% taxable): $7,000 x 50% = $3,500
- Dividend income (1.38 gross-up): $1,000 x 1.38 = $1,380
- Interest income: $1,000

Total income: $50,000 + $3,500 + $1,380 + $1,000 = $55,880

Step 4: Taxable Income: $55,880 - $2,000 (RRSP contribution) = $53,880

Step 5:

Federal Tax:

The federal tax brackets for 2023 are as follows:

- $0 to $53,359 of income: 15%

- More than $53,359 to $106,717: 20.5%

Federal tax payable: $53,359 x 15% + ($53,880 - $53,359) x 20.5% = $8,110.66

Provincial Tax (BC):

BC tax brackets for 2023:

- $0 to $45,654 of income: 5.06%

- $45,654.01 to $91,310 of income: 7.70%

Provincial tax payable: $45,654 x 5.06% + ($53,880 - $45,654) x 7.70% = $2,943.50

Step 6 -7:

Total Income Tax:

Add the federal and provincial taxes and subtract the dividend tax credit:

$8,110.66 + $2,943.50 − $1,380 x 15% = **$10,847.16**

Tax Savings with RRSP:

By contributing $2,000 to your RRSP, you've saved $564 in tax. Calculation below:

$2,000 x (20.5% + 7.7%) = $564

The higher your marginal tax rate, the more income tax you save with RRSP contributions.

Note: This is a simplified example, and various factors, credits and deductions can impact your final tax liability

If I lost you in the above nerdy calculations. Not to worry. Here are the key points:

- **Dividend Income and Capital Gains:** These are generally more tax-efficient than employment income or interest income.
- **RRSP Contributions:** it reduces your tax payable substantially especially when you are in a high-income tax bracket.

While tax calculations might not be the most thrilling topic, understanding these basics can help you save a nice chunk of change. And remember, every penny saved is a penny earned!

What Happens After You File Your Tax Return?

So, you've filed your taxes. What happens next? Here's a step-by-step breakdown of what you can expect after hitting that "submit" button:

1. CRA Receives and Reviews Your Tax Return: After you file, the CRA will receive and begin processing your tax return. This is an automated process, so it's usually quite fast. However, if there are any discrepancies, unusual claims, or if you've been flagged for review, the CRA may take a closer look and potentially conduct an tax audit, which could slow things down.

2. Notice of Assessment (NOA): Once your tax return is processed, you'll receive a Notice of Assessment (NOA). This document is crucial — it's like your tax report card. The NOA outlines your income, the tax you paid, any credits you received, and whether you owe money or are getting a refund. The NOA will also show your Registered Retirement Savings Plan (RRSP) contribution room available for the next year. This is important information if you're planning to make RRSP contributions to reduce your taxable income. It's important to carefully review your NOA to ensure everything matches up with the tax return you filed. If there are discrepancies, you might need to file an adjustment request.

3. Refund or Payment: If your Notice of Assessment (NOA) shows that you've overpaid your taxes, you'll receive a refund. If you filed online and chose direct deposit, the refund usually arrives within two weeks. However, it may take longer if you filed a paper return or didn't set up direct deposit. On the other hand, if you owe money, the Canada Revenue Agency (CRA) expects payment by the due date, typically April 30th unless specified otherwise on your NOA. To avoid interest charges, it's wise to pay any outstanding balance as soon as possible.

4. Interest and Penalties: If you owe taxes and haven't paid them by the deadline, the CRA will start charging interest on the unpaid balance. This point can't be stressed enough: filing your taxes on time is crucial to avoid any unnecessary penalties. By staying on top of your deadlines, you can save yourself from the additional stress of accumulating interest and penalties.

5. Keep Your Documents Safe: Once everything is processed and you've either received your refund or paid your taxes, it's time to put your documents in a safe place. The CRA recommends keeping your tax records for at least six years, as they may request to review them during that period. This includes your NOA, tax slips, receipts, and any other relevant documents.

Conclusion

Navigating the world of taxes doesn't have to be overwhelming. With a little understanding and the right tools, you can manage your taxes efficiently and even find ways to save. Now that you have a grasp on personal income tax and the importance of filing on time, we'll move on to explore key tax components for businesses in the next chapter. This will be especially useful if you're a business owner or are considering starting your own business. So, stay tuned — understanding taxes is an investment that pays off in the long run!

TAX TACTICS FOR BUSINESS OWNERS

Key Tax Considerations for Businesses

Reading Guide Reminder: This chapter is tailored for business owners or those considering whether to incorporate their business. If that doesn't apply to you, feel free to skip ahead — it won't affect your overall planning. You can always revisit this chapter if and when it becomes relevant to your situation.

Introduction

Have you ever wondered how your choice of business structure — whether as a sole proprietor or a corporation — affects your tax obligations? Now that we've explored the ins and outs of personal taxes, it's time to shift our focus to the tax landscape for businesses. Understanding these tax implications is crucial for making decisions that can significantly impact your bottom line. In this chapter, we'll delve into the key tax components for businesses, with a particular focus on Sole Proprietorships and Corporations.

Sole Proprietorship: The Simple Start

A sole proprietorship is the most straightforward business structure. It's owned and operated by one person, and it doesn't require formal registration. Your business income is reported on your personal tax return, which means you'll be taxed at your personal income tax rate. While this simplicity is appealing, it also means that you, as the owner, are personally liable for all business debts and obligations. Essentially, your business and personal finances are one and the same.

Corporations: The Separate Entity

A corporation, on the other hand, is a separate legal entity from its owners. It's owned by shareholders and managed by directors and officers, who can all be the same person — yes, you can be your own boss, employee, and shareholder! Unlike a sole proprietorship, a corporation requires formal registration and has more complex legal and tax requirements. The corporation itself is taxed on its profits, and then shareholders are taxed on any dividends they receive. While this may seem like double taxation, there are strategic advantages to incorporating, which we'll explore later.

Taxes for Corporations: A Closer Look

For simplicity, we'll focus on Canadian-Controlled Private Corporations (CCPC). These are private companies controlled by Canadian citizens and residents, which do not include publicly traded companies listed on stock exchanges.

Federal Business Tax Rates

The basic federal business tax rate is a daunting 38%, but don't panic just yet—there are deductions available:

- **10% Federal Tax Abatement**: This applies to income earned inside Canada.

- **13% General Tax Reduction**: This is available for most businesses, excluding investment corporations and personal services businesses (which are essentially individuals providing services to one main client).

After these deductions, the net federal tax rates look more reasonable:

- **Basic business income**: **15%**
- **Small business deduction tax rate**: **9%**

The Small Business Deduction

The Small Business Deduction (SBD) is a significant tax advantage, applying to the first $500,000 of active business income. This reduces the net federal tax rate to just 9% for that portion of your income. Income exceeding this $500,000 threshold is taxed at the general business rate of 15%.

Provincial or Territorial Tax Rates

In addition to federal taxes, corporations are also subject to provincial or territorial taxes. These rates vary by location and are divided into two categories:

- **Lower Rate**: Applies to income eligible for the federal small business deduction, i.e. the first $500,000 business income.
- **Higher Rate**: Applies to income exceeding the small business deduction amount.

For instance, in British Columbia, the lower rate is 2%, and the higher rate is 12%. In Ontario, the lower rate is 3.2%, and the higher rate is 11.5%.

Let's consider an example:
If your business income in BC is $600,000, your total business income tax would include:

- **Federal Tax**: $500,000 x 9% + ($600,000 - $500,000) x 15% = $60,000
- **BC Provincial Tax**: $500,000 x 2% + ($600,000 - $500,000) x 12% = $22,000
- **Total business income tax**: $60,000 + $22,000 = $82,000

Your total business income tax in this case is $82,000, resulting in an average tax rate of 13.67% ($82,000 / $600,000).

Impact of Passive Income on Small Business Deduction (SBD)

One important tax rule to keep in mind is the Passive Income Rule. According to this rule, if your corporation earns more than $50,000 in passive income in a year, the amount eligible for the Small Business Deduction starts to decrease. Once passive income reaches $150,000, the deduction disappears entirely. As a result, higher corporate tax rates will apply to your entire business income, reducing the tax deferral benefits of incorporation. This rule is designed to address the practice of retaining cash within the corporation and investing it to generate additional income. By doing so, business owners can defer personal income taxes while allowing their money to grow within the corporation. To mitigate the impact of the passive income rule, a common strategy is to invest the company's cash in capital gain-oriented investments, such as growth stocks, rather than in dividend- or interest-generating investments. This approach helps reduce regular passive income and allows greater control over the timing of capital gains realization.

Passive Income Tax Rate

Investment income is considered **passive income** (unlike active business income) and is taxed at a higher rate than active business income. In Canada, the combined federal and provincial tax rate on passive income can be over 50%, depending on the province. Corporate passive income generally includes:

- Interest income
- Dividend income
- Capital gains
- Rental income
- Royalties

Capital Dividend Account

When a corporation generates capital gains, only 66.7% of those gains are taxable, while the remaining 33.3% is non-taxable. This non-taxable portion is added to a special account within the corporation called the Capital Dividend Account (CDA). The CDA is an important tool because it allows the corporation to pay out tax-free dividends to its shareholders. In addition to capital gains, the CDA also receives the tax-free portion of the death benefit from a corporate-owned life insurance policy. This amount can also be distributed tax-free to shareholders.

The CDA is a valuable mechanism for improving tax efficiency and is particularly beneficial for estate planning. It allows business owners to transfer corporate assets to their shareholders or estates without triggering significant tax liabilities. This makes it an effective strategy for preserving and passing on wealth within a corporation.

Lifetime Capital Gains Exemption

The Lifetime Capital Gains Exemption (LCGE) is a valuable tax benefit that allows business owners to shelter a portion of their capital gains from taxation when they sell their business. As of June 2024, the exemption limit is $1.25 million. This exemption can be particularly advantageous for business owners looking to sell their business and retire. However, there are many detailed rules and requirements around this. It's better to consult a financial or tax professional at least 2 years before your planned business sale to ensure you are eligible for this tax exemption.

Should you incorporate your business to save on Tax? - The Theory of Tax Integration

Now, let us tackle a common question: "Does setting up a corporation and paying yourself dividends instead of operating as a sole proprietorship save you big on taxes?" The government has implemented something called the Theory of Tax Integration to ensure that the total tax cost is roughly the same, whether you earn income as a sole proprietorship or corporation.

Here's how it works: When a corporation pays taxes at the lower small business rate, the dividends paid to shareholders are considered "non-eligible dividends" and are taxed at a higher rate than "eligible dividends" (typically paid by public companies). This ensures that the overall tax paid, both at the corporate and personal levels, is comparable to what would be paid on salary income or sole proprietorship income.

Comparing Taxes: Sole Proprietorship vs. Corporation

Let's compare the income tax payable for a sole proprietorship versus a corporation in BC:

- Sole Proprietorship: On a $600,000 income, personal income tax would amount to $277,321.
- Corporation: Here, the tax is paid in two layers. The first layer is the corporate income tax, which would be $82,000. The second layer is the personal income tax on the dividend payout, totalling $206,165. Together, this adds up to $288,165.

The difference is not significant — just 1.8% more if you incorporate your business and pay yourself through dividends. This demonstrates that the theory of tax integration in Canada, while not perfect, is fairly effective.

The tax payable for a sole proprietorship is quite similar to that of a business owner who incorporates but chooses to pay themselves entirely in salary instead of dividends. Therefore, there isn't a significant tax saving whether you opt for a full salary or dividends.

However, If you're incorporated, you have the advantage of controlling the timing and amount of salary or dividend payments, which can help create tax efficiency. In the earlier example, we assumed all business income was paid out as dividends in the same year, but in reality, business owners rarely do this. Instead, you can defer dividend payments if you expect a high personal income for the year to avoid pushing yourself into a higher tax bracket. This flexibility allows you to strategically manage your income, optimizing your tax situation and minimizing your overall tax burden.

Did you know? Unlike salary income, dividend income does not generate any RRSP contribution room. If all your income comes from dividends, you won't accumulate any RRSP room for that year. Therefore, a balanced approach, combining salary and dividends, might be more beneficial for long-term financial planning.

To Incorporate or Not to Incorporate?

Deciding whether to incorporate your business involves weighing the pros and cons. Incorporation offers advantages like controlling dividend timing, deferring personal taxes, and separating personal and business finances. However, it also adds complexity and costs. The government's tax integration and passive income rules ensure that the tax advantages of incorporation are not as significant as they might seem at first glance.

Incorporating your business is not a one-size-fits-all decision. It requires careful consideration of your business's unique circumstances and long-term goals. Consulting with a tax professional can help you make the best choice for your situation.

Conclusion

As we conclude this chapter, you're now equipped with a solid understanding of the key tax components for businesses. Whether you're flying solo or leading a corporate empire, understanding these structures and rules can help you navigate the tax landscape more effectively. In the next chapter, we'll explore a tax concept known as the Alternative Minimum Tax (AMT). This tax mechanism is designed to ensure that individuals with significant income, who might otherwise reduce their tax liability through various deductions and credits, still pay a minimum level of tax. By being aware of MAT, you can better anticipate its impact and plan accordingly to minimize any potential surprises.

(12)

NAVIGATING THE AMT (ALTERNATIVE MINIMUM TAX)

What the Alternative Minimum Tax Means for You

Reading Guide Reminder: This chapter is especially relevant for those who experience significant capital gains, such as from selling a business, investment properties, or a substantial investment portfolio. If that doesn't apply to you at the moment, feel free to skip ahead — it won't affect your overall financial planning. You can always revisit this chapter if and when it becomes relevant to your situation.

Introduction

In 1986, the Canadian government introduced the Alternative Minimum Tax (AMT) as a catch all to ensure that everyone, particularly those with high capital gains income, contributes their fair share of taxes. It's the CRA's effort to make sure no one is left behind — a backup plan designed to catch those who might otherwise slip through the cracks thanks to various deductions and credits. This chapter will guide you through the essentials of AMT, helping you understand how it works and how it might affect your tax planning.

How It Works: Two Methods to Calculate Taxes

When it comes to calculating taxes, the government uses two methods to ensure fairness:

1. **Regular Calculation**: This is the standard method that most of us are familiar with. Your tax is calculated based on your total income, minus eligible deductions and credits.
2. **Alternative Calculation**: Under the Alternative Minimum Tax (AMT) rules, your taxes are recalculated to determine what you would owe if certain tax benefits were limited.

Each year, your taxes are calculated using both the regular method and the Alternative Minimum Tax (AMT) method. The CRA will require you to pay whichever amount is higher. For most people, the regular calculation results in higher taxes, so the AMT doesn't usually apply. However, if you've claimed significant deductions and credits, or triggered significant capital gains, the AMT might kick in, and you'll end up paying the difference.

AMT as "Tax Paid in Advance"

If you find yourself paying AMT, don't think of it as a permanent loss. Instead, consider it a "tax paid in advance." You can potentially recoup this amount over the next seven years if your regular tax payments exceed your AMT during that time. However, if your regular tax payable never exceeds the AMT, it becomes a permanent part of your tax liability. This is why careful planning is crucial, especially when dealing with capital gains.

How AMT is Calculated

The AMT rate is set at 20.5%, with an exemption threshold aligned with the start of the fourth federal tax bracket, which is approximately $173,000 in 2024. This threshold will be adjusted for inflation over time. The AMT primarily targets individuals with high capital gains income, ensuring that they contribute a minimum amount of tax. If your capital gains are below $173,000, you won't be subject to AMT.

Here's a simplified comparison of how capital gains are treated under regular income tax and the Alternative Minimum Tax (AMT) regime:

Description	Regular income tax	AMT regime
General rate, including capital gains below $250,000 (for individuals only)	50%	100%
General rate, including capital gains above $250,000 (for individuals only)	67%	100%
Donation of capital property (other than publicly listed securities) to a registered charity	50%	100%
Qualified small business corporation (QSBC) shares	50%	100%
Donation of publicly listed securities	0%	30%
Net capital loss carryforward rate	50%	50%
Lifetime capital gains exemption rate	50%	70%
Stock option benefit inclusion rate	50%	100%

Let's break this down with a simple example. Imagine you have a capital gain of $250,000 in 2024, and your average tax rate is 22%. For simplicity, let's ignore any other income.

Regular Tax Calculation:
$250,000 x 50% (inclusion rate) x 22% = $27,500
Alternative Minimum Tax Calculation:
($250,000 - $173,000) x 100% x 20.5% = $15,785

Since the regular tax calculation results in a higher tax liability ($27,500) than the AMT calculation ($15,785), you would owe the regular tax amount of $27,500.

The AMT is expected to affect only about 32,000 Canadians annually and is projected to generate nearly $3 billion in additional revenue over five years starting in 2024. This is a significant measure for ensuring tax fairness and boosting government revenue.

The Takeaway

While the AMT is designed to ensure that everyone pays their fair share of taxes, it can complicate tax planning, particularly if you're selling a business or claiming the Lifetime Capital Gains Exemption (LCGE). To navigate this tax maze effectively, it's essential to keep a close eye on your deductions and credits and consider seeking professional advice.

Conclusion

In this chapter, we've delved into the complexities of the Alternative Minimum Tax (AMT) and how it ensures that everyone pays a minimum level of tax, even when significant deductions and credits are claimed. We also explored how AMT works as a "tax paid in advance," potentially allowing you to reclaim some of it in future years. Remember, tax rules are constantly evolving, and staying informed is key to optimizing your tax situation.

As we wrap up this chapter, we're shifting our focus toward practical strategies for managing and minimizing your tax burden. In the next chapter, we'll explore actionable tips and strategies to help you keep more of your hard-earned money. Stay tuned as we uncover ways to optimize your tax situation and make smarter financial decisions.

(13)

SMART TAX MOVES

Tax Strategies for Canadians: How to Keep More of What You Earn

Introduction

Have you ever wondered if there's a way to make taxes work more in your favour? After navigating the complex terrain of the Canadian tax system, exploring the ins and outs of income tax filing, and delving into key tax components for businesses and the concept of Alternative Minimum Tax (AMT), you might be asking yourself this very question. By now, you should have a good understanding of how taxes work in Canada and the various obligations that come with them. But knowing the tax system is only half the battle. The next step is learning how to use this knowledge to your advantage. In this chapter, we'll dive into some practical tax-saving strategies that can help you make the most of the tax rules and enhance your financial well-being.

1. Maximize Your RRSP Contributions

The Registered Retirement Savings Plan (RRSP) is one of the most powerful tools available to Canadians for tax-deferred growth. Contributions to your RRSP are tax-deductible, which means they can reduce your taxable income in the year you contribute. Here's how to make the most of it:

101

- **Contribute the Maximum Allowable Amount:** Each year, you can contribute up to 18% of your previous year's income, up to a specified limit. The more you contribute, the more you can reduce your taxable income.
- **Delay Withdrawals:** Funds within an RRSP grow tax-free until you withdraw them, typically in retirement when your tax rate may be lower. Consider delaying withdrawals until you're in a lower tax bracket to minimize the tax hit.
- **Spousal RRSPs:** If one spouse earns significantly more than the other, contributing to a spousal RRSP can help balance retirement income and reduce the overall tax burden during retirement.

2. Utilize Your TFSA for Tax-Free Growth

The Tax-Free Savings Account (TFSA) allows you to earn investment income and capital gains without paying any tax. Contributions are not tax-deductible, but withdrawals are entirely tax-free, making it an excellent vehicle for both short-term and long-term savings.

- **Maximize Annual Contributions:** Each year, the government sets a contribution limit. Contributing the maximum allowable amount ensures that all your investment income is sheltered from tax.
- **Invest Wisely:** Since withdrawals are tax-free, a TFSA is an ideal place for growth-oriented investments, such as stocks or high yield bonds. Consider prioritizing higher-yield investments in your TFSA to take full advantage of the tax-free growth.

3. Prioritize Capital Gains and Canadian Dividends Over Interest Income

When it comes to investing, not all income is taxed equally. Understanding the tax implications of different types of income can significantly impact your tax liability:

- **Capital Gains:** As we have discussed, only 50% of capital gains are taxable, making them more tax-efficient than interest income, which is fully taxable. Whenever possible, focus on investments that generate capital gains.
- **Canadian Dividends:** Dividends from Canadian corporations' benefit from the dividend tax credit, which can reduce the effective tax rate on this income. Prioritizing investments that pay Canadian dividends can provide better after-tax returns.
- **Minimize Interest Income:** Since interest income is fully taxable at your marginal rate, it's generally less tax-efficient. Consider holding interest-bearing investments, such as bonds or GICs, in your RRSP or TFSA to shelter the income from taxes.

4. Strategic Income Splitting

Income splitting involves distributing income within a family to take advantage of lower tax brackets. While direct income splitting is limited, there are several legal strategies to achieve this:

- **Spousal Loans:** If one spouse is in a lower tax bracket, consider a spousal loan at the CRA-prescribed rate to allow investment income to be taxed at the lower rate. This strategy works best when there is a substantial difference in the marginal tax rates of the two spouses and when the prescribed interest rate is low, maximizing the tax-saving potential.
- **Retirement Income Splitting:** In Canada, many types of retirement income can be split between spouses. If you and your partner are retired and one of you has a higher income, you can consult a tax professional to learn how to split your retirement income.
- **Family Trusts:** A family trust can allocate income to family members in lower tax brackets, though this strategy is complex and requires careful planning.

5. Pay Yourself a Combination of Salary and Dividends

If you're a business owner, how you pay yourself can have significant tax implications. A mix of salary and dividends can be a tax-efficient way to draw income from your corporation:

- **Salary:** Paying yourself a salary allows you to contribute to the Canada Pension Plan (CPP) and build RRSP contribution room. It's also tax-deductible for your business, reducing corporate income tax.
- **Dividends:** Dividends are taxed at a lower rate than salary because of the dividend tax credit. However, they don't generate CPP contributions or RRSP room.
- **Balance Your Income:** Striking the right balance between salary and dividends can minimize your overall tax burden while providing the benefits of both income types.

6. Be Strategic About the Timing of Income

The timing of income can impact the amount of tax you pay. Here's how to be strategic:

- **Defer Income:** If you anticipate being in a lower tax bracket next year, consider deferring bonuses or other income until the following year to reduce your overall tax liability.
- **Consider Corporate Deferral:** If you own a corporation, leaving income in the corporation rather than drawing it as a salary or dividend can defer personal tax liability until a later, more opportune time.

7. Leverage Tax Credits and Deductions

Canada offers various tax credits and deductions that can reduce your taxable income. Some key ones to consider include:

- **Charitable Donations:** If there are charitable causes you would like to support, donations to registered charities are eligible for tax credits. Bunching donations into a single year can maximize this credit.
- **Medical Expenses:** You can claim a tax credit for eligible medical expenses that exceed a certain percentage of your income. Keep detailed records to ensure you claim all eligible expenses.
- **Home Office Deduction:** If you are required to work from home, you may be eligible to deduct certain expenses related to your home office, reducing your taxable income.
- **Smith Maneuver:** The Smith Maneuver is a legal tax strategy that allows homeowners to make interest on their residential mortgage tax-deductible. It involves converting your mortgage into an investment loan by re-borrowing against the equity in your home to invest, making the interest on the loan deductible. This strategy can help accelerate mortgage repayment while providing tax benefits.

8. Review Your Tax Strategy Regularly

Tax laws change, and your financial situation evolves. Regularly reviewing your tax strategy with a qualified accountant or financial advisor ensures you're taking advantage of all available opportunities and adjusting your plan as needed.

Conclusion

Tax planning is a crucial component of financial management. Whether it's maximizing your RRSP and TFSA contributions, prioritizing capital gains and dividends over interest income, or strategically balancing salary and dividends as a business owner, these strategies can significantly reduce your tax burden and boost your savings. Filing your taxes on time, taking advantage of income splitting, and leveraging tax credits and deductions are all steps you can take to ensure you're not paying more than you need to.

However, be aware that tax rules are constantly changing, keeping our 200,000 accountants in Canada gainfully employed and perpetually busy. Therefore, it's wise to consult with professionals who can tailor strategies to your specific situation. They can help you navigate the complexities and ensure you're taking full advantage of the tax-saving opportunities available to you.

As we transition to the next section of this book, we'll explore how to make the most of the money you have saved. After all, it's not just about keeping more of what you earn; it's also about putting your money to work to secure your financial future.

"Not-so-fun fact" about the Canadian tax system: You've probably heard of "income splitting," which often means balancing incomes between spouses to lower overall taxes. In Canada, many rules, like the attribution rules, restrict this practice. Unlike in the U.S., where spouses can file tax jointly to equalize income and pay less tax, Canadian working couples can't split their income for tax benefits. However, if you're retired, you can split income with your spouse. Divorced? The spouse paying alimony can deduct those payments and pay less tax. So, it's only married working couples who can't split income to save on taxes. Seems a bit unfair, eh? Maybe one day the government will change the rules when they need to win votes — or even boost the birth rate by making married life a little more tax-friendly! Until then, Canadian working couples will have to find other ways to keep their taxes in check.

Part Three

GROWING YOUR FINANCIAL GARDEN

Planting the Seeds of Wealth: Cultivate, Nurture, and Watch It Grow

Part 3 focuses on growing your wealth through smart budgeting, investing, and saving strategies. It covers everything from the basics of budgeting and building an emergency fund to investment options like mutual funds, ETFs, and segregated funds. You'll also explore lesser-known investment vehicles, learn about registered accounts like RRSPs and TFSAs, and understand how to assess and manage market risk. This part serves as a comprehensive guide to growing your wealth, helping you make informed decisions that align with your financial goals.

(14)

BUDGETING 101

Our Personal Finance GPS: The Key to Financial Freedom

Introduction

Have you ever found yourself wondering, "Where does all my money go?" If you've ever reached the end of the month and realized that despite all your hard work, you're still living paycheque to paycheque, you're not alone. Budgeting might not sound like the most exciting task, but it's the secret sauce to taking control of your finances and building wealth. Unless you are a trust fund baby, or married into wealth, the key to financial freedom is spending less than you earn. So, how do you manage your money effectively without feeling restricted? One simple and effective approach is the 50/30/20 rule, a budgeting method that helps you allocate your income in a balanced way — covering your essentials, indulging in some wants, and saving for your future. Let's dive in and see how it works.

50% for Needs:

This portion of your budget is allocated to essential expenses — like rent or mortgage payments, utilities, groceries, transportation, insurance, and minimum debt repayments. These are the non-negotiable costs that keep your life running smoothly.

30% for Wants:
This category is for non-essential spending that brings you joy — dining out, entertainment, hobbies, vacations, and shopping. These are the things that make life enjoyable, but they should be indulged in within reason.

20% for Savings:
The final portion of your income is dedicated to savings and paying off debt beyond the minimum payments. This could include building an emergency fund, contributing to retirement accounts, paying down debts faster, and investing in long-term goals.

The Dilemma of Need vs. Want

You might start to wonder, "Is the cost related to my pet a need or a want?" Let me tell you about our little bundle of joy, Pistachio Macaroni Al Dente.

We adopted this little guy in November 2023, and he's definitely made an impact on our budget. There's a pet store in my neighbourhood that I used to walk past every day without a second glance. Now? I practically live there!

We spend about $150 a month on Pistachio for food, insurance, treats, toys, and more. But really, can you put a price on unconditional love? Having a pet does mean making compromises — a new leash for him might mean one less necklace for me. (Just kidding... maybe.) P.S. if you ever meet Pistachio, please don't mention that we adopted him.

Whether you consider certain costs a need or a want doesn't matter much, as long as you're saving at least 20% of your income. That's the main goal here.

Besides our beloved fur babies, there's another group of cute but

costly little beings: kids. And no, we're not talking about baby goats—
we mean the tiny humans constantly demand the latest and greatest of
everything. Managing your own needs and wants is challenging
enough, but throw in your rebellious offspring and things get even
more complicated. I am sure every parent can relate to this struggle.
So, to all the parents out there: we get it. Just try your best!

Practical Steps to Implement the 50/30/20 Rule

1. Calculate Your Income: First, know how much money is coming
in each month. This includes your after-tax salary, any side hustles, or
other regular income sources. This is the total amount you have available to spend and save.

2. Identify and Categorize Expenses: List all your expenses and
divide them into needs, wants, and savings. Review your bank statements and receipts to ensure you don't miss anything.

3. Allocate Savings or Trim Expenses: If you're saving 20% or
more of your after-tax income, congratulations! Ensure you're putting
that money to good use by considering options like:

- Setting up a Preauthorized Automatic Contribution to your
  Group RSP through work (prioritize this, as it often comes
  with employer matching contributions).
- Setting up automatic contributions to your RRSP, TFSA, or
  regular investment accounts.

Automated savings plans are the way to go. They take the decision-
making out of the equation, so your money is automatically moved
from your checking account to your investment accounts before you
even see it, reducing the temptation to spend.

If you can't save 20% of your income or are facing a deficit, it's time to
reassess:

- **Living Beyond Your Means:** If your wants are overpowering your budget, it's time to rein in some spending. Opt for cooking at home instead of dining out, or cancel those unused subscriptions.
- **High Cost of Living:** If expenses are just too high, consider relocating to a more affordable area or increasing your income by gaining new skills, finding a higher-paying job, or picking up an extra job.
- **High Debt Payments:** If debt is eating into your budget, it's crucial to develop a debt management plan as we discussed in chapter 7.

4. Review and Revise: Life changes, and so should your budget. Regularly review your budget and make adjustments for new expenses, changes in income, or shifts in financial goals.

By following the 50/30/20 rule, you create a balanced budget that allows you to live comfortably, enjoy life, and build a secure financial future.

Conclusion

Budgeting isn't about restrictions; it's about aligning your money with what makes you happy. By dedicating 30% of your income to your wants, you're giving yourself permission to indulge in what brings you joy without guilt. Budgeting also cultivates mindfulness in your financial decisions, helping you make the most of what you have.

Ultimately, the discipline you develop through budgeting helps you build an asset that works for you even in your sleep, paving the way to financial freedom and shielding you from unexpected surprises. In the next chapter, we'll dive into how to build an emergency fund, a critical step in securing your financial foundation. Stay with us, because financial peace of mind is worth the journey.

15

YOUR FINANCIAL SAFETY NET

Building an Emergency Fund: Preparing for Life's Storms

Introduction

Have you ever wondered how you would handle an unexpected financial crisis? Before diving into long-term investments or other financial ventures, it's essential to have a safety net in place. That's where an emergency fund comes in — it's your financial buffer, ready to catch you when life throws those inevitable curveballs. Whether it's an unexpected medical bill, a sudden job loss, or an urgent home repair, an emergency fund is your first line of defence. It helps you avoid the pitfalls of high-interest debt or selling off investments at the worst possible time. Let's explore why building this safety net is so important.

Why Is an Emergency Fund Important?

An emergency fund is about more than just money; it's about peace of mind. Imagine skydiving — would you jump without a parachute? Your emergency fund is that parachute. It provides a reassuring sense of security, knowing that you have a financial cushion to fall back on when things don't go as planned.

Beyond peace of mind, an emergency fund helps you avoid the trap of high-interest debt. Without it, you might find yourself relying on credit cards or loans to cover unexpected expenses, which can quickly spiral into overwhelming debt due to hefty interest rates. And let's not forget about life's big challenges — like job loss or health issues. An emergency fund can cover your living expenses while you search for a new job or help pay for medical bills, bridging the gap until insurance kicks in.

How Much Do You Need?

So, how much should you aim to save? Ideally, your emergency fund should cover three to six months' worth of living expenses. To figure out how much that is, take a close look at your monthly budget (remember that handy tool from the previous chapter?) and multiply your essential expenses by three or six. This should include rent or mortgage payments, utilities, groceries, transportation, insurance, and any other non-negotiable costs that keep your life running smoothly.

Where to Keep It?

Your emergency fund needs to be easily accessible — because emergencies don't send advance notices. A simple savings account or a high-interest e-savings account works well. The goal is to ensure you can access your funds quickly when you need them, without facing penalties or waiting for investments to sell.

How to Build Your Emergency Fund

Building an emergency fund might seem daunting at first, but with a little patience and a clear strategy, you'll be on your way to financial security in no time.

1. Set a Goal: Start by calculating your monthly living expenses, then set a target to save three to six times that amount. Break this down into smaller milestones to make the task less overwhelming.

2. Automate Your Savings: One of the easiest ways to build your emergency fund is to set up automatic transfers from your checking account to your savings account. By automating the process, you remove the temptation to spend the money elsewhere, and it becomes a habit—just like paying a bill.

3. Trim Unnecessary Expenses: Take a hard look at your spending and identify areas where you can cut back. Do you really need that daily coffee shop latte, or could you make it at home? Could you dine out less frequently or cancel those unused subscriptions? These small changes can add up to meaningful savings over time.

4. Use Windfalls Wisely: Whenever you receive unexpected money, such as a tax refund, work bonus, or gift, consider putting it straight into your emergency fund. This can give your savings a nice boost without impacting your regular budget.

5. Be Patient: Remember, building an emergency fund is a marathon, not a sprint. It takes time, and that's okay. Think of it as planting a seed that will eventually grow into a sturdy financial tree, providing shade and shelter in times of need.

An emergency fund isn't for splurging on vacations or luxury items —it's your financial lifeline. Once you've reached your savings goal, you can start focusing on other financial dreams, such as investing for retirement or saving for a down payment on a home.

Conclusion

By establishing a solid emergency fund, you're not just protecting yourself from the unexpected — you're paving the way for a more secure and stress-free financial future. In the next chapter, we'll explore the various investment options available to you, helping you grow your money wisely and strategically.

16

INVESTMENT 101

The ABCs of Investing: Making Your Money Work for You

"The fundamental cause of the trouble is that in the modern world, the stupid are cocksure while the intelligent are full of doubt." – Bertrand Russell

Introduction

Have you ever felt overwhelmed by the idea of investing, as if you're about to step into a maze with potential risks at every corner? You're not alone. Investing can seem daunting, but it doesn't have to be. In this chapter, we'll break down some of the most common investment vehicles and guide you in making decisions that align with your financial goals. Here's a golden rule to keep in mind: the greater the risk you take with your investment, the higher the potential return. And if anyone promises high returns without any risk? Be cautious — they're either misinformed or trying to take you for a ride. Let's dive in and demystify the world of investing.

1. Guaranteed Investment Certificates (GICs)

GICs are like the sturdy, reliable old friend of investments. These are low-risk, fixed-term investments offered by banks and credit

116

unions. When you invest in a GIC, you're lending money to the bank for a set period in exchange for a guaranteed return. GICs come in different flavours: some offer fixed rates, while others have variable rates that may rise or fall with the prime rate.

One of the biggest perks of GICs is that your principal—the initial amount you invested — is protected. Plus, GICs are typically insured by the Canada Deposit Insurance Corporation (CDIC), covering up to $100,000 per issuer. So even if the bank goes belly-up, your money is safe.

GICs are ideal for short-term savings goals (1-3 years) and for those who prioritize security over high returns. However, the trade-off for safety is often lower returns compared to other investment options. And if you need to withdraw your money before the term ends, you might have to forfeit some or all of the interest.

2. Bonds

Bonds are like IOUs from the government or corporations. When you buy a bond, you're essentially lending money to the bond issuer in exchange for regular interest payments and the return of your principal at a set maturity date.

Government bonds from credible countries are the safest, backed by the "full faith and credit" of the issuing government. Corporate bonds are a bit riskier but offer higher interest rates to compensate. The riskier the issuer, the higher the interest rate they'll need to offer to attract investors.

Bonds are considered "fixed income" investments because they provide predictable returns. They're generally safer than stocks, making them a good choice for conservative investors or those nearing retirement. However, bond prices can fluctuate with interest rates, potentially leading to capital gains or losses.

Bonds come with a variety of terms that might sound like jargon at first:

- **Maturity Date:** The date when the bond issuer repays the bond's principal.

- **Par Value:** The amount you lent to the issuer, also known as the bond's face value.
- **Coupon Rate:** The interest rate paid by the bond, usually annually or semi-annually.
- **Bond Issuer:** The entity that borrows the money by issuing the bond, such as a corporation or government.
- **Yield to Maturity (YTM):** The total rate of return you can expect if you hold the bond until maturity.
- **Credit Rating:** Bonds are rated by agencies like Moody's or Standard & Poor's based on the issuer's creditworthiness. Higher ratings (e.g., AAA) indicate lower risk.

Price movement of a bond and its investment income:

Bonds don't just sit there earning interest; they can also generate capital gains or losses. Here's the deal: after a bond is issued, its coupon rate stays the same, but if you need cash and decide to sell your bond, you might not get back its original value (par value).

Why? Because interest rate environment changes. For example, in March 2022, the Bank of Canada raised its policy interest rate, and new bonds started offering higher coupon rates. As an investor, if you had the choice between buying a bond with a higher coupon and one with a lower coupon for the same price, you'd naturally opt for the higher rate. This means that if you hold an older bond with a lower rate, you would need to reduce its selling price to make it appealing to buyers. When these discounted bonds mature, buyers can benefit from both the interest payments and the difference in the bond price — a nice capital gain. On the flip side, sellers might experience a capital loss. This dynamic explains why bond investors saw losses in their portfolios in 2022.

Since capital gains are taxed more favourably than interest income, purchasing bonds with lower coupon rates at a discount, with the potential for capital gains, can be a tax-efficient strategy — particularly when you're in a high tax bracket.

3. Stocks (Equities)

Stocks represent ownership in a company. When you buy a stock, you're buying a tiny piece of the company, making you a shareholder. Stocks can be exhilarating because of their potential for high returns through capital gains and dividends. However, they also come with higher risks compared to GICs and bonds.

Stocks are volatile. Prices can swing wildly based on the company's performance, market conditions, and investor sentiment. If the company does well, your stock's value may increase. However, if the company struggles or goes bankrupt, stockholders are last in line for any payouts, meaning you could lose your entire investment.

Common terms you hear related to stocks:

Understanding some common stock-related terms can help you navigate the stock market:

Bull vs. Bear Markets

A bull market is like a charging bull — full of energy and pushing prices up. Investors are feeling good, and optimism is in the air. Think of it as the stock market on a caffeine high. Conversely, a bear market is like a hibernating bear — slow, sluggish, and dragging prices down. Investors feel like they're stuck in a financial winter, and pessimism takes over. Where do these terms come from? One popular story is that they mimic the animals' attack styles: a bull thrusts its horns upward (rising market), while a bear swipes its paws downward (falling market). So, when prices are rising, it's a bull market; when they're falling, it's a bear market.

IPO: The Stock Market's Grand Opening

An IPO, or **Initial Public Offering**, is like a company's debutante ball. It's when a company's shares are traded publicly for the first time. Microsoft had its IPO in 1986 and raised $61 million. That's the magic of an IPO — it gives companies access to a ton of cash from investors who buy their shares.

For investors, getting in on an IPO is like getting a pass to invest early in a company that could hit it big. However, it's not all glitz and glam. The company's future performance is uncertain, and stock prices can be as unpredictable as a cat on a hot tin roof. So, while it's exciting, it's also a bit of a rollercoaster ride.

Market Cap: Measuring a Company's Size with Style

Market capitalization, or "market cap," is the total value of a company's outstanding shares. Think of it as the company's price tag. For example, Microsoft's market cap is around 3 trillion US dollars as of March 2024. Investors use market cap to gauge a company's size, instead of just looking at sales or assets. A high market cap means the company is a big player in the market. While larger firms may have slower growth rate compared to start-up's, they often enjoy advantages such as easier access to financing, stable revenue streams, and leveraging brand recognition.

Here's a breakdown of the different sizes:

- **Large-cap stocks:** These are the titans of the stock market, usually with market caps over $10 billion. They're well-established, less volatile, and come with stable earnings. Think of giants like Apple (AAPL) and Microsoft (MSFT).
- **Mid-cap stocks**: These companies have market caps between $2 billion and $10 billion. They're often in growth mode, offering higher returns but also more risk than large-caps. Examples include Etsy (ETSY) and Zillow (Z).
- **Small-cap stocks**: These are the adventurous young companies with market caps below $2 billion. They have high growth potential but come with higher risk. Examples include Beyond Meat (BYND) and Carvana (CVNA).

So, when you're eyeing stocks, think about their market cap to gauge their size and growth potential. Do you want to ride with the giants or take a chance on the up-and-comers? While there's a lot more to market cap and growth rates than we can cover here, this gives you a simplified snapshot.

The P/E Ratio

The price-to-earnings (P/E) ratio shows how much investors are willing to pay for each dollar of a company's earnings. A high P/E ratio might mean a stock is overvalued, or it could mean investors expect big things in the future. For example, Microsoft's P/E ratio is 37.9 as of March 2024. In simpler terms, if you bought a Microsoft share at 37.9 price to earnings ration, it would take 37.9 years for Microsoft to earn back the cost of that share. So, think of the P/E ratio as a reality check on whether you're paying too much for a company's future growth or not!

Long and Short

You might have heard some investors use terms like "long" and "short," but they're not about length.

To "long" a stock means buying it with the plan to sell it later at a higher price. You're basically betting that the stock price will go up. This is the strategy that the majority of investors use when they purchase stocks.

For example:
You buy Apple shares at $100.
You sell them at $170 later.
You profit $70 per share by going long on Apple.

On the flip side, to "short" a stock means selling a stock you don't actually own (you borrow it from your broker) with the plan to buy it back later at a lower price. You're betting that the stock price will go down.

For example:
You borrow Apple shares from your broker, sell the shares at $170.
You then buy them back at $100 later.
You return the shares to your broker, profit $70 per share by shorting Apple.

Here's the kicker: predicting stock price movements is incredibly difficult. The risk with shorting a stock is theoretically unlimited. If you go long, the most you can lose is the amount you invested. In our example, that's $100 per Apple share. But if you short a stock, your potential loss is unlimited. If Apple's price skyrockets to $1,000, you would have to buy it back at $1,000, taking a $900 per share loss. So, while shorting might sound savvy, it can be a wild and risky ride!

GameStop frenzy

You might have heard about the GameStop frenzy of early 2021. It all started when a group of retail investors, organized through online forum, noticed that hedge funds had heavily shorted GameStop's stock. Sensing an opportunity, these individual investors banded together to buy up shares of the struggling video game retailer, driving its stock price to astronomical heights. The hedge funds, betting on GameStop's demise, found themselves on the wrong side of the trade as the stock soared. As they rushed to buy back GameStop stocks to cover their short positions and limit their losses, it drove the stock price even higher due to the massive buying pressure, leading to the classic "Short Squeeze" phenomenon. Some major hedge funds took heavy hits from their short positions against GameStop:

- Melvin Capital: Lost 49% of its investments in early 2021, needing a $3 billion bailout.
- Citron Capital: Experienced 100% losses on its GameStop positions amid the stock's surge.

This emphasized the potential risk involved shorting a stock. Overall, the GameStop frenzy underscored the evolving dynamics of the stock market and the significance of informed investing strategies.

Common Stock Indices

Stock indices are like the report cards of the financial world. They track the performance of a group of stocks, giving you a snapshot of how a particular segment of the market is doing. They're not investment portfolios themselves but rather benchmarks for comparing your investments.

Some of the most well-known indices include:

- **S&P 500:** Tracks 500 large-cap U.S. stocks and is often seen as a barometer of the U.S. stock market's overall health. Since its establishment (also known as inception) in 1957, this index has achieved an average annual compounded return of approximately 9.8%.
- **Dow Jones Industrial Average (DJIA):** Includes 30 large, publicly traded companies in the U.S., representing a range of industries. Since its inception in 1896, this index has achieved an average annual compounded return of approximately 8.7%. However, because the index is weighted in a way that doesn't accurately reflect the market, its return rate may not be the most reliable benchmark for comparison.
- **NASDAQ Composite:** Focuses on technology related companies, including over 2,500 stocks. Since its inception in 1971, this index has achieved an average annual compounded return of approximately 10.7%.
- **S&P/TSX 60:** Tracks the 60 largest companies on the Toronto Stock Exchange, representing Canadian market leaders. Since its inception in 1998, this index has achieved an average annual compounded return of approximately 7.7%.
- **FTSE 100:** Tracks the 100 largest companies on the London Stock Exchange, a key benchmark for the U.K. market. Since its inception in 1984, this index has achieved an average annual compounded return of approximately 7.4%.
- **Nikkei 225:** Represents 225 large companies on the Tokyo Stock Exchange, providing insight into the Japanese market. Since its inception in 1950, this index has achieved an average annual compounded return of approximately 8.4%.

- **MSCI World Index:** Covers large and mid-cap stocks across 23 developed markets, offering a global market perspective. Since its inception in 1986, this index has achieved an average annual compounded return of approximately 9.77%.

Some indices have more ups and downs than others, such as the NASDAQ Composite, but the higher annual returns often compensate for the extra risk investors take on.

4. Real Estate: Building Wealth with Bricks and Mortar

Investing in real estate is often seen as a solid, tangible way to build wealth. When you buy property, whether it's a house, condo, or commercial building, you're purchasing a physical asset that you can see, touch, and improve. Unlike stocks, where your ownership is represented by digital shares, real estate gives you something concrete.

The Pros and Cons of Real Estate Investing

Real estate can be a rewarding investment, offering the potential for steady income and long-term appreciation. However, it's not without its challenges. Here's a closer look at what to expect:

Pros:

1. **Potential for Monthly Cash Flow**: If you rent out your property, it can generate a steady stream of income. This monthly cash flow can cover your mortgage payments, property taxes, and maintenance costs, with some left over as profit. Over time, as you pay down the mortgage, your cash flow can increase, providing a reliable source of income.

2. **Appreciation**: Real estate tends to increase in value over the long term. While there are market fluctuations, property values generally rise, especially in desirable locations. This appreciation can result in significant profits when you sell the property down the road.

3. **Tangible Asset**: Unlike stocks or bonds, real estate is a physical

asset that you can see and use. This tangibility provides a sense of security for many investors who like knowing that their investment isn't just a number on a screen.

4. **Leverage**: Real estate allows you to leverage your investment. By using a mortgage to finance part of the purchase, you can control a larger asset with a smaller initial investment. If property values increase, your return on equity can be substantial.

Cons:

1. **Requires Significant Upfront Investment**: Real estate typically requires a large initial outlay of capital. Down payments, closing costs, and renovation expenses can add up quickly. This high barrier to entry can make it difficult for some investors to get started.

2. **Interest Rate Risk**: If you take out a mortgage, fluctuations in interest rates can impact your monthly payments. Rising rates can increase your costs, especially if you have a variable-rate mortgage, squeezing your profit margins.

3. **Less Liquidity**: Real estate is not as liquid as stocks or bonds. Selling a property can take months, and there are no guarantees you'll get the price you want. This lack of liquidity means you can't easily convert your investment into cash when you need it.

4. **High Transaction Costs**: Buying and selling real estate involves significant transaction costs, including real estate agent commissions, legal fees, and closing costs. These expenses can eat into your profits, especially if you sell the property shortly after purchasing it.

5. **Ongoing Maintenance and Management**: Properties require regular maintenance, from repairs and renovations to paying property taxes and insurance. If you rent out your property, you'll also need to manage tenants, handle vacancies, and deal with potential issues like non-payment or property damage. Alternatively, hiring a property management company can reduce your workload but will cut into your profits.

Risks and Rewards: Comparing Real Estate to the Stock Market

Real estate investing offers the potential for consistent income and long-term appreciation, but it comes with risks, particularly the need for significant upfront capital and ongoing maintenance. Compared to the stock market, real estate investments can be less volatile, but they also require more hands-on involvement.

Long-Term Returns: Historically, real estate in Canada has provided solid returns, often matching or slightly exceeding inflation rates. However, the long-term returns on real estate are generally lower than those of the stock market. For instance, over the past several decades, the average annual return for real estate in major Canadian cities has been around 3% to 4% after inflation, while the Canadian stock market has averaged around 6%.

Real estate offers stability and the potential for consistent income through rental properties, making it a valuable addition to a diversified investment portfolio. However, it's essential to be aware of the upfront costs, risks, and responsibilities involved. Before diving into real estate, ensure you're prepared for the long-term commitment it requires and consider how it fits into your overall financial strategy.

Conclusion

By understanding the basics of GICs, bonds, stocks, and real estate, you're well on your way to making informed financial decisions. Remember, diversification is key — spreading your investments across different assets can help balance risk and reward.

In the next chapter, we'll explore managed investment options like mutual funds, ETFs, and segregated funds. These are great tools for those who prefer a hands-off approach to investing or want to benefit from professional management. Keep reading to discover how these options can fit into your financial strategy!

17

MASTERING MANAGED INVESTMENTS

Demystifying Mutual Funds, ETFs, and Segregated Funds

Introduction

Have you ever wondered if there's a way to grow your wealth without having to become a financial expert yourself? With so many investment options out there, it can be overwhelming to know where to begin. Managed investments like mutual funds, ETFs, and segregated funds offer a practical solution. They provide professional guidance, making investing accessible to everyone, whether you're a beginner or a seasoned investor. But with each investment charging a fee, is it really worth it? In this chapter, we'll break down these investment vehicles into simple, understandable terms so you can decide if they're the right fit for your financial goals.

1. Mutual Funds

Mutual funds are like the financial world's version of a buffet. You contribute to a pool of money along with other investors, and a professional manager uses that pool to buy a diversified mix of stocks, bonds, or other securities. With mutual funds, you get a little bit of everything, and someone else handles the cooking — meaning you don't have to worry about selecting individual investments.

One of the main attractions of mutual funds is diversification. Instead of putting all your money into one stock or bond, mutual funds spread your investment across various securities. This reduces risk and can lead to more stable returns over time. However, this convenience comes at a cost: fees. These fees, including management fees and other expenses, can significantly impact your returns. It's essential to understand these fees and how they affect your overall investment performance.

Key Features of Mutual Funds:

Mutual funds pool money from multiple investors to create a diversified portfolio. They are managed by professional fund managers who make investment decisions based on the fund's objectives.

Investment Strategy Limitations:

Mutual funds have built-in rules that protect your investment by limiting certain high-risk strategies:

- **Concentration Limits:** Mutual funds are required to diversify their holdings to avoid putting too much money into any one stock or sector. For instance, no single security can comprise more than 10% of the entire mutual fund. This diversification helps reduce the risk and impact of poor performance by any single investment.
- **No Leverage:** Mutual funds typically cannot borrow money to amplify returns, which reduces risk but also limits potential gains.
- **No Short Selling:** Mutual funds generally can't bet on the decline of a stock's value, which could limit their ability to hedge against market downturns.
- **No Derivatives:** Mutual funds often avoid complex financial instruments like options and futures, keeping their investment strategy straightforward.

These restrictions keep your investment safer but can also limit the mutual fund's ability to capitalize on certain market opportunities. While mutual funds might not offer the high-risk, high-reward potential of other investments, they provide a stable and diversified option for most investors.

Fund Facts: Think of Fund Facts as the dating profile for a mutual fund. It's a document that gives you all the essential details you need before committing your money. You'll find the fund's investment objectives, past performance, risk level, fees, and info about the fund manager. It's designed to help you make an informed decision, like a mutual fund's elevator pitch, but without the awkward small talk.

Understanding Fees:
When investing in mutual funds, it's crucial to understand the different types of fees, such as the Management Expense Ratio (MER). The MER is the percentage of your investment used to cover the fund's management and operational costs. Different mutual fund series come with different fee structures:

- **Series A:** Typically sold through financial advisors with an MER ranging from 2% to 2.5%. This fee includes a trailing commission paid to the advisor or the distribution firm.
- **Series F:** These funds have lower MERs (around 1% to 1.5%) but require you to pay your advisor separately. They are sold through fee-based advisors.
- **Series D:** For the Do It Yourself investor, these funds have MERs between 1.5% and 1.7%, sold through discount brokerages or online trading platforms.

Load Fees:
Load fees are extra charges that might apply when you buy or sell mutual funds. These can include front-end loads (paid when you buy) and back-end loads (paid when you sell). While load fees are becoming less common, always check with your advisor before buying any investments to avoid unnecessary costs.

Asset Allocation:
Mutual funds manage risk by diversifying their investments across different asset classes like stocks, bonds, and cash equivalents. This strategy is known as asset allocation and is tailored to match the investor's risk level:

- **Conservative Funds:** Focus on bonds and cash, offering lower risk and stable returns.
- **Balanced Funds:** Combine stocks and bonds for a moderate risk-return balance.
- **Growth Funds:** Primarily invest in stocks, offering higher potential returns but with increased risk.

Summary

Mutual funds offer convenience, diversification, and professional management, making them a popular choice for many investors. However, be mindful of the fees and limitations, and choose funds that align with your financial goals and risk tolerance.

2. Exchange-Traded Funds (ETFs)

ETFs have skyrocketed in popularity due to their low costs, transparency, and flexibility. ETFs are similar to mutual funds in that they offer a diversified portfolio, but they trade on stock exchanges like individual stocks. This means you can buy and sell them throughout the trading day, giving you more control over your investment.

ETFs management styles:

- **Passive ETFs**: These are the laid-back cousins of the ETF family, aiming to replicate the performance of a specific index or benchmark. They hold the same securities in the same proportions as the index, typically resulting in lower management fees.

- **Active ETFs:** On the flip side, active ETFs are managed by portfolio managers who actively buy and sell securities aiming to outperform the market or achieve a specific investment goal. Naturally, this active management comes with higher fees compared to their passive counterparts.

The average Management Expense Ratio (MER) for ETFs hovers around 0.31%, with individual MERs ranging from a rock-bottom 0.03% to a still-reasonable 0.95%, depending on the asset class, management style, and geographic region. ETFs offer a smorgasbord of investment options across various asset classes, sectors, and regions, making them a well-liked choice for those looking to diversify their investment portfolios.

Summary

ETFs combine the diversification of mutual funds with the flexibility of trading like stocks, offering a low-cost, transparent, and flexible investment option.

3. Segregated Funds

Segregated funds, or "seg funds," are a unique blend of insurance and investment, offered exclusively by insurance companies in Canada. They function similarly to mutual funds but come with added benefits like principal guarantees and death benefits, making them a popular choice for conservative investors.

Key Features of Segregated Funds:

- **Principal Guarantee:** A portion of your initial investment (usually 75% to 100%) is guaranteed, protecting you from market downturns.
- **Death Benefit:** Your beneficiaries receive a guaranteed payout, either a predetermined percentage of your initial investment or the current market value, whichever is higher.

While these guarantees provide peace of mind, they come at a cost. Seg funds typically have higher fees than mutual funds, with MERs often exceeding 3%.

Mutual Funds vs. Segregated Funds:

When choosing between mutual funds and segregated funds, consider your financial goals and risk tolerance. Mutual funds offer more flexibility and lower fees, making them ideal for slightly more growth-oriented investors. Segregated funds, with their guarantees and insurance benefits, are better suited for conservative investors seeking capital protection. Additionally, segregated funds allow you to designate beneficiaries, which can be an efficient way to pass assets to your heirs.

Conclusion

Managed investment options like mutual funds, ETFs, and segregated funds provide a range of choices for investors with different goals and risk appetites. Understanding the features, benefits, and costs of each can help you make informed decisions that align with your financial objectives. In the next chapter, we'll explore some of the less common investment options, such as annuities, hedge funds, and cryptocurrencies. These options might not be for everyone, but they offer unique opportunities for those willing to venture off the beaten path. Stay tuned!

18

UNLOCKING HIDDEN TREASURES

The Not-So-Common Investment Options: What Else is Out There?

Introduction

Have you ever wondered if there are investment options beyond the usual stocks, bonds, ETFs and mutual funds? While these are the bread and butter of many portfolios, there's a whole world of alternative investments that offer unique opportunities — and risks. In this chapter, we'll explore some of these less common but potentially rewarding investment options: annuities, hedge funds, and cryptocurrencies. Whether you're planning for a steady income in retirement or looking for a high-risk, high-reward opportunity, there's something here for everyone.

1. Annuities: The Steady Paycheque for Retirement

An annuity might not be the most exciting investment, but it's a reliable companion when planning for retirement. Imagine having a steady paycheque that continues to roll in, even after you've hung up your work boots. That's what an annuity promises — a consistent income stream that can last for a specified period or even for the rest of your life.

Who Are Annuities For?

Annuities are ideal for individuals who want the security of a guaranteed income stream and are concerned about the risk of outliving their savings. If you're someone who values financial predictability, especially in retirement, an annuity could be your go-to option.

How Do Annuities Work?

The process is simple: you make a lump-sum payment or a series of payments to an insurance company. In return, the company provides you with regular payments, known as annuitization, which can start immediately (immediate annuity) or at a later date (deferred annuity). The amount you receive depends on several factors, including your initial investment, age, the type of annuity, and the prevailing interest rates.

Where Can You Buy Annuities?

You can purchase annuities through insurance companies, and they come in various flavours: fixed, variable, or indexed. Each type offers different benefits, so it's essential to choose one that aligns with your financial goals.

Example of How an Annuity Works:

Let's say Sarah is 65 and wants to ensure she has a steady income throughout her retirement. She invests $200,000 in an immediate fixed annuity. Based on interest rates and her life expectancy, the insurance company calculates that Sarah will receive $1,200 every month for the rest of her life. This arrangement gives Sarah financial security and peace of mind, knowing she has a reliable income to cover her living expenses in retirement.

Key Features of Annuities:

Annuities offer tax-deferred growth, flexible payout options, and the ability to customize based on your needs and preferences. However, there's a trade-off: because of the guaranteed payment feature, the actual return on your principal might not be as high as other investments like stocks, and it's heavily influenced by the interest rate environment. Think of an annuity as trading in your roller coaster stock ride for a steady, reliable Ferris wheel—less thrilling, but you know exactly what to expect.

2. Hedge Funds: The Sophisticated Investor's Playground

Hedge funds often evoke images of high-stakes financial maneuvers and enormous profits (or losses). But what exactly are hedge funds, and are they right for you?

What Are Hedge Funds?

Hedge funds are investment vehicles managed by professionals who use a variety of strategies to generate returns. Unlike mutual funds, hedge funds have much more freedom in their investment approaches —they can use leverage, derivatives, and short-selling to achieve their goals.

A Brief History:

Hedge funds have been around since the 1940s when Alfred W. Jones pioneered a strategy to hedge against market risk by buying undervalued stocks and short-selling overvalued ones. In many ways, he's the grandfather of modern hedge funds.

Who Are Hedge Funds For?

Hedge funds are typically designed for accredited investors, institutions, and high-net-worth individuals who can handle higher risks in exchange for the possibility of higher returns. These are not your everyday investments; they're geared towards those who are comfortable with complexity and volatility.

Absolute Return Objective:

Unlike mutual funds, which aim to beat benchmark indexes, hedge funds focus on generating returns regardless of market conditions. For instance, if the stock market drops by 20%, a mutual fund that loses only 16% might be considered successful. But a hedge fund losing even 2% at the same time would be seen as a failure because it's expected to make money no matter what.

Fees:

Hedge funds often come with hefty fees, including a management fee based on assets under management (AUM) and a performance fee based on profits. These fees are higher than those for mutual funds, but investors pay them for the chance to achieve absolute returns — if the fund delivers.

Famous Hedge Funds:

Some hedge funds have achieved legendary status, such as:

- **Bridgewater Associates:** Founded by Ray Dalio, known for its macroeconomic approach, managing about $153 billion in 2022.
- **Renaissance Technologies:** Founded by James Simons, famous for its quantitative trading strategies, managing about $106 billion in 2022.
- **Citadel:** Founded by Ken Griffin, recognized for its multi-strategy approach, managing about $62 billion in 2022.
- **Soros Fund Management:** Founded by George Soros, famous for global macro investing, managing about $25 billion in 2022.

The Bottom Line:

Hedge funds offer sophisticated investors the potential for attractive returns but come with higher fees and risks. It's essential to do your homework and know your risk tolerance before diving into the hedge fund pool.

3. Cryptocurrency: The Digital Frontier

Cryptocurrency, led by Bitcoin and Ethereum, represents a new investment asset class in finance. These digital currencies operate on decentralized networks, using blockchain technology to secure transactions.

What Is Cryptocurrency?

Cryptocurrency is a type of digital or virtual currency that uses cryptography for security. Unlike traditional currencies issued by governments, cryptocurrencies operate on decentralized networks, meaning no single entity controls them. Below are the 2 most prominent cryptocurrencies to date:

Bitcoin:

Launched in 2009 by the mysterious Satoshi Nakamoto, Bitcoin was the first cryptocurrency and remains the most well-known. It's often referred to as "digital gold" because of its limited supply and store of value.

Ethereum:

Rolled out in 2014, Ethereum introduced a game-changing feature—smart contracts. These self-executing contracts allow developers to build decentralized applications (DApps) on the Ethereum platform, expanding its use beyond just a currency.

Investing in Cryptocurrency:

Investing in cryptocurrencies is like venturing into the Wild West of finance. It's a new, volatile asset class with the potential for significant rewards — but also great risks. Prices can swing wildly in short periods, leading to substantial gains or losses.

Key Considerations Before Investing:

- **Volatility:** Cryptos are known for their dramatic price fluctuations. One minute you're up, the next minute you're down.
- **Lack of Regulation:** The crypto space is still largely unregulated, which can be both an opportunity and a risk.
- **Research:** It's crucial to understand what you're investing in, the technology behind it, and the market dynamics.
- **Risk Management:** Only invest what you can afford to lose. Treat it like a high-stakes game and avoid betting your life savings on it.

The Bottom Line:

Cryptocurrencies represent an exciting but risky frontier in the investment world. Approach them with curiosity and caution, and you might just strike digital gold—or at least have an interesting story to tell.

4. Other Investment Options You Might Come Across

Beyond hedge funds and cryptocurrencies, there's a whole universe of investment options waiting to be explored. Here are a few more to consider:

Real Estate Investment Trusts (REITs):

Want a piece of the real estate pie without buying property? REITs let you invest in a portfolio of properties, offering a way to earn rental income and potential capital gains. It's like owning a slice of the Empire State Building without having to deal with tenants.

Structured Notes:
These are like the bespoke suits of the investment world — custom-designed to meet specific investor needs. They combine bonds and derivatives to offer unique risk-return profiles.

Derivatives:
Think of derivatives as the power tools of investing. These financial instruments derive their value from an underlying asset, like stocks or commodities. They can be used for hedging or speculative purposes but require careful handling—they're not for the faint of heart.

Private Equities:
Investing in private companies can offer substantial returns, but it's a bit like betting on a dark horse. These investments are typically illiquid and require a longer time horizon.

Private Debts:
This involves lending money to private companies. It's like being the bank, but with potentially higher returns (and higher risks) than traditional bonds.

Conclusion

The world of investing offers a wide array of options, from the steady reliability of annuities to the high-stakes excitement of cryptocurrencies. Each of these investment vehicles comes with its own set of risks, returns, and tax implications. The right choice for you will depend on your financial goals, risk tolerance, and time horizon. As you consider diversifying your portfolio, remember that the key to successful investing is knowledge, preparation, and a clear understanding of your financial objectives.

In the next chapter, we'll delve into some of the more common registered investment accounts — RRSPs, RIFs, and TFSAs — where tax advantages and long-term savings strategies come into play. Whether you're planning for retirement or building a nest egg, these accounts are essential tools in your financial toolkit. Stay tuned as we explore how to maximize their benefits!

19

REGISTERED ACCOUNTS UNWRAPPED

RRSPs, RRIFs, and TFSAs: Your Ticket to Tax-Advantaged Growth

Introduction

Have you ever found yourself scratching your head when it comes to understanding investment accounts like the RRSP, RRIF, and TFSA? You're not alone. These accounts come with a range of benefits, understanding them is crucial for making the most of your financial future. In this chapter, we'll break down these common registered investment accounts in a way that's simple and practical. By the end, you'll feel confident in navigating these essential financial tools.

Registered vs. Non-Registered Accounts

Before we dive into the specifics, let's clarify the two main categories of investment accounts in Canada: registered and non-registered.

- **Registered Accounts:** These accounts, registered with the federal government, offer significant tax advantages. The income earned within these accounts isn't taxed until withdrawal, and in the case of a TFSA, it's never taxed. A key feature of registered accounts is the ability to designate beneficiaries. This means you can specify who will receive the funds upon your passing, allowing your savings to transfer directly to them without going through probate, simplifying the process for your loved ones. We'll discuss probate in more detail in later chapters.

- **Non-Registered Accounts:** These are your regular investment accounts. Non-registered accounts don't offer the tax benefits of registered accounts, meaning you pay taxes annually on any income generated. However, they give you more flexibility in how and when you invest or withdraw your money.

Now that we've covered the basics, let's delve into the specifics of RRSPs, RRIFs, and TFSAs — three of the most common registered accounts in Canada.

Registered Retirement Savings Plan (RRSP)

The RRSP is a cornerstone of retirement planning in Canada. It's designed to help you save for retirement while providing immediate tax benefits.

How RRSPs Work:

When you contribute to an RRSP, the contribution is tax-deductible. For instance, if you earn $100,000 and contribute $10,000 to your RRSP, this can reduce your taxable income to $90,000. This often results in a significant tax refund, making RRSPs an attractive option for high-income earners.

The real power of an RRSP comes from tax-deferred growth. Unlike non-registered accounts, where you pay taxes on your investment income each year, RRSPs allow your investments to grow without annual tax deductions. The strategy here is to contribute more during your high-income years to enjoy tax breaks, then withdraw the money in retirement when your income (and tax rate) is lower.

Eligibility and Contribution Limits:

Anyone with earned income who files tax in Canada can contribute to an RRSP until December 31 of the year they turn 71. The contribution limit is the lesser of 18% of your previous year's earned income or the annual maximum set by the government (e.g., $31,560 for 2024). Your RRSP contribution limit can be found on your CRA Notice of Assessment.

Investment Options:

RRSPs can hold a variety of investments, including cash, GICs, stocks, bonds, mutual funds, and ETFs. However, certain risky investments like short-selling or derivatives are generally not allowed in RRSPs.

Contribution Deadline

You actually can contribute to an RRSP at any time during the year as long as you have contribution room. However, if you want to deduct you RRSP contribution for a specific tax year, you must make contributions during that calendar year, or up to 60 days into the following year. For example: you must make a contribution before Feb 29th, 2024 to deduct this contrition amount from your 2023's taxable income.

Over contribution

There is Over-Contribution penalty for RRSP. However, there is a buffer. Everyone has a lifetime allowance of $2,000 for over-contributions. Generally, you will have to pay a penalty tax of 1% per month on excess contributions that exceed your RRSP deduction limit by more than $2,000. It's important to note that your work pension shares the same RRSP contribution room as your regular RRSP contributions. Therefore, you should be mindful not to over-contribute, as you may inadvertently exceed your contribution limit by not factoring in your pension contributions.

Withdrawal Rules and Penalties:

Withdrawing money from your RRSP is not as straightforward as making an ATM withdrawal. When you withdraw funds from your RRSP, the CRA wants its share immediately. This means your RRSP provider (like your bank or broker) will withhold taxes and send them straight to the Canada Revenue Agency (CRA) on your behalf. It's the CRA's way of making sure they get paid, just in case you forget to settle up at tax time.

Here's How Withholding Taxes Work:

Amount of RRSP Withdrawal	All Provinces Except Quebec	Quebec
Up to and including $5,000	10%	5%
$5,000.01 to $15,000	20%	10%
More than $15,000	30%	15%

For example, when you withdraw $5,000 from your RRSP, the CRA will withhold $500 (10%), so you'll get $4,500. When you withdraw $20,000, the CRA will withhold $6,000 (30%), so you'll get $14,000.

But that's not the end of the tax story. When you file your tax return, you must declare the withdrawal amount as taxable income. The CRA will then figure out your actual tax based on your total income. If they withheld too much, you'll get a refund. If they didn't withhold enough, you'll owe more.

Importantly, once you withdraw funds, you permanently lose that contribution room, meaning you can't put that money back in later to continue receiving the tax-deferred benefit.

RRSPs are designed for retirement savings, so think twice before raiding the piggy bank before retirement. For shorter-term cash needs, consider using a TFSA or non-registered account. Save the RRSP for when you're really ready to kick back and enjoy your retirement.

Spousal RRSPs:

Spousal RRSPs are an excellent strategy for couples to balance retirement savings and reduce overall tax burdens. The higher-earning spouse can contribute to a Spousal RRSP in the name of the lower-earning spouse, receiving the tax deduction while the lower-earning spouse eventually withdraws the funds at a potentially lower tax rate.

RRSP Conversion to RRIF:

By the end of the year in which you turn 71, you must convert your RRSP into a Registered Retirement Income Fund (RRIF) or use it to purchase an annuity. This conversion is a seamless transition from saving to spending in retirement, but it comes with mandatory withdrawal requirements, which we will discuss in the RRIF section.

Home Buyers' Plan (HBP) and Lifelong Learning Plan (LLP):

The RRSP also offers programs like the Home Buyers' Plan (HBP) and Lifelong Learning Plan (LLP), allowing you to withdraw funds for buying your first home or pursuing education without immediate tax consequences. However, these withdrawals must be repaid within a specific timeframe to avoid tax penalties.

Registered Retirement Income Fund (RRIF)

We mentioned previously that you can't hold an RRSP forever. Once you hit 71, you have to convert it to a RRIF. So, what exactly is a RRIF, and how does it work? Let's dive in.

How RRIFs Work:

A RRIF is similar to an RRSP but with one key difference: you can no longer contribute, and you must withdraw a minimum amount each year. These withdrawals are considered taxable income, but the advantage is that your investments can continue to grow tax-deferred within the RRIF.

Minimum Withdrawals:

The minimum withdrawal amount is calculated based on the value of your RRIF at the end of the previous year and your age (or your spouse's age). Using your spouse's age, if they are younger, can reduce the required minimum withdrawals, allowing your investments to grow longer in a tax-deferred environment.

Excess Withdrawals and Withholding Tax:

If you withdraw more than the minimum required amount, the excess is subject to withholding tax, similar to RRSP withdrawals. However, careful planning can help you manage these withdrawals efficiently to avoid unnecessary taxes.

Beneficiaries and Estate Planning:

Like RRSPs, you can designate a beneficiary for your RRIF. If your spouse is the beneficiary (or successor annuitant to be more accurate), the RRIF can be transferred to them tax-free upon your passing, ensuring your retirement savings continue to provide for your family.

Tax-Free Savings Account (TFSA)

Despite its name, the Tax-Free Savings Account (TFSA) is much more than just a savings account. Introduced in 2009, the TFSA is one of the most flexible and tax-efficient investment vehicles available to Canadians.

How TFSAs Work:

Contributions to a TFSA are not tax-deductible, but any income earned within the account—whether interest, dividends, or capital gains—is completely tax-free. Withdrawals are also tax-free and do not affect your contribution room for future years.

Contribution Limits and Eligibility:

The government sets an annual contribution limit for TFSAs, and any unused room carries forward indefinitely. As of 2024, the cumulative limit for someone who has been eligible since the TFSA's inception in 2009 is $95,000. You can contribute to a TFSA as soon as you reach the age of majority and have a valid SIN. Even if you haven't contributed before, you can still catch up on all the missed contribution room. Over-contribute, though, and you'll face a hefty penalty of 1% per month on the excess amount. If you want to find out your contribution room, you can check it on the CRA website. The CRA tracks your contribution room and reports this amount through the "My Account" function on their website.

Investment Options:

TFSAs can hold a wide range of investments, including cash, GICs, stocks, bonds, mutual funds, and ETFs. However, similar to RRSPs, certain high-risk investments are generally not permitted.

Withdrawals and Flexibility:

One of the most attractive features of a TFSA is the flexibility in withdrawals. You can withdraw money at any time for any reason, and the withdrawn amount is added back to your contribution room in the following year. This makes TFSAs an excellent choice for both short-term savings and long-term investments.

No Age Limit:

Unlike RRSPs, there's no age limit for contributing to a TFSA. You can keep contributing and enjoying tax-free growth for life.

Beneficiaries and Successor Holders:

You can designate a beneficiary or successor holder (only spouse eligible) for your TFSA, ensuring that your savings can be passed on tax-free. This makes TFSAs a valuable component of estate planning as well.

Conclusion

RRSPs, RRIFs, and TFSAs are powerful tools in your financial toolkit, each serving distinct purposes in your journey toward financial security. Whether you're planning for retirement, looking to grow your investments tax-free, or converting savings into a steady income stream, these registered accounts offer valuable tax advantages and flexibility.

Understanding how to use these accounts effectively can make a significant difference in achieving your financial goals. In the next chapter, we'll explore other registered investment accounts, including the FHSA, RESP, LIRA, and RDSP, each offering unique benefits tailored to specific needs. Stay tuned to learn how to further optimize your financial strategy!

BEYOND THE BASICS

Diving into LIRA, FHSA, RESP, and RDSP: Beyond the Usual Suspects

Reading Guide Reminder: This chapter is especially relevant if you've left a previous job with pension options or if you have specific investment goals, such as saving for your first home, funding your children's education, or planning for a family member with disability needs. If none of these situations apply to you right now, feel free to skip ahead —you can always revisit this chapter when it becomes more relevant to your life.

Introduction

Have you ever wondered what happens to your pension when you leave your job? Or how you can save for your first home, your child's education, or even a secure future for a loved one with a disability? This chapter is dedicated to exploring those questions by diving into the various other registered investment accounts available in Canada. While the RRSP and TFSA might be the stars of the show, there are other important accounts that can play a crucial role in your financial planning. Let's break down the Locked-In Retirement Account (LIRA), First Home Savings Account (FHSA), Registered Education

Savings Plan (RESP), and Registered Disability Savings Plan (RDSP) so you can see how they might fit into your life.

Locked-in Retirement Accounts (LIRA) — Securing Your Pension

When you leave a job, especially one that offered a pension plan, you might be given the option to take a lump sum payout, known as the "commuted value" of your pension. If you receive this payout as cash, the entire amount will be considered taxable income for that year, leading to a hefty tax bill. However, the good news is that you can transfer this amount into a Locked-In Retirement Account (LIRA) and defer the taxes. The trade-off? The money is "locked-in," meaning you can't access it freely until you retire.

What is a LIRA?

A Locked-In Retirement Account (LIRA) functions much like an RRSP but is specifically designed to hold pension funds until retirement. When you transfer money from an employer pension plan into a LIRA, the funds are "locked-in" to ensure they're preserved for your retirement. Unlike an RRSP, you can't make personal contributions to a LIRA, and you generally cannot withdraw funds until you reach a specific age, usually between 55 and 65, depending on the rules in your plan's jurisdiction. This ensures that the funds are available when you retire.

Plan Jurisdiction and Maturity Options

The rules governing your LIRA depend on where you earned your pension. For example, if your pension plan was in Ontario, then Ontario's pension rules apply, even if you move to another province later on. One of the most common options for your LIRA upon retirement is to convert it into a Life Income Fund (LIF), which works similarly to a RRIF but with a maximum withdrawal limit in addition to the minimum withdrawal amount to ensure the money lasts throughout your retirement.

Unlocking Your LIRA

In certain cases, you might be able to unlock a portion or all of your LIRA under specific circumstances such as financial hardship, a shortened life expectancy, or if the account balance is below a certain threshold.

Summary

Your LIRA is a vital part of your retirement plan, especially if you're transitioning from an employer with a pension plan. It's crucial to understand the rules and options available to you, as well as the implications of unlocking these funds early. Treat your LIRA like a treasure chest — one that you protect until it's time to enjoy the rewards in retirement.

First Home Savings Account (FHSA) — Your Key to Homeownership

Buying your first home is an exciting milestone, but it often requires significant savings. Enter the First Home Savings Account (FHSA), a registered account designed specifically to help first-time homebuyers contribute up to $40,000 tax-free. It's like combining the best features of an RRSP and a TFSA into one account specifically for your first home purchase.

How Does the FHSA Work?

The FHSA allows you to contribute up to $8,000 per year, with a lifetime limit of $40,000. Contributions are tax-deductible, meaning they reduce your taxable income, similar to an RRSP. The real magic happens when you withdraw the money to buy your first home —

those withdrawals, including any investment income, are tax-free, just like a TFSA.

Who is Eligible?

To open an FHSA, you must be a Canadian resident, at least 18 years old, and a first-time homebuyer, meaning you haven't owned a home you lived in during the current year or the previous four years. The account can remain open for up to 15 years, giving you plenty of time to save.

Using the FHSA and Home Buyers' Plan (HBP) Together

One of the great features of the FHSA is that you can use it in conjunction with the Home Buyers' Plan (HBP) within your RRSP. The HBP allows you to withdraw up to $60,000 from your RRSP to buy your first home, provided you pay it back over 15 years. By using both the FHSA ($40,000 lifetime contribution room) and HBP, you could access up to $100,000, plus any investment growth in the FHSA, for your home purchase.

Summary

The FHSA is a powerful tool for first-time homebuyers, offering the dual benefits of tax-deductible contributions and tax-free withdrawals. It aims to help you reach your homeownership goals faster and with less financial strain.

Registered Education Savings Plan (RESP) — Investing in Your Child's Future

Higher education is expensive, and it's only getting pricier. That's where the Registered Education Savings Plan (RESP) comes in. It's a government-backed savings plan that allows your contributions to grow tax-deferred, with the added bonus of government grants to boost your savings.

How Does a RESP Work?

A RESP lets you save for your child's post-secondary education, and while your contributions aren't tax-deductible, the investment income grows tax-free until it's withdrawn. When the money is eventually used for education, the investment income is taxed in your child's hands — since students typically have low income, the tax payable on the withdrawal is often minimal or non-existent due to the tax-free Basic Personal Amount.

Government Grants and Contribution Limits

One of the biggest benefits of a RESP is the Canada Education Savings Grant (CESG), where the government matches 20% of your contributions, up to $500 per year, with a lifetime maximum of $7,200 per child. If you missed making contributions in previous years and didn't receive the grant, you can catch up—however, you can only catch up one year at a time. For example, if you didn't contribute last year and missed out on the $500 government grant, you could contribute $5,000 this year to receive a $1,000 grant (covering both this year and last year's missed grant). While there's no annual contribution limit, the lifetime contribution limit is $50,000 per child.

Withdrawals and Tax Implications

Withdrawals from an RESP can include the original contributions, government grants, and any investment earnings. The taxable portion of the withdrawal includes the grants, and investment earnings, while the original contributions are non-taxable. When the time comes to use the money, withdrawals can take the following 3 formats:

- **Educational Assistance Payments (EAPs):** These withdrawals include the taxable portion, such as investment earnings and government grants. They are taxed in the hands of the students, but because students typically have low incomes, it often results in little to no tax.

- **Refund of Contributions:** This allows you to withdraw your original contributions at any time. However, be mindful of the timing to avoid triggering a repayment of the CESG. It's generally a good idea to prioritize taking EAPs before withdrawing your contributions to make the most of the grant money.

- **Accumulated Income Payments (AIPs):** If no beneficiaries attend post-secondary education, you can withdraw the earnings. However, the earnings will be taxed at your regular marginal tax rate plus an additional 20% penalty.

Summary

A RESP is an excellent way to invest in your child's future, providing tax-deferred growth and government contributions to help fund their education. Just be sure to plan your contributions and withdrawals carefully to maximize the benefits and avoid any potential pitfalls such as grant repayment to the government or tax penalty on accumulated investment income.

Registered Disability Savings Plan (RDSP) — Securing the Future for a Loved One with a Disability

The Registered Disability Savings Plan (RDSP) is a powerful tool designed to provide long-term financial security for people with disabilities. It offers tax-deferred growth, access to government grants and bonds, and the ability for family members to contribute, making it a cornerstone of financial planning for those with disabilities.

How Does an RDSP Work?

An RDSP is a savings plan set up to provide financial security for people with disabilities. Contributions to the RDSP aren't tax-deductible, but the money grows tax-free until it's withdrawn. When withdrawals are made, they can be used for any purpose, but the money must benefit the individual with the disability.

Eligibility and Contributions to an RDSP

Contributions are allowed while the beneficiary is a Canadian resident and eligible for the Disability Tax Credit. Contributions can be made until the end of the year the beneficiary turns 59, with a lifetime limit of $200,000. There's no annual contribution cap.

Government grants, known as the Canada Disability Savings Grant (CDSG), can boost RDSP savings. Contributions must be made by the end of the year the beneficiary turns 49 to qualify for the CDSG. Additionally, the Canada Disability Savings Bond (CDSB) may be paid into the plan, even without contributions, until the beneficiary turns 49. These deadlines ensure long-term savings and retention of grants and bonds in the RDSP for at least 10 years before the beneficiary turns 60, at which age the beneficiary will start withdrawing from RDSP. As you will see later in the Repayments of Grants and Bonds section that the timing of withdraw can trigger government grant claw back.

Government Grants and Bonds

One of the major advantages of an RDSP is the government's contribution through the Canada Disability Savings Grant (CDSG) and the Canada Disability Savings Bond (CDSB). The CDSG can match your contributions by up to 300%, depending on your family income, while the CDSB offers up to $1,000 per year to low-income families, even if no contributions are made. For every beneficiary, the maximum lifetime CDSG can be received from the government is $70,000, and the maximum CDSB is $20,000.

Repayments of Grants and Bonds

Early withdrawals from an RDSP usually trigger a repayment of the "assistance holdback amount" (AHA), which includes all grants and bonds received in the past 10 years. The proportional repayment rule states that for every $1 withdrawn, $3 of grants or bonds received in the past 10 years must be repaid, up to the AHA limit. Repayments follow the order grants and bonds were received.

Withdrawals and Taxation

Withdrawals from an RDSP can include the original contributions, government grants, bonds, and any investment earnings. The taxable portion of the withdrawal includes the grants, bonds, and investment earnings, while the original contributions are non-taxable. There are two types of payments from an RDSP:

1. Disability Assistance Payments (DAPs):

- One-time or unscheduled payments to the beneficiary or their estate.
- DAPs can be requested by the holder, but not all RDSP issuers allow them. Confirm if your RDSP issuer permits DAPs before opening an RDSP. Taking a DAP before age 60 might trigger a proportional repayment of grants and bonds to the government.

2. Lifetime Disability Assistance Payments (LDAPs):

- Regular, scheduled payments to the beneficiary until the plan ends or the beneficiary passes away.
- Must start by the end of the year the beneficiary turns 60, but the holder can request earlier payments.

Summary

The RDSP is an essential savings tool for individuals with disabilities, providing significant government contributions and tax-deferred growth. However, navigating the rules and maximizing the benefits can be complex, so it's advisable to consult with a financial professional to ensure you're making the most of this valuable account.

Conclusion

Navigating the world of registered investment accounts can seem daunting, but each one offers unique benefits tailored to specific life goals. Whether you're planning for retirement, buying your first home, saving for your child's education, or securing the future for a loved one with a disability, these accounts are designed to help you reach your financial goals with added tax advantages.

In the next chapter, we'll dive into a topic that might give you pause — market risks. We'll take a look at some major market events since the 1970s and explore how understanding risk can help you build a more resilient investment strategy. Stick with us as we turn our focus to the ups and downs of the market and what they mean for your investments.

21

RISKY BUSINESS

A sense of Market Risk: The Rollercoaster of Investing

Introduction

Ever wondered why investing in the stock market feels like riding a rollercoaster? One moment you're climbing to exhilarating heights, and the next, you're plunging into a gut-wrenching drop. This is the essence of market risk — the uncertainty that comes with investing in financial markets. Understanding market risk is crucial for any investor, whether you're just starting or you've been in the game for years.

Let's take a walk down memory lane and revisit some of the most significant market crashes over the past 50 years. These events, while terrifying at the time, hold valuable lessons for any investor looking to navigate the volatile world of financial markets.

The Wild Ride of the S&P 500

To get a clear sense of market risk, look no further than the Standard & Poor's 500 (S&P 500) index, which has been on a wild journey over the last five decades. If you had invested $10,000 in the S&P 500 back in 1970, by June 2024, your investment would have grown to an impressive $665,000. That is, of course, if you managed to hold on tight and not panic sell during any of those nail-biting market crashes. Along the way, the market experienced several drastic downturns — each with its own dramatic backstory.

Let's get a visual sense of the market movement, and then dive into these stories of market mayhem and see what we can learn:

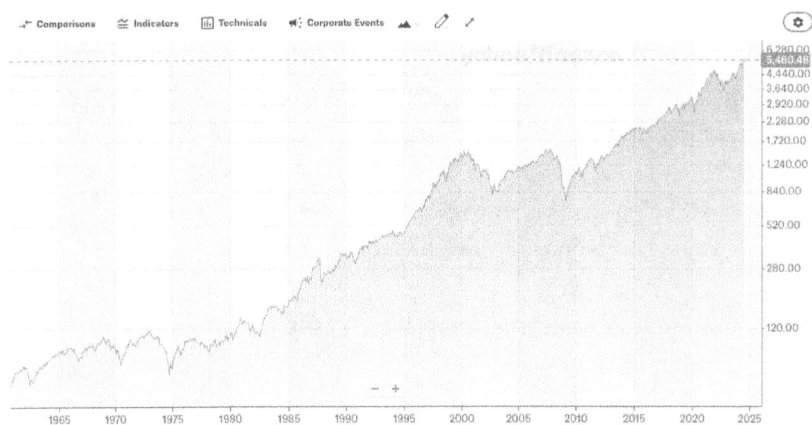

Source: Yahoo Finance. (2024, June 10). S&P 500 stock price, news, quote & history. *Yahoo Finance*. https://finance.yahoo.com/quote/%5E-SPX/chart/

As you can see, over time, the stock market has shown an upward trend, despite experiencing occasional sharp downturns. Each major dip has its own dramatic story: from the 1970s Oil Shock and Black Monday to the Dot-com Bubble burst, the 2008 financial crisis, and the COVID-19 pandemic crash. While these moments caused panic, they also offered valuable lessons and demonstrated the market's resilience as it always bounced back.

The 1970s Oil Shock: Gas Pains

In the 1970s, an oil embargo by the Organization of the Petroleum Exporting Countries (OPEC) sent oil prices soaring. The sudden spike in oil prices made everyone realize just how dependent they were on oil, leading to widespread economic stagnation.

Maximum Drawdown: Around 48%. This represents the deepest decline from the peak during this crisis.

Maximum drawdown is like the worst drop on a roller coaster. Imagine you're at the top of the ride, feeling great because the market (or your investment) is doing really well. Maximum drawdown measures the deepest fall from this high point to the lowest point before things start to improve again.

In simpler terms, it's the biggest loss you experience from the peak of your investment to the bottom. It's a way to see how much you could lose during a bad time before your investment starts to go up again. It's important because it shows the potential risk and helps you understand how bumpy the investment ride can get.

- **Causes:** Political maneuvering and supply cuts by oil-producing nations.
- **Reactions:** Gasoline prices skyrocketed, leading to long lines at gas stations and a push for alternative energy sources. Governments scrambled to implement conservation measures.
- **Rebound Time:** It took about 3-4 years for the market to recover as the crisis gradually eased by the late 1970s.

Black Monday (1987): The Sudden Crash

On October 19, 1987, the stock market took a nosedive, sparking widespread fears of another Great Depression. Known as Black Monday, this was one of the most dramatic one-day crashes in market history.

- **Maximum Drawdown:** About 22% in a single day.
- **Causes:** A combination of program trading, overvaluation, and panic selling.
- **Reactions:** The Federal Reserve quickly intervened by cutting interest rates to stabilize the market. This event also

led to changes in how markets and regulators respond to sudden drops.
- **Rebound Time:** The market bounced back within roughly 2 years, recovering by 1989.

The Dot-com Bubble Burst (2000): The Tech Wreck

Fast forward to the late 1990s saw tech companies multiplying like rabbits. The internet was new and shiny, and everyone wanted a piece of the digital pie, leading to astronomical stock prices. Investors poured money into tech startups with more ideas than profits.

- **Maximum Drawdown:** About 22% for the S&P 500, and a staggering 78% for the NASDAQ index, which was heavily weighted with tech stocks.
- **Causes:** Over-investment in tech companies, many of which lacked viable business models. The frenzy was driven by speculation, with investors buying stocks simply because everyone else was.
- **Reactions:** When reality set in, the bubble burst. Stock prices plummeted, and many tech companies vanished, leaving investors with significant losses.
- **Rebound Time:** It took about 4 years for the markets to stabilize, with recovery around 2004.

The 2008 Financial Crisis: A Housing Nightmare

The financial crisis of 2008 was a result of risky lending practices and the collapse of the housing market. Banks were handing out subprime mortgages like candy, leading to a housing bubble that eventually burst with catastrophic consequences.

- **Maximum Drawdown:** About 57%, one of the most severe drops in recent history.
- **Causes:** Subprime mortgages, complex financial products

like mortgage-backed securities, and widespread greed in the financial sector.

- **Reactions:** The collapse of Lehman Brothers and other financial institutions triggered a global recession. Governments and central banks had to step in with bailouts and stimulus packages to prevent total economic collapse.
- **Rebound Time:** The market took roughly 5-6 years to regain its footing, with recovery by 2013-2014.

The COVID-19 Pandemic Crash (2020): The Unseen Enemy

Finally, we reach the COVID-19 pandemic. This was a plot twist no one saw coming. The pandemic brought the world to a standstill in early 2020. As economies worldwide ground to a halt, the stock markets reacted with unprecedented speed.

- **Maximum Drawdown:** About 57%, mirroring the severity of the 2008 financial crisis.
- **Causes:** A global pandemic that disrupted economies and supply chains, leading to widespread uncertainty and fear.
- **Reactions:** Stock markets plummeted as governments and central banks rushed to respond with stimulus checks, furlough schemes, and interest rate cuts.
- **Rebound Time:** Remarkably fast, about 1-2 years, with markets rebounding by late 2021.

Ket Takeaways

As you can see, about every 10 to 13 years, a major economic crisis comes along and shakes up the market. Each time, the market tends to lose nearly half its value, wiping out years of gains. Each crisis brings its own unique chaos, but the common thread is human optimism followed by a harsh dose of reality. Yet, through it all, markets bounce back, and the economic rollercoaster ride continues. These events, while terrifying, offer crucial lessons in resilience and the importance of staying the course.

If you can withstand a 50% decline in your portfolio without panic selling, an ETF tracking the S&P 500 could be a wise long-term investment. However, it's essential to have a long-term perspective and the emotional fortitude to ride out the downturns. If the idea of losing half your savings makes you anxious, consider diversifying your investments across different asset classes like bonds or alternative investments such as private debt.

For people in retirement, especially those who need to withdraw money from their portfolio regardless of market conditions, it's often better to focus on a portfolio that generates income, such as dividend-paying stocks, interest-paying bonds, and GICs etc. This strategy allows you to avoid selling your shares during market downturns and instead live off the income your investments generate, thereby preserving your capital and ensuring it continues to produce income for the future.

Conclusion

Understanding and managing market risk is key to finding your financial comfort zone. By aligning your investments with your risk tolerance, when the next economic downturn hits, you can sleep soundly, knowing your financial ship is steady. Next up, we'll explore how to better understand your personal risk tolerance and find your financial comfort zone. Knowing where you stand on the risk spectrum will help you make informed decisions about your investments and navigate the markets with greater confidence.

22

FINDING YOUR FINANCIAL SWEET SPOT

Assessing Your Risk Tolerance: What Kind of Investor Are You?

Introduction

Ever wondered why some people love the thrill of roller coasters while others prefer a calm carousel ride? The same concept applies to investing — everyone has their own level of comfort when it comes to risk. This comfort level is known as risk tolerance, and understanding it is crucial for making smart investment decisions that align with your financial goals and peace of mind.

Risk tolerance is essentially your ability and willingness to endure the ups and downs of the market. It's influenced by a mix of factors, including your personality, life experiences, financial situation, and even your age. Typically, the older you get, the less risk you're willing to take, because you have less time to recover from potential losses before you need to tap into your savings.

Finding Your Risk Tolerance: Where Do You Fit?

Your risk tolerance can be thought of as your financial comfort zone — what you can handle without losing sleep at night. To figure out your risk tolerance, you can ask yourself some of the following questions:

- **What is my investment time horizon?** How long do I plan to keep my money invested before I need to access it? The longer your time horizon, the more risk you might be able to tolerate.
- **How would I feel if my investment lost 10%, 20%, or 30% in value?** Would I be comfortable waiting for the market to recover, or would I feel the need to sell and cut my losses? Your emotional response to potential losses is a key indicator of your risk tolerance.
- **What are my financial goals?** Am I investing for short-term goals (like buying a house in a few years) or long-term goals (like retirement in 20-30 years)? Different goals may require different levels of risk.
- **How stable is my current financial situation?** Do I have an emergency fund, stable income, and minimal debt? If your financial situation is strong, you might be able to tolerate more risk. If not, you may prefer safer investments.
- **Am I more focused on protecting my principal or maximizing returns?** Would I prefer slow and steady growth, or am I looking for potentially higher returns, even if it means taking on more risk?

Here's a look at different levels of risk tolerance:

Low Risk Tolerance: If you answered the earlier questions and find yourself focused on short-term goals or protecting your principal, you likely have a low-risk tolerance. You're drawn to safer investments like savings accounts and government bonds. While these options may not offer massive growth, they provide stability and peace of mind, knowing your money is secure.

Moderate Risk Tolerance: If you're in a stable financial position and focused on long-term goals, you probably have a moderate risk tolerance. You're comfortable with a balanced mix of stocks and bonds, which allows for some growth while maintaining stability. It's like trying something new, but not straying too far from your comfort zone.

High Risk Tolerance: If you're confident about your financial situation and eager to maximize your returns, you likely have a high-risk tolerance. You're willing to invest in riskier options like stocks or even leverage your investments to achieve higher returns. While the ride might be bumpy, you're prepared to handle the ups and downs for the potential rewards.

Choosing the Right Investment Strategy

Once you've identified your risk tolerance, it's time to pick an investment strategy that matches your comfort level. Here's how different strategies might look:

Conservative Strategy: This is the safe and steady route. A conservative strategy focuses on low-risk investments like bonds, guaranteed investment certificates (GICs), and cash. It's the investment equivalent of driving a reliable family sedan — steady, predictable, and unlikely to cause any major surprises. A typical conservative portfolio might be 20% equities, 75% fixed income, and 5% cash. This approach is perfect for those who prefer to play it safe and avoid sleepless nights worrying about market volatility.

Balanced Strategy: If you like a little excitement but still want some stability, a balanced strategy could be your best bet. This approach mixes stocks and bonds, aiming to balance risk and potential reward. Think of it as having a well-prepared meal with a mix of flavours — satisfying, with just enough spice to keep things interesting. A balanced portfolio might look like 58% equities, 40% fixed income, and 2% cash. This strategy works well for those who want growth but aren't comfortable with taking on too much risk.

Growth Strategy: For those who love to chase high returns and don't mind taking on more risk, a growth strategy might be the way to go. This approach leans heavily on stocks and other high-risk investments, aiming for significant growth. It's like driving a sports car — fast and thrilling, but with the potential for some sharp turns. A growth portfolio might be composed of 80% equities, 18% fixed income, and 2% cash. This strategy is ideal for investors who are in it for the long haul and can handle the ups and downs of the market.

Conservative and growth investment strategies are like different vehicles taking you from A to B. The conservative strategy is akin to driving a reliable family sedan, offering steady and predictable performance. On the other hand, the growth strategy resembles the exhilarating ride of a sports car, offering higher potential returns but also greater volatility and risk. Much like driving a sports car requires skill and caution, investing in a stock-heavy growth portfolio demands a tolerance for fluctuations in value and a longer time horizon to ride out market ups and downs. While the family sedan provides a comfortable and safe journey, the sports car offers the thrill of speed and the potential for adrenaline-pumping gains, but also the risk of occasional bumps along the way.

Other Common Investment Strategies

Beyond the basic strategies, there are other approaches to consider that can help you manage risk while pursuing your financial goals:

Core and Satellite Strategy: This approach is like building a solid sandwich with a touch of flair. You invest 70-80% of your funds in safe, low-cost core investments like index funds, high-quality bonds, and large-cap stocks. These serve as the foundation of your portfolio. The remaining 20-30% is allocated to higher-risk, higher-return satellite investments, such as sector-specific funds, small-cap stocks, emerging markets or private equity etc. This strategy is great for those who want stability with a little excitement on the side. Regularly checking and adjusting your investments helps maintain the right balance, making this method particularly appealing for long-term investors.

Dollar Cost Averaging: This strategy helps you avoid the pitfalls of trying to time the market. Dollar cost averaging involves investing a fixed amount of money at regular intervals, regardless of market conditions. For example, if you invest $500 every month, you buy more shares when prices are low and fewer shares when prices are high. This approach smooths out the cost of your investments over time, reducing the impact of market volatility. It's like setting your investment plan on autopilot—no need to worry about whether the market is up or down.

Income-generating portfolio: This strategy is ideal for investors who need regular cash flow from their investments, such as retirees or those not actively working. By focusing on investments that generate steady income — like dividend-paying stocks, interest-paying bonds, GICs or structured products — you can meet your cash flow needs without having to sell off assets, even during market downturns. This approach preserves your capital, ensuring that your portfolio continues to generate income over time. It's a practical strategy for those who value stability and consistent returns, making it a reliable choice for long-term financial security.

Conclusion

Choosing an investment strategy that aligns with your risk tolerance is like picking the right vehicle for your journey. Whether you prefer the steady ride of a family sedan or the thrilling speed of a sports car, understanding your risk tolerance ensures you're comfortable with the bumps and curves along the way. Before you decide on your investment strategy, ask yourself: Would a 20% drop in your portfolio cause you to lose sleep? Do you need to access your money in the near future? Are you aiming for a specific financial goal, and are you willing to take on the corresponding risk to achieve it? Investing doesn't have to be overly complicated. It's about making choices that fit your comfort level and align with your financial objectives. And remember, the key to successful investing is to stay the course and avoid making emotional decisions when the market gets rocky.

In the next chapter, we'll explore the Five Keys to Successful Investing and Savings, including the importance of starting early, investing regularly, contributing enough, investing strategically, and maintaining good relationships. These principles will help you build a strong foundation for long-term financial success. Stay tuned!

23

THE FIVE GOLDEN RULES

5 Keys to Successful Investing and Saving: How to Win at the Money Game

Introduction

Have you ever wondered what the secret sauce is for building wealth? You might think it's about picking the hottest stocks or timing the market just right, but in reality, successful investing and saving are more about consistency, discipline, and a few simple principles that anyone can follow. In this chapter, we'll dive into the five keys that can set you on the path to financial success. Whether you're just starting out or looking to refine your approach, these tips are timeless.

1. Start Early: Time is Your Best Friend

Think of starting early as planting a tree. The sooner you plant it, the bigger it grows over time. The same principle applies to investing. Time allows your investments to benefit from compounding returns, turning even small contributions into significant wealth over the years.

For example, imagine you and your friend Bob are both 25 years old. You save $10,000 and invest it in your TFSA, while Bob procrastinates and doesn't start until he's 35. If both of you achieve an annual return of 6.5%, by the time you both reach 65, your $10,000 would have grown to around $124,160, while Bob's would only grow to about

$66,143. By starting just 10 years earlier, your investment nearly doubles his, even with the same initial amount. If you haven't started investing yet, now is the perfect time to begin.

2. Invest Regularly: Consistency is Key

Regular investments are like watering that tree. It's not just about starting early; it's also about being consistent. Setting up a regular investment schedule — whether monthly, quarterly, or annually — helps you build your portfolio steadily over time. Automating these contributions ensures that you don't miss out on opportunities to grow your wealth.

Let's say you add a $500 monthly contribution to that $10,000 you invested at age 25. By the time you're 65, with the same 6.5% annual return, your investment could grow to over $1.27 million, compared to just $124,160 with the initial lump sum alone. Needless to say, investing regularly is key to building significant wealth over time.

3. Contribute Enough: Commit to Your Future

It's not just about contributing regularly; it's also about contributing enough. To build substantial wealth, you need to commit a significant portion of your income to investments. The exact amount will vary depending on your financial goals, income, and time horizon, but it's important to increase your contributions as your income grows. This helps you keep pace with inflation and maintain your standard of living in the future.

For instance, while $1.27 million might seem like a lot now, inflation could erode its purchasing power over 30 or 40 years. As your income increases, it's wise to review your goals and adjust your contributions accordingly. This way, you ensure that your investments will meet your future needs.

4. Invest Strategically: Make Informed Choices

Investing isn't just about putting money away — it's about doing so strategically. This means making well-informed investment choices, diversifying your portfolio to spread risk, and aligning your investments with your risk tolerance.

Imagine As you steadily built your portfolio, Bob felt a 6.5% annual return was too small. He heard from his neighbour that a stockbroker recommended a gold mining company, Super Gold Co., which was about to go public and promised to increase in value a hundredfold. Excited by this hot tip, Bob pulled his $15,000 from his TFSA and invested in the private gold company, hoping to get rich quickly. He encouraged you to join him, but you were hesitant since you knew nothing about mining. However, after Bob's persistent persuasion, you invested $500 in Super Gold Co. alongside Bob.

Five months later, as predicted, the company went public and its price skyrocketed. Bob's $15,000 turned into a whopping $1,000,000, and he retired on the spot. Your $500 turned into $33,000, making you wish you'd invested more so you could retire too. Oh well, no time machine can fix that, but at least your portfolio got a nice boost. As good friends sometimes do, you and Bob drifted apart, because you belong to different economic classes now, at least that's what Bob thinks.

You continued with your diversified portfolio, increasing your savings, and eventually grew your portfolio to $2,000,000 by age 60. With this success, you decided to step back from work and enjoy a semi-retired life supported by your investments. Curious about Bob's life post-early retirement, you gave him a call, hoping to reconnect now that you both had more free time.

To your surprise, you discovered that Bob didn't diversify his portfolio after his big win. His $1,000,000 dwindled back down to $10,000, forcing him to return to work. Retirement was no longer in his near future. You didn't know what to say, feeling a mix of sympathy and relief that your cautious approach had paid off in the long run.

Moral of the story: do not go after the flashy new things when it comes to investing. Do your research before committing serious money and always diversify. Sure, you will not become rich overnight, but at least you won't wake up to find your life savings have vanished like a magician's rabbit. Slow and steady wins the race.

5. Maintain Good Relationships: Love and Money

Your financial success isn't just about money — it's also about the relationships you maintain, especially in a romantic partnership. Investing time and effort in keeping your relationship strong is as important as any financial strategy. Divorce or separation can be one of the most expensive events in your life, potentially cutting your net worth in half and significantly affecting your retirement plans. Open communication and mutual support are key to ensuring both your emotional and financial well-being.

Conclusion

These five keys — starting early, investing regularly, contributing enough, Invest Strategically, and maintaining good relationships—work together to help you achieve your financial goals and build wealth over time. By following these principles, you can navigate the ups and downs of the market with confidence, knowing that you're on a path to financial success.

As you reflect on these keys, remember that investing is a long-term journey. The market may have its rollercoaster moments, but with the right strategies, you can ride out the bumps and steadily grow your wealth. In the next part of the book, we'll shift gears and dive into retirement planning, covering how much you need to retire comfortably, how company pensions and government benefits like CPP and OAS fit into your plan, and how to ensure financial security in your later years. Stay with us as we continue this journey to financial freedom!

Part Four

RETIREMENT – THE FINAL FRONTIER

Preparing for the Golden Years: It's Never Too Early (or Too Late!)

Retirement planning is the focus of Part 4, where we discuss how much you need to retire comfortably and what to do if you find yourself short on retirement income. This section provides a cheat sheet for understanding government pensions like CPP and OAS and demystifies work pensions, including defined benefit and defined contribution plans. We also explore additional retirement savings options, such as group RRSPs and individual pension plans. The goal of this part is to ensure you're prepared for retirement, no matter where you are in your financial journey.

RETIREMENT ROADMAP

How Much Do You Need to Ride Off into the Sunset?

Introduction

Have you ever wondered how much you'll really need to retire comfortably? Back in the 1940s, retirement at 62 was practically a brief pause before the final act, with life expectancy barely reaching 63. You could see why retirement planning wasn't a big concern back then. Fast forward to today, and retiring at 65 is just the beginning of a whole new adventure. With people living well into their 80s and 90s, you could spend as much time in retirement as you would in your working years. It's like signing up for an extended vacation with no return ticket — exciting, but only if you've planned it right.

With a horizon stretching 20 to 30 years into the unknown, planning isn't just a suggestion; it's a survival strategy. After all, no one wants to spend their golden years counting pennies and watching the clock tick by. So, let's dive into how much you really need to save to make those retirement dreams a reality.

Why Retirement Planning Matters

Financial Security and Dignity: Retirement planning ensures you have enough money to live comfortably when you're no longer earning a paycheque. It also saves you from having to rely on your children's financial support. Think of it as building a nest egg that will keep you warm and cozy when your working years are behind you.

Peace of Mind: Knowing you have a solid plan in place can alleviate the stress and anxiety that often accompanies thoughts of the future. It's like having a roadmap guiding you to a worry-free retirement.

How Much Do You Need to Save for Retirement?

1. The Quick Answer

A good rule of thumb is to aim to save around 25 times of your current annual income. This number is a quick and easy way to estimate how much you'll need to maintain your lifestyle in retirement.

For example, if you're earning $100,000 a year before tax, multiplying that by 25 gives you a target of $2.5 million. If your investments generate a modest 4% annual return, that would provide you with around $100,000 a year in income. By withdrawing only the income earned each year, you preserve the principal, ensuring that you can continue drawing this income indefinitely without depleting your savings. This creates a reliable financial safety net, giving you peace of mind that you will never run out of money, no matter how long you live.

What if you don't have a regular income? In that case, aim to save about 30 times your annual expenses instead. This accounts for the potential taxes payable on your investment income.

2. The Detailed Plan

If you want to dive deeper and create a more personalized plan, here's how you can calculate exactly how much you'll need.

Step 1: Figure Out How Much Income You'll Need Annually in Retirement

Typically, you'll need around 80% of your current expenses in retirement. Why less? You'll likely spend less on work-related costs like commuting, lunches, and clothing, and you may have paid off your mortgage or car loan by then. However, if you anticipate higher expenses during retirement, you can increase this to 100% or even 120% of your current expenses.

Step 2: Calculate Your Annual Government Pension Benefits

This includes what you can expect from the Canada Pension Plan (CPP) and Old Age Security (OAS).

Step 3: Determine Your Work Pension Benefits

If you have a pension plan through your job, estimate how much you'll receive annually from that.

Step 4: Determine the Shortfall

Subtract your government and work pension benefits from the annual income you calculated in Step 1. The difference is your cash flow shortfall — the amount you'll need to cover with your own savings.

Step 5: Account for Inflation

Inflation is the sneaky culprit that can erode your purchasing power over time. Assume an annual inflation rate of 2% and adjust your shortfall accordingly. For instance, if you determine you'll need $50,000 annually, inflation means that in 20 years, you'll need $74,297 to maintain the same standard of living.

Step 6: Estimate How Long You'll Spend in Retirement

This depends on when you plan to retire and your life expectancy. It's wise to plan for longevity, so consider estimating based on living until 95 or even 100 years old.

Step 7: Calculate the Present Value of Savings Needed at Retirement

Use a financial calculator to determine how much you need to have saved by the time you retire. For instance, if your inflation-adjusted shortfall is $74,297, you plan to retire at 65 and spend 30 years in retirement, assuming a 4% return on your investments, you'd need to save approximately $1,284,746 by age 65.

Step 8: Determine How Much You Need to Save Annually Now
Here's where you figure out how much you need to save each year to reach your goal. For example, if you're 40 years old with $100,000 already saved, assuming a 6% annual return, you'll need to save around $15,594 annually (or $1,300 monthly) to reach $1,284,746 by age 65. We used a higher expected return rate here, 6% vs. 4%, because, during your working years, you may be more willing to take on additional investment risk to achieve a higher rate of return compared to during retirement.

Step 9: Monitor and Adjust
Life is full of surprises, so regularly review your retirement plan and make adjustments as needed. Maybe your investment strategy changes, or you receive an unexpected windfall. Keep your plan flexible to adapt to these changes.

Conclusion

By following these steps, you can build a retirement plan that acts like a sturdy bridge, carrying you safely into your golden years. Remember, retirement isn't just about reaching the end of your working life; it's about enjoying the freedom that comes with knowing you're financially secure.

As you move forward, the next chapter of the book will guide you through what to do if your retirement savings fall short. It's never too late to make adjustments and secure your future. So, stay tuned as we explore how to make the most of your resources and ensure a comfortable retirement, no matter where you currently stand.

25

CLOSING THE INCOME GAP

What to Do When You Don't Have Enough Retirement Income

Introduction

Are you worried that your retirement savings might not be enough to carry you through your golden years? It's a common concern, but there are practical steps you can take to improve your financial situation, even if you're already retired or close to retirement. Running short on retirement income can feel stressful, but with some strategic adjustments, you can navigate this challenge and still enjoy a comfortable and fulfilling retirement.

Let's explore some options that can help you boost your income, reduce expenses, and secure your financial future.

Pick Up a Part-Time Job

One of the most straightforward ways to supplement your retirement income is by picking up a part-time job. This doesn't mean you have to dive back into the 9-to-5 grind. Instead, consider jobs that align with your interests and skills, or those that offer flexibility and a sense of purpose.

For example, if you have a wealth of experience in a particular field, you might consider becoming a part-time consultant. This allows you to leverage your expertise while working on your own terms. Alternatively, you could explore roles like a librarian, where you can share your love of books, or a position at a local golf course, where you can stay active and enjoy the outdoors. Not only will these jobs provide additional income, but they can also keep you engaged and socially connected.

Downsize Your Home

Another effective strategy for freeing up cash and reducing expenses is downsizing your home. If you're living in a large house that requires significant maintenance and upkeep, moving to a smaller, more manageable property can provide multiple financial benefits.

By downsizing, you can lower your utility bills, reduce property taxes, and cut down on maintenance costs. Plus, selling a larger home and purchasing a smaller one may leave you with a significant amount of equity that you can reinvest or use to support your retirement lifestyle. It's a win-win: less space to worry about and more cash in your pocket.

Get a Home Line of Credit

If you own your home and have built up substantial equity, a home equity line of credit (HELOC) could be a valuable resource. This option allows you to borrow against the equity in your home, providing you with flexible access to funds when you need them.

A home line of credit can be a great way to cover unexpected expenses or supplement your income without the need to sell your home. Keep in mind that, unlike downsizing, you're not freeing up equity in a lump sum, but rather accessing it as needed, which can help with cash flow management. However, it's important to use this credit responsibly and avoid over-borrowing to ensure your financial stability.

Use a Reverse Mortgage: Tapping into Home Equity in Retirement

For those who want to stay in their homes but don't qualify for a HELOC due to insufficient income, a reverse mortgage might be the answer. This financial product allows you to convert part of your home's equity into cash, without having to sell the property. Essentially, it provides you with a steady income stream based on the value of your home.

How does a Reverse Mortgage work?

We know how a mortgage works, but what is reverse mortgage? When you have a mortgage, your bank lends you money in a lump sum, and then you pay the principal and interest back gradually over years. The equity in your home is increasing as you pay it off gradually. A reverse mortgage, just as the name suggests, is the reverse of how a traditional mortgage works. Instead of making payments, you will receive payments from a reverse mortgage. The equity in your home is decreasing as you take money out. You do have interest accruing on the payments you taken out as well. The interest rate on reverse mortgage is generally higher than a traditional mortgage or home line of credit.

Reverse mortgages can be an attractive option for some homeowners, especially those who are retired and looking to tap into their home equity without having to sell their property. One of the biggest advantages of a reverse mortgage is that there are no monthly payments required, which can significantly ease financial pressure.

However, it's important to be aware of the downsides as well. Interest accumulates over time on the amount you borrow, which can significantly increase the total debt owed. High fees are another drawback, as reverse mortgages often come with closing costs and other associated charges. Additionally, taking out a reverse mortgage can have a potential impact on your inheritance, as the debt will need to be repaid when you sell the home or pass away, which could reduce what you leave behind for your heirs.

Conclusion

Finding yourself short on retirement income can be daunting, but remember, it's never too late to take steps to improve your situation. By exploring options like part-time work, downsizing, a home line of credit, or a reverse mortgage, you can create a strategy that aligns with your financial needs and lifestyle goals. Don't let financial worries overshadow your retirement years. With thoughtful planning and the right tools, you can secure a comfortable and fulfilling future.

As you continue your journey through retirement planning, the next chapter will help you understand your retirement income sources, focusing on the Canada Pension Plan (CPP) and Old Age Security (OAS). These government benefits are crucial components of your retirement income, and understanding how they work can further enhance your retirement planning. Let's explore how you can make the most of these essential resources.

26

THE CPP & OAS CHEAT SHEET

Understanding Your Government Pensions: A Lifeline for Retirees

Introduction

Have you wondered how much pension you will receive from the government when you retire? For many Canadians, a reliable portion of their retirement income comes from government programs like the Canada Pension Plan (CPP) and Old Age Security (OAS). Understanding these programs is essential for creating a secure and comfortable retirement plan. This chapter will help you get a clear picture of what to expect from CPP and OAS.

Canada Pension Plan (CPP)

The Canada Pension Plan (CPP) is like a savings account that you, your employer, and the government contribute to throughout your working life. When you retire, you can draw from this account to provide a steady stream of income. The amount you will receive depends on how much and how long you've contributed, as well as when you will start collecting your pension.

As of 2024, the maximum CPP monthly payment at age 65 is $1,364.60. While this may seem modest, it remains a crucial compo-

185

nent of your retirement plan. Typically, each year of full-time work increases your monthly CPP by about $35, or $420 annually. If you've worked full-time for 39 years or more, you would qualify for the full $1,364.60 monthly payment. And don't worry — your CPP is indexed to inflation, so it maintains its value over time.

When Should You Start CPP?

The standard age to start receiving CPP is 65, but you have the flexibility to start as early as 60 or as late as 70. Your decision will affect the amount you receive:

- **Starting early:** If you begin at 60, your payments decrease by 0.6% per month, or 7.2% annually, up to a maximum reduction of 36%. For instance, if you are entitled to a CPP payment of $1,000 at age 65, starting early at age 60 would reduce your payment to $640.
- **Starting late:** If you delay until 70, your payments increase by 0.7% per month, or 8.4% annually, up to a maximum increase of 42%. For instance, if you are entitled to a CPP payment of $1,000 at age 65, starting late at age 70 would increase your payment to $1,420.

There's no additional benefit waiting beyond age 70 to start your CPP. If you're considering delaying, 70 is your upper limit. So, should you wait to start collecting CPP? Well, it depends on your situation.

Factors to Consider:

- **Health and Longevity:** If you're in good health and expect a long life, delaying CPP might make sense as it ensures larger payments over time.
- **Financial Needs:** If you need the income sooner, starting early might be the best option, even though it means smaller monthly payments.

To get an estimate of what you'll receive, you can request a CPP Statement of Contributions from the government. This document will show you how much you've contributed and give an estimate of your future payments.

Old Age Security (OAS)

Old Age Security (OAS) is another cornerstone of retirement income in Canada. Unlike CPP, OAS is a non-contributory program, meaning you don't have to pay into it during your working life to receive benefits. Instead, your eligibility is based on how long you've lived in Canada after the age of 18.

To receive the full OAS pension, you must have lived in Canada for at least 40 years after turning 18. If you've lived here for less than that but more than 10 years, you can still receive a partial OAS pension. For example, if you've lived in Canada for 20 years after age 18, you would receive 50% of the full OAS amount.

Maximum Payments and Adjustments:

Here is what you can expect to receive from OAS in 2024:

Age	Maximum Monthly Payment	Annual Net World Income Must Be Less Than:
65 to 74	$713.34	$134,626
75 and over	$784.67	$137,331

As of 2024, the maximum monthly OAS payment is $784.67, and like CPP, this amount is adjusted for inflation.

If you start receiving OAS at age 65, you'll get the standard payment. However, similar to the Canada Pension Plan (CPP), you have the flexibility to start as early as 60 or delay it until age 70 for your OAS. The age at which you choose to start will impact the amount you receive.

- **Starting early:** You can start before 65, but your payments will be reduced by the same percentage, 0.6% each month, or 7.2% annually, up to a 36% reduction.
- **Start Late:** If you wait until age 70, your OAS payments will increase by 0.6% per month, or 7.2% annually, up to a 36% increase.

Here are some important things to know about Old Age Security (OAS):

OAS Claw back (Pension Recovery Tax): If your annual income exceeds a certain threshold, which is $81,761 in 2024, you may be required to repay some or all of your OAS pension. This repayment is commonly known as the OAS clawback. For every dollar of income above the threshold, you'll need to repay 15 cents of your OAS. This can quickly add up if your income is significantly above the threshold.

Bonus for the 75-and-Over Club: When you turn 75, your OAS payment automatically increases by 10%. Consider it a little bonus for reaching that milestone!

Integrating CPP and OAS into Your Retirement Plan

While CPP and OAS might not cover all your retirement expenses, they form a solid foundation. Together, they provide a steady income stream that you can supplement with other savings, like RRSPs, TFSAs, or workplace pensions.

Conclusion

By understanding how CPP and OAS work, and by making strategic decisions about when to start receiving these benefits, you can maximize your retirement income and plan for a secure financial future.

As you move forward with your retirement planning, the next chapter will delve into understanding your work pensions, specifically the differences between Defined Benefit and Defined Contribution pension plans. These are crucial elements of your retirement income, and understanding them will help you piece together a more complete and robust retirement strategy.

27

WORK PENSIONS UNLOCKED

DB vs. DC Plans: Cracking the Code on Work Pensions

Introduction

Do you know what kind of pension plan your job offers? Ever met someone who doesn't even know if they have a pension plan through work, let alone what type it is?

I once worked with a very successful entrepreneur who, after ten years at her previous job, had no clue she had a pension. During our discussion, I discovered she had no LIRA (Locked-In Retirement Account) in any financial institution. If you recall our conversation on different investment account types, LIRA account is used to hold your pension funds after you leave your employer. After some serious sleuthing through her old statements, guess what? We unearthed a Defined Contribution pension plan worth over $200,000! She had no idea. Thankfully, she was able to claim it and move the funds over, securing a hefty part of her retirement savings.

It's not uncommon for people to go through their working lives without fully understanding the details of their work pensions. Yet, the difference between a Defined Benefit (DB) and a Defined Contribution (DC) pension plan could be the difference between a predictable

190

income in retirement and a more uncertain financial future. This chapter will break down the differences, benefits, and potential pitfalls of both types of plans, so you can approach your retirement planning with clarity and confidence.

Defined Benefit Pension Plan vs. Defined Contribution Pension Plans

Pension plans are a critical part of retirement planning, but they often go unnoticed until it's time to retire. There are two main types of pension plans: Defined Benefit (DB) and Defined Contribution (DC) plans. Each type comes with its unique features, and understanding them is crucial to making informed decisions about your retirement.

Defined Benefit Pension Plans

Think of Defined Benefit plans as a guaranteed income stream for your retirement. These plans promise a specific monthly benefit upon retirement, calculated based on your salary history and the number of years you've worked for your employer. The key advantage of a Defined Benefit plan is that the employer bears all the investment risks. You get a predictable retirement income, regardless of how the market performs.

Example:
Let's take Susan, who has a Defined Benefit plan at work. Her employer offers 2% of her final five-year average salary for each year of service. Suppose Susan's final five-year average salary is $80,000, and she has worked for the company for 30 years.

Her annual pension would be calculated as follows:
2% × $80,000 × 30 years = $48,000 per year.

This means Susan will receive $48,000 per year, or $4,000 per month, once she retires. This amount is guaranteed, providing Susan with a reliable income for the rest of her life.

Retirement Options with a Defined Benefit Plan:

When you retire with a Defined Benefit plan, you typically have two options:

1. **Opt for a lifetime monthly pension:** This choice gives you a reliable monthly income for the rest of your life. If you pass away, your surviving spouse may continue to receive a portion of your pension until their passing, depending on the specific terms of the plan.
2. **Choose the commuted value:** This option gives you a lump sum representing the current value of your future pension payments. You can transfer this amount into a Locked-In Retirement Account (LIRA) and manage the investments yourself or with the help of a financial advisor. Keep in mind, though, that this approach shifts the investment risk to you.

Defined Contribution Pension Plans

In contrast to Defined Benefit plans, Defined Contribution (DC) plans do not promise a specific payout at retirement. Instead, both you and your employer contribute to the plan, and these contributions are invested. The amount you end up with at retirement depends on the performance of these investments. With a Defined Contribution plan, you bear the investment risk instead of your employer.

Scenario: Susan's DC Plan Adventure

Imagine Susan is enrolled in a Defined Contribution plan instead of a Defined Benefit plan. Both she and her employer contribute 5% of her $80,000 annual salary to the plan, making a total annual contribution of $8,000. The value of her retirement fund will grow based on the performance of the investments she chooses.

- **Conservative Growth:** If her investments grow at an annual rate of 5%, her retirement fund could reach $530,000 after 30 years. This amount will provide her with a limited income in retirement, depending on how long she lives and her withdrawal rate. If Susan decides to withdraw $4,000 a month ($48,000 /year), assuming her investments continue to grow at 5% annually, she will deplete her funds in about 16.5 years.
- **Optimistic Growth:** If her investments grow at a rate of 9% annually, her fund could balloon to $1,090,460 by retirement, offering her more financial security and flexibility in retirement. With this larger sum, Susan can withdraw $48,000 annually. Even after 30 years of withdrawals, she ends up with a whopping $1,523,840 still in her portfolio.

These scenarios illustrate how much the performance of her investments can affect Susan's retirement income. The key takeaway is that with a Defined Contribution plan, your retirement income is not guaranteed. It depends on your contributions and how well your investments perform.

Retirement Options with a Defined Contribution Plan:

When it's time to retire, you must transfer your Defined Contribution plan's value to a LIRA. From there, you can decide how to invest your savings, either by yourself or with the help of a financial advisor. The amount you ultimately receive in retirement depends on the performance of these investments.

Comparison of Defined Benefit and Defined Contribution Plans

The main difference between Defined Benefit and Defined Contribution plans lies in who bears the risk and the predictability of your retirement income. DB plans offer a predictable income regardless of market conditions, making them a secure option. On the other hand, Defined Contribution plans are more flexible but come with the risk that your retirement income could fluctuate based on investment performance.

Pros and Cons of Each Plan

Defined Benefit Plans:
Pros:

- Provides a guaranteed income for life, reducing retirement planning anxiety.
- Typically managed by professionals, so you don't have to make investment decisions.
- Employers bear the investment risks.

Cons:

- Less portable, which can be a disadvantage if you change jobs frequently.
- The benefits are tied to the employer's financial health; if the company goes under, your pension might be at risk.
- Often considered more expensive for employers to maintain.

Defined Contribution Plans:
Pros:

- Highly portable, which is great if you change jobs often.
- Offers more control over how your money is invested.
- Potentially higher returns if investments perform well.

Cons:

- No guaranteed retirement income; it all depends on your investment choices and market performance.
- Requires more financial literacy to manage effectively.
- Your retirement income could be significantly lower if the markets perform poorly or if you don't contribute enough.

Which Employers Tend to Offer DB and DC Plans?

In Canada, the type of pension plans an employer offer can depend on the industry, company size, and financial stability. Defined Benefit Plans are often offered by public sector employers, large corporations, and unionized environments. Whereas Defined Contribution Plans are more common in the private sector, especially among newer, smaller businesses, start-ups, and industries with high employee turnover.

Over the years, there's been a shift from Defined Benefit to Defined Contribution plans, particularly in the private sector. Employers prefer DC plans because they limit the company's pension obligations and shift the investment risk to employees. DB plans are increasingly rare in the private sector but remain common in the public sector, such as positions within the government.

Conclusion

Understanding the type of pension plan you have is crucial for effective retirement planning. Whether you have a Defined Benefit or Defined Contribution plan, each has its own set of advantages and risks. If you're unsure about your pension details, check with your employer and integrate this valuable retirement resource into your broader retirement planning. Your future self will thank you for the effort you put in today.

As we continue our exploration of retirement income sources, the next chapter will discuss other retirement income options, such as Group RRSPs and Individual Pension Plans. These additional tools can further strengthen your retirement savings, though they may not be accessible to everyone. Let's explore them in detail to ensure you're fully prepared for a financially secure retirement!

28

BEYOND THE BASICS

Exploring Group RRSPs and Individual Pension Plans: More Ways to Save for Retirement

Reading Guide Reminder: This chapter is particularly useful if your employer offers a group RRSP savings option or if you're a business owner planning for retirement. If these scenarios don't apply to you at the moment, feel free to skip ahead — you can always come back to this chapter when it becomes more relevant to your situation.

Introduction

Have you ever wondered are there other ways to save for retirement? This chapter will introduce you to two additional retirement income sources: Group RRSPs and Individual Pension Plans (IPPs). However, these tools are not available to everyone.

Group RRSPs: A Win-Win for Employers and Employees

Group Registered Retirement Savings Plans (Group RRSPs) are an increasingly popular retirement savings option offered by employers. They provide a convenient way for employees to save for retirement, with the added bonus of potential employer contributions. Here's how they work and why they could be a great addition to your retirement portfolio.

How Group RRSPs Work

A Group RRSP is essentially a collection of individual RRSP accounts managed as part of a group plan by an employer. The beauty of this setup is its simplicity and the immediate tax benefits for employees. Contributions are made through automatic payroll deductions, which means the money is invested before it even hits your bank account, making it an easy and painless way to save for the future.

1. Employee Contributions: Employees decide how much to contribute from their salary. This amount is deducted directly from their paycheque. It's a "set it and forget it" approach to saving.

2. Employer Participation: Many employers sweeten the deal by matching employee contributions up to a certain percentage. This match is essentially free money, making it one of the best benefits an employer can offer. For employees, it's like receiving an instant raise that directly boosts their retirement savings.

3. Investment Management: Contributions are typically invested in a range of options selected by the employer, such as mutual funds, or ETFs. Employees often have the flexibility to choose where their money goes within the provided options, allowing them to align their investments with their risk tolerance and retirement goals.

Who Offers Group RRSPs?

Group RRSPs are commonly offered by medium to large-sized enterprises as part of an employee benefits package. However, they are also becoming more popular among smaller businesses that want to stay competitive in attracting and retaining talent.

Institutions That Manage Group RRSPs

Group RRSPs are usually managed by financial institutions like major Canadian banks or insurance companies such as Sun Life Financial or Manulife Financial. These institutions provide the infrastructure and investment options for the Group RRSP, often at lower management fees than individual RRSP accounts due to the bulk nature of the group plan.

In short, Group RRSPs offer a structured, efficient way for employees to save for retirement, with the added bonus of employer contributions and a variety of investment choices. If your employer offers a Group RRSP, make sure you take full advantage of that, especially if they match contributions. It's an easy, effective way to ensure you're building a strong financial foundation for your retirement.

Individual Pension Plans (IPPs) for Business Owners

If you're a private business owner or a high-earning incorporated professional, you might not have access to the traditional pension plans that employees enjoy. But don't worry — there's a powerful tool tailored just for you: the Individual Pension Plan (IPP). This plan could potentially boost your retirement savings, especially if you're over age 40 and looking for ways to enhance your financial security in retirement.

What is an IPP?

An Individual Pension Plan (IPP) is usually set up by an employer for a single employee, often the business owner themselves. It's a defined benefit pension plan, which means it promises a specific retirement income based on factors like your salary and years of service. It allows for larger, tax-deductible contributions than an RRSP, particularly as you get older. This can be a game-changer for high-earning individuals who want to maximize their retirement savings while enjoying tax benefits and protection from creditors. You can set up an IPP between the ages of 18 and 71, but it becomes more advantageous after age 40. Before you reach 40, you might be better off with an RRSP due to its simplicity and lower cost. After 40, the IPP contributions can exceed RRSP limits because IPPs promise a set benefit at retirement.

Below is a comparison of IPP and RRSP maximum contribution **amount** after age 40 for 2023:

Age	IPP Contribution	RRSP Contribution	IPP Advantage
40	$33,030	$30,780	$2,250
45	$36,280	$30,780	$5,500
50	$39,850	$30,780	$9,070
55	$43,770	$30,780	$12,990
60	$48,080	$30,780	$17,300
65	$50,700	$30,780	$19,920

Why is it good to have a higher contribution limit? A higher contribution limit allows you to put more of your retirement savings into a tax-sheltered account. This offers two key benefits: first, it reduces your current income tax, and second, it allows more of your money to grow tax-deferred. In an Individual Pension Plan (IPP), the closer you are to retirement, the higher your contributions can be to meet your retirement goals, making it an excellent option for those who are late to saving. However, IPPs come with specific rules and restrictions under provincial and federal pension legislation, such as the need for regular actuarial evaluations, which can add extra costs.

Who can Benefit from an IPP?

An IPP is particularly beneficial if you are:

- **Aged 40 or older:** The contribution limits increase significantly with age, allowing you to save more for retirement.

- **A High-Earner:** The higher your income, the more you can contribute to an IPP compared to an RRSP, making it a powerful tool for maximizing your retirement savings.
- **Incorporated:** The IPP must be sponsored by an incorporated company that employs you. Your salary must be reported on a T4 tax slip; income from self-employment, partnerships, or dividends does not qualify.

Key Advantages of an IPP

1. Tax Deferral: Contributions to an IPP are tax-deductible for the corporation, reducing your corporation's taxable income while deferring taxes on the funds until retirement.

2. Small Business Deduction Eligibility: By funding an IPP, you can reduce passive assets in your corporation, helping maintain eligibility for the reduced corporate income tax rate on active business income.

3. Asset Protection: IPPs offer protection from creditors, as the assets in the IPP are held in a separate legal entity.

Considerations Before Setting Up an IPP

1. Costs: Setting up an IPP typically costs between $3,000 and $4,000, with ongoing annual maintenance costs of about $2,000. If you wind up the plan upon retirement or sell the business, expect to pay additional fees.

2. Lock-In Rules: Funds in an IPP are locked in, meaning they must be used for retirement purposes and cannot be accessed for other needs.

3. Funding Requirements: Regular contributions are mandatory, which can be a financial burden if your business experiences cash flow issues.

Do You Need an IPP?

Before you decide to set up an IPP, consider whether it aligns with your overall financial strategy. Ask yourself:

1. Prioritization: Do you prioritize retirement savings over reinvesting the funds back to your business?

2. Financial Stability: Does your company have the cash flow required to make significant contributions to an IPP?

3. Existing Retirement Savings: If you've been consistently contributing to an RRSP and are confident in your retirement savings, an IPP might not be necessary.

In conclusion, while IPPs offer significant advantages for retirement planning, they require careful consideration. Make sure the benefits outweigh the costs and align with your long-term financial goals before diving in.

Conclusion

We've just taken a whirlwind tour through additional sources of retirement income: Group RRSPs and Individual Pension Plans (IPPs). These tools can play a vital role in enhancing your retirement savings strategy, whether you're an employee or a business owner. The key is to understand how each option fits into your overall plan and to take advantage of the opportunities they offer. As we transition into the next part of the book, we'll explore how to protect your wealth through various methods, including insurance, trusts, and fraud prevention. After all, growing your wealth is only half the battle — keeping it safe is just as important. Let's dive into how you can secure your financial future and protect your hard-earned assets.

Part Five

PROTECTING YOUR FORTUNE

Safeguarding What You've Built: Insurance, Risk Management, and More

In Part 5, we shift focus to protecting the wealth you've worked hard to build. This section covers the essential role of insurance in your financial plan, including health, disability, and life insurance. You'll learn about creative strategies for using whole life insurance and understand the importance of creditor insurance and trusts in protecting your assets. We also discuss how to protect yourself from fraud and financial exploitation. The purpose of this part is to provide you with the tools and knowledge to safeguard your financial future against life's uncertainties.

29

THE INSURANCE PLAYBOOK

Protecting Your Wealth: The Essential Role of Insurance

Introduction

You've mapped out your financial future, started saving regularly, and have a clear picture of the lifestyle you want to maintain. But life is full of unexpected twists and turns, and even the best-laid plans can be derailed by unforeseen events like accidents or illnesses. Imagine being unable to work due to an injury or illness — your carefully constructed savings plan could crumble, and you might even risk losing your home if you can't keep up with payments. This is where insurance and risk management come into play.

You might have been approached one way or another by an insurance agent in the past. Insurance agents are often eager to sell you policies, sometimes without assessing your actual needs. They may dive straight into the benefits of their products without considering if those products are appropriate for you. I remember getting a call during my second year of university from an agent who was selling a Critical Illness policy. The agent did a great job explaining the benefits and features of the policy. However, there was one glaring problem: I was still dependent on the Bank of Mom and Dad with no income of my own. How could spending a large chunk of my monthly allowance on

205

insurance be a financial priority? Despite this, I almost signed up —
proof of how convincing these sales pitches can be.

My goal today is to arm you with essential knowledge about insurance so that you'll be better prepared to ask the right questions and
make sound financial choices if you ever find yourself in a similar
situation.

What is Insurance For?

Insurance is essentially a tool for managing the various risks we
encounter in life — whether it's a car accident, an illness or a natural
disaster. When it comes to handling these risks, people generally use
four main strategies, each with its own approach and mindset.

1. Avoiding Risks:

First, there's the idea of avoiding risks altogether. This is like deciding
to steer clear of high-risk activities, such as extreme sports, simply to
minimize the chances of getting into an accident. It's a straightforward
approach: if you don't put yourself in harm's way, there's no risk to
worry about. By avoiding situations with inherent risks, you're essentially aiming to eliminate any possibility of something bad happening.

2. Mitigating Risks:

Then, we have the concept of mitigating risks. Think of it like
installing a security system at home to reduce the likelihood of a
burglary or damage. Mitigation is all about taking proactive steps to
lessen the impact or likelihood of potential risks. It's like putting on a
raincoat before stepping out into a drizzle — you can't stop the rain,
but you can certainly avoid getting drenched. This approach makes
potential risks more manageable and less daunting.

3. Retaining Risks:

On the other hand, some folks opt for retaining risks. Imagine
deciding not to buy disability insurance after weighing its cost against
the chances of actually becoming disabled. In this case, you're
choosing to keep the risk to yourself, accepting that if something does
go wrong, you'll handle the consequences on your own. It's like

deciding to leave your umbrella at home on a sunny day — you've calculated the odds and are comfortable with the risk.

4. Transferring Risks:

Finally, there's transferring risks, which is where insurance really shines. Picture purchasing car insurance so that if an accident occurs, the financial burden doesn't fall entirely on your shoulders. Instead, the insurance company steps in to cover the losses. This strategy is all about shifting the financial responsibility for certain risks to someone else — typically an insurer — giving you peace of mind and a safety net should the unexpected happen.

Whether you're avoiding, mitigating, retaining, or transferring risks, each strategy offers a different way to deal with life's uncertainties. The key is to find the balance that works best for you and your comfort level with risk.

In essence, insurance is a way for you to transfer risks. It offers a means to manage the various risks we encounter in everyday life by transferring the financial consequences of unforeseen events to insurance companies. In exchange, we pay premiums. Most of the insurance types available help manage different risks, with the exception of Whole Life Insurance, which is often used for tax planning and wealth transfers. But we'll get into that later.

It's important to understand that insurance doesn't reduce the chances of accidents, injury, illness, or death. Instead, it helps mitigate the negative financial impact when accidents happen. By having insurance, you ensure that unexpected events don't become financial disasters.

By understanding these concepts, you'll be better equipped to navigate the world of insurance and make informed decisions that align with your financial goals. So, whether you're avoiding, mitigating, retaining, or transferring risks, having a plan to keep your financial goals on track, no matter what happens, is crucial.

Common Types of Insurance in Canada

Here are some of the most common types of insurance in Canada, each designed to protect different aspects of your life:

Auto Insurance: This covers damages and liability in case of car accidents, theft, or vandalism. Premiums depend on your driving history, car type, and location. On average, Canadians pay between $1,000 and $3,000 per year. If you drive like you're in an action movie, expect to pay more.

Home Insurance: Protects your home and belongings from events like fires, theft, and damage. If you're getting a mortgage, banks usually require this insurance as a safety net to ensure they can recover their money if your house is destroyed. Annual premiums range from $800 to $3,000, depending on your home's location, size, and coverage type.

Travel Insurance: This covers medical expenses, trip cancellations, and other travel-related mishaps. Prices vary based on age, trip length, and coverage. It can range from a few dollars a day to several hundred for a longer adventure. Think of it as paying a little now to avoid paying a lot later if you end up in a foreign hospital.

Long-Term Care Insurance: This provides coverage for the costs associated with long-term care services, whether in a nursing home or through in-home care. This type of insurance is increasingly important as people live longer and may need extended care in their later years.

Critical Illness Insurance: This pays a lump sum if you're diagnosed with a major illness like cancer, stroke, or a heart attack. This helps cover unexpected costs, from treatments to lifestyle changes. Premiums vary based on age, health, coverage amount, and the number of illnesses covered. Expect to pay more as you age.

Disability Insurance: Replaces a portion of your income if you become disabled and can't work. Premiums depend on your occupation, age, health, and policy terms. If you're in a high-risk profession, this coverage is crucial.

Life Insurance: Provides financial support to your loved ones in case of your untimely demise. Prices vary based on age, health, and coverage amount. Term life insurance is usually more affordable, while whole life insurance is much more expensive offering lifelong coverage and can be part of a broader financial plan.

Creditor Insurance: This covers your loan repayments to your banks or credit unions. If you face disability, critical illness, or death, this insurance will cover your loan balance or make the payments for you. Prices vary based on age, health, and loan balance.

Key Insurance Terminology

Understanding insurance jargon is key to help you navigate the insurance world and make informed decisions:

1. **Policyholder:** The owner of the insurance policy, responsible for paying the premiums. This can be a person, a corporation, or even a trust.

2. **Beneficiary:** The person or entity who gets the benefit payout from the insurance policy.

3. **Benefit Amount (Face Amount):** The sum of money the insurance company pays out under the policy terms.

4. **Life Insured**: The individual whose life is covered by a life insurance policy. This could be the same as the policyholder, but not always.

5. **Insurer:** The insurance company providing the coverage.

6. **Premium:** The amount you pay for the insurance coverage. Think of it as a subscription fee for peace of mind.

7. **Exclusion**: Specific situations or conditions not covered by the insurance policy. For example, pre-existing health conditions are often exclusions for disability insurance.

8. **Underwriting:** The process insurers use to evaluate risk and determine policy terms, including premiums and exclusions. It's like a background check for your health.

9. **Claim**: A request for payment under the terms of the insurance policy. For example, submitting a claim after the life insured passes away.

10. **Renewal:** The continuation of an insurance policy after its initial term. It's like hitting the refresh button on your coverage.

12. **Rider**: An optional add-on to a standard insurance policy for extra

coverage. For example, you might add a term life insurance rider to a whole life insurance policy for additional coverage during your working years. Imagine your insurance policy is a motorcycle - the vehicle that gets you to places, and you're the driver who controls and steers the policy. Adding a passenger represents an additional rider on your policy, providing extra benefits. Just as carrying a passenger uses more fuel, adding riders to your insurance policy increases the cost.

Conclusion: Protecting Your Financial Future

Insurance isn't just about protecting your assets — it's about securing your financial future against life's unexpected events. With the right insurance in place, you can face the future with confidence, knowing that you've taken steps to safeguard your financial goals.

As we move into the next chapter on health and disability insurance, including long-term care, disability insurance, and critical illness coverage, keep in mind that a well-rounded insurance plan is a crucial component of a comprehensive financial plan. Let's dive deeper into how these specific types of insurance can protect you and your loved ones from financial hardship.

● 30

HEALTH & DISABILITY INSURANCE DEMYSTIFIED

Long-Term Care, Disability, and Critical Illness: What You Need to Know

Introduction:

In this chapter, we'll break down three critical types of insurance that could mean the difference between financial stability and financial disaster: Long-Term Care Insurance, Disability Insurance, and Critical Illness Insurance. Understanding these can help you prepare for the unexpected and ensure that your financial plans remain on track, no matter what life throws your way.

Long-Term Care Insurance: Planning for the Later Years

Long-term care insurance is designed to cover the costs associated with care you might need as you age. This type of insurance can help pay for expenses related to daily activities such as bathing, dressing, eating, and mobility. It also covers community services like adult day care, transportation, or the costs of residing in a nursing home, assisted living facility, or other care settings.

Recently, my mother had to undergo an open-heart surgery in the fall of 2023. She had been experiencing chest pain and difficulty breathing for months. Despite visiting several hospitals, none of the doctors could pinpoint the cause. Some speculated it was Dysautonomia, a nervous system disorder that affects autonomic functions like blood pressure and heart rate. Others thought it might be stress-related. It wasn't until they conducted an angiogram that they discovered four of her coronary arteries were severely blocked, and that she had likely suffered from a heart attack at some point. It was heartbreaking to see the scars from the surgery, both on her chest and legs, where they had taken veins to replace the blocked arteries.

Her recovery was long and challenging. She couldn't get out of bed on her own, needed help with basic activities like going to the bathroom and preparing meals, and required constant care. Initially, a medical caregiver assisted her in the hospital, and once she was discharged, my sister took over. I flew back to China to help care for her and to support my sister, providing some much-needed relief. Although my mother eventually recovered after five months, the experience made me think about the future. What happens when she gets older and needs ongoing care? Does she have a plan? What can I do to prepare for it?

These are important questions we all have to ask ourselves. As Canada's senior population grows, so too will the number of loved ones called into caregiving roles. While caregiving is necessary and can be rewarding, it can also strain the caregiver's career, finances, and personal life. It's not uncommon for caregivers to experience significant stress and sleep deprivation while caring for a family member. How do you navigate these challenges?

Perhaps long-term care insurance has a place in your planning, or maybe it doesn't due to its high cost in certain situations. Let's explore how long-term care insurance works and when it might be worthwhile to consider it in your financial planning.

How Does Long-Term Care Insurance Work?

Long-term care insurance policies generally activate when you can no longer perform a specified number of daily living activities independently or if you develop a cognitive impairment, such as dementia. Typical daily living activities covered include:

- Bathing
- Dressing
- Eating
- Using the toilet
- Getting in and out of bed or chairs
- Managing incontinence

Once you qualify for benefits, the insurance will typically cover a portion of the care costs, either on a daily or monthly basis. These benefits usually have a cap, either in terms of a lifetime maximum or for a specified number of years. The benefit levels may vary depending on whether you receive care at home, in a nursing home, or another facility.

For example, a policy might pay $150 per day for home care or $200 per day for nursing home care. While you can choose higher benefit levels, this will increase your premiums. Additionally, many policies offer inflation protection, which allows benefits to increase over time, though this feature also raises costs.

Considerations When Choosing Long-Term Care Insurance

1. Cost of Premiums:

- **Age and Health:** The cost of long-term care insurance increases as you get older. Existing health issues can also hike up premiums or even result in denial of coverage.
- **Premium Increases:** Like many insurance products, long-term care premiums can rise over time, especially with traditional policies. Missing premium payments often results in the loss of coverage.
- **Inflation Protection:** This feature increases your benefits

over time to keep up with rising care costs but at a higher premium.

2. Risk of Unused Benefits:

"Use It or Lose It": One drawback of traditional long-term care insurance is that if you never need long-term care, the premiums you've paid are essentially lost. The insurance company retains these funds to cover other policyholders' claims.

3. Long-Term Care Hybrid Policies:

- **Combining Coverage:** Hybrid policies, which combine long-term care insurance with another benefit like life insurance or an annuity, have become popular in response to the risk of unused benefits. Typically, hybrid policies involve a lump-sum benefit payment or a series of fixed annual payments. This approach eliminates the risk of rising premiums and ensures that some benefits will be paid out, whether for long-term care or as a life insurance benefit to your heirs.
- **Cost and Benefits:** Hybrid policies tend to be more expensive than traditional ones, and the life insurance payout is usually reduced or eliminated if you use the long-term care benefits. However, they provide peace of mind, knowing you will receive some form of benefit regardless of your care needs.

Long-term care insurance can be a valuable tool in planning for the future, but it's crucial to carefully consider the options and potential drawbacks before making a commitment.

Disability Insurance: Your Financial Lifeline

Disability insurance is your financial safety net if you become unable to work due to injury or illness. It replaces a portion of your income when you can't work, helping you cover essential expenses like rent, mortgage, and food.

How Disability Insurance Works

When you're sidelined by a covered disability and can't work, disability insurance steps in to provide a portion of your pre-disability income as a regular benefit, typically paid monthly. The benefit can last for a certain period, until you recover, or up to age 65, depending on your policy terms. The benefit amount usually ranges from 40% to 80% of your income.

Income Requirement

To qualify for disability insurance and receive benefit payments, you need to be employed and earning an income. If you are not working, disability insurance does not apply to you.

Waiting Period

The waiting period, or "elimination period," is the time you must wait after becoming disabled before receiving benefit payments. This period can vary from a few days to several months, depending on your policy. The waiting period is crucial because it determines how soon you'll get financial support. Shorter waiting periods generally mean higher premiums, while longer waiting periods can lower the cost. Because benefits don't kick in until after the waiting period, having an emergency fund is essential to cover expenses in the meantime. This fund acts as a financial buffer until your disability benefits start.

All Source Maximum

Disability insurance benefits are capped at 85% of your pre-disability income to encourage you to return to work. This cap ensures you're more motivated to earn your full income rather than rely on comfortable disability benefits. When someone is disabled, they might receive income from several sources, including:

- Employment Insurance payment from the government
- Workers' Compensation
- Disability Tax Credits
- Group disability plans provided by employers
- Personal disability insurance policies

Each of these sources contributes to your total income during disability, but the combined amount cannot exceed 85% of your pre-disability income.

Avoid Being Over-Insured

Having too much disability insurance is like buying a fancy sports car and never driving it — it's a waste. If your total coverage from all sources exceeds 85% of your pre-disability income, you won't receive the full benefit amounts from each policy, even though you're paying premiums for them. To avoid this, review your disability coverage from all sources. If you find you're over-insured, consider reducing your personal disability insurance to lower your monthly premiums.

Common Riders in Disability Insurance

Own Occupation Rider: This rider allows you to receive benefits if you can't perform your specific job, even if you can work in a different field. For example, if a surgeon's hand tremor prevents surgery but not teaching, they'd still get benefits and wouldn't be forced to take a lower-paid job.

Future Increase Option (FIO) Rider: This rider lets you increase your coverage as your income rises without needing more medical exams. Perfect for young professionals or those climbing the career ladder, it ensures your benefits keep pace with your growing salary.

In summary, disability insurance is your financial safety net when illness or injury disrupts your ability to work. Customizable riders allow you to tailor your coverage to fit your needs. This insurance provides financial stability during tough times, protecting your savings and the lifestyle you've built.

Next Steps

Disability insurance can be expensive, so it's important to assess your actual needs before committing to a policy. If you're part of a union or work for a large company, you may already have adequate coverage. Take the time to review your existing insurance to determine if additional coverage is necessary. By avoiding over-insurance, you can save on premiums and allocate your resources more effectively to other financial priorities.

Critical Illness Insurance: A Safety Net for the Unexpected

Critical illness insurance tackles the big, scary question: What if you're diagnosed with a severe illness? How will you cover the treatment costs and keep up with your living expenses? This insurance provides a lump-sum payment to help with the financial burden of life-altering illnesses.

A dear friend of mine, Tim, recently went through a distressing experience with his mother, Sonya. It all started when Sonya developed a severe toothache, leading them to a dentist who performed a root canal procedure. To prevent infection, the dentist prescribed aspirin. After a few days of taking it, Sonya began experiencing unusual symptoms—swelling in her face and hands, along with frequent urination at night. Concerned, Tim took her to the emergency room. After hours of waiting, the doctor diagnosed her with seasonal allergies and prescribed anti-allergy medication.

However, Sonya's symptoms persisted. Another visit to a walk-in clinic resulted in a diagnosis of a urinary tract infection (UTI), and she was prescribed antibiotics. Tim, still uneasy, insisted on a urine test, even though the doctor was confident it was just a UTI. Unfortunately, Sonya's condition continued to worsen, with new symptoms like nausea and itching. Two days later, they received an urgent call from the clinic doctor late at night, who told them to go to the emergency room immediately. It turned out that Sonya was suffering from acute kidney failure. Tragically, due to the delayed diagnosis and the added strain from unnecessary antibiotics, her condition had progressed to chronic kidney failure, which is much more challenging to treat.

This story is heartbreaking and frustrating, especially knowing that Tim and Sonya did everything they could by consulting multiple doctors, yet her condition worsened due to misdiagnoses. Sonya's situation was further complicated because she was on a visitor visa in Canada, meaning her medical treatment, which cost thousands of dollars a day, wasn't covered by the provincial health system. Fortunately, they had travel medical insurance to cover the treatment costs, but this didn't extend to other expenses, such as caregiving. For most people, such a situation could also mean a loss of income while still facing regular or even increased living costs.

This is where critical illness insurance could play a vital role. It provides a financial cushion during serious health crises, covering more than just medical expenses. However, like any insurance, it comes with nuances, such as which illnesses are covered and the associated costs. In the following section, we'll explore the basics of critical illness insurance to help you determine if it's a worthwhile addition to your financial plan.

How does Critical Illness Insurance Work

If you're diagnosed with one of the specified critical illnesses covered by your policy — like cancer, stroke, dementia, or a heart attack — critical illness insurance delivers a one-time, tax-free lump-sum payment. This payout is meant to cover medical expenses, out-of-country treatment if needed, everyday bills, or any other financial needs, letting you focus on recovery without the added stress of financial worries.

Common Riders Available in Critical Illness Insurance

• **Return of premium rider:** Think of it as a money-back guarantee. If you stay healthy and don't make a claim, you get all your premiums paid back after a certain period specified in the policy. However, this rider will likely add 20% - 30% more to the cost of your premium.
• **Disability waiver of premium rider:** If you become disabled and can't work, this rider waives your premium payments while keeping your coverage intact.
• **Additional illness rider:** Expands the list of covered conditions beyond the standard ones, giving you broader protection.

Considerations When Choosing Critical Illness Insurance

Critical illness policies can be a cost-effective safety net, especially when obtained through an employer, with some plans starting as low as $25 a month. However, they only cover a limited range of specified illnesses under specific conditions. For example, a cancer diagnosis might not qualify for a payout unless the cancer is deemed life-threatening or has spread significantly.

The scope of coverage directly affects the premium cost. A 45-year-old woman might pay $40 monthly for a cancer-only policy with $25,000 in coverage. This cost could double if she includes additional illnesses like heart conditions and organ transplants in her plan.

Seniors should approach these policies with caution due to potential restrictions. Some policies may not offer payouts to individuals over a certain age, such as 75, or they might have an "age reduction schedule," which reduces the payout amount as the policyholder ages. These stipulations mean that while the premiums are lower, the coverage is narrowly defined and might not meet the policyholder's expectations in every medical scenario.

If you decide to take out a critical illness policy, carefully read the terms and conditions and work with an experienced advisor to find the right coverage for you. This way, you'll have a financial safety net that truly meets your needs, giving you peace of mind in uncertain times.

Conclusion: Preparing for the Unexpected

Health and disability insurance are vital components of a well-rounded financial plan. While you can't predict when illness or injury will strike, you can prepare for the financial implications. By understanding the roles of long-term care insurance, disability insurance, and critical illness insurance, you equip yourself with the tools to protect your financial future.

I realize the stories we've discussed so far have been quite heavy, and I apologize for being a bit of a downer. My goal is to raise awareness about the unexpected events that can occur in life and how you can prepare for them. But let's not forget, life is also full of wonderful moments, especially when you're in good health. It's important to focus on maintaining your well-being so you can continue to enjoy those moments. Countless studies have shown that good sleep, a balanced diet, and nurturing relationships with family and friends can significantly boost your immune system and help you stay healthy. So, while we prepare for the unexpected, let's also make an effort to extend our good health and relish the things that bring us happiness.

As we move into the next chapter, "Life Insurance: Demystifying the Mystery," we'll dive into how life insurance fits into your overall financial plan. Stick with me, because understanding life insurance could be the key to ensuring your loved ones are taken care of, no matter what life throws your way.

31

LIFE INSURANCE UNCOVERED

From Mystery to Mastery: Understanding Life Insurance

Introduction:

Do You Really Need Life Insurance? Life insurance, as one of the highest commission-generating financial products, there is no mystery why an agent wants to sell you a life insurance. But the question is: Do you really need it and why? Many people find themselves with multiple life insurance policies without fully understanding their purpose. They might remember which friend sold them the policy but have no idea why they have it. The truth is, there's nothing wrong with having multiple policies — provided each one serves a specific purpose and offers genuine benefits.

Life insurance is a crucial component of a solid financial plan, but it's essential to understand what you're signing up for and why. In this chapter, we'll unravel the mystery of life insurance, helping you understand what it is, why you might need it, and how to choose the right policy for your needs.

What Exactly is Life Insurance?

Life insurance is designed to answer a fundamental question: If you were to pass away, how would your family, who depends on you financially, manage? How would they pay for their food, mortgage, and education costs? Unlike disability and critical illness insurance, which protect you while you're alive, life insurance provides a financial safety net for your loved ones when you're no longer around.

Key Facts About Life Insurance:

- A life insurance policy remains active as long as the policyholder pays the required premiums, whether upfront or on an ongoing basis.
- Life insurance comes in various forms, including term and permanent policies.
- Upon the insured's death, it is crucial to contact the life insurance company promptly to initiate the claims process and facilitate the payout.
- Beneficiaries, who can be individuals or organizations, must be designated for your life insurance policy.
- Beneficiaries can receive life insurance payouts in different ways, such as a lump sum, instalment payments, or through annuities.

Important Questions to Consider

When contemplating life insurance, here are some critical questions to ask yourself:

1. Do You Need Life Insurance? Why?

To determine if you need life insurance, consider scenarios where it's essential:

- **Parents with Minor Children:** Life insurance provides financial security if a parent passes away, covering the loss of income or caregiving costs until the children become self-sufficient.

- **Parents with Special-Needs Adult Children:** It ensures ongoing care for adult children who require lifelong support.
- **Adults Who Own Property Together:** Life insurance can cover ongoing property expenses like mortgage payments and taxes for surviving partners.
- **Wealthy Families or Business Owners Facing Estate Taxes:** It prevents estate shrinkage due to taxes by providing necessary funds.
- **Businesses with Key Employees:** Insuring key personnel helps mitigate financial losses if they pass away.

If you're single with no dependents, you might not need life insurance. However, if anyone depends on you financially, life insurance can provide crucial support after you're gone.

2. How Much Coverage Do You Need?

The first step in determining how much coverage you need is to assess your family's financial needs if you were to pass away. Consider expenses such as:

- **Funeral Costs:** Typically, $15,000 – $25,000
- **Liabilities:** Mortgage balance, personal loans, and lines of credit
- **Education Costs for Children:** Around $50,000 per child
- **Income Replacement:** Calculate the present value of 60-80% of either spouse's income until retirement (typically age 65)
- **Estate Taxes:** Estimate capital gains taxes on investment properties, privately owned corporations, non-registered investment accounts, and estate taxes on RRSP/RRIF account balances.

Next step, review any existing coverage you have through work or personal policies, and factor these into your new insurance needs to avoid being over-insured. Many employees have group life insurance through work, usually in the form of term life insurance. It's essential to consider existing coverage when applying for new insurance to ensure you're adequately insured but not over-insured.

3. What Type of Insurance Do You Need?

Before deciding which type of insurance you need, it's important to understand the different types of life insurance available. Life insurance generally comes in two main types: **term** and **permanent**. Each serves different purposes, so understanding the distinctions will help you make an informed choice.

a) Term Life Insurance

Term life insurance is temporary and lasts for a certain number of years. It's ideal for covering financial responsibilities like income replacement during your working years, mortgage balances, or education costs for children. While premiums are affordable, coverage ends when the term expires.

Advantages and disadvantages of term life insurance:
Advantages: Term life insurance is budget-friendly, with very affordable premiums in early years.
Disadvantages: Coverage is temporary, and premiums become more expensive when renewing as the insured ages.

b) Permanent Life Insurance

Permanent life insurance includes **Whole Life** and **Universal Life** policies. These cover the insured's entire life and include a cash value component that grows tax-deferred. Although premiums are higher, these policies offer lifetime coverage and investment benefits.

Whole Life Insurance:

Whole life insurance lasts your entire life. It includes a cash value component, similar to a savings account. You can think of it like two baskets where your annual insurance premium goes into:

Basket 1: It stores the portion for the pure cost of insurance. It covers the costs of the insurance company's operations and benefit payouts to other policyholders. This basket gets emptied out every year as you grow older.

Basket 2: This basket holds the remaining portion of your premium, which is the premium you paid minus the pure cost of insurance in basket one. Instead of being emptied out every year, this portion is invested by the insurance company, growing tax-deferred. It forms the cash value of the whole life policy. Policyholders don't control how these funds are invested. Over time, this cash value grows and adds to the total death benefit paid out to your beneficiaries.

Advantages and disadvantages of whole life insurance

Advantages:

1. It offers lifetime coverage, meaning you don't have to worry about it expiring at a certain age.

2. The cash value within the policy grows tax-deferred over time, eventually being paid out tax free when the insured person passes away.

Disadvantages:

1. Whole life insurance comes with higher premium, which can be prohibitively expensive

2. The return on premiums can be low, depending on the insurance company and life insured age and health situation

Universal Life Insurance:

Universal life insurance is another type of permanent life insurance with a cash value component that earns investment returns. Like whole life insurance, it has two baskets to store your premium as well:

Basket 1: Stores the portion for the pure cost of insurance, which gets emptied out every year as you grow older.

Basket 2: Stores the cash value portion, which is invested by the insurance company, growing tax-deferred. However, unlike whole life, policyholders of universal insurance can decide where to invest this cash value within the options provided by the insurance company. Meaning, if the policyholder has a higher risk tolerance, they could choose to invest in more growth oriented investment. However, the cash value is not always paid out together with the face amount.

Universal life insurance offers either a level or increasing death benefit.
1. Level Death Benefit: The cash value stays with the insurance company upon your passing, and only the original death benefit is paid out.
2. Increasing Death Benefit: The cash value is paid out to your beneficiary along with the face amount, but this option requires higher premiums.

Advantages and disadvantages of universal life insurance
Advantages:
1. They offer flexible payment options and lifelong coverage, which can give you peace of mind knowing that you're protected no matter what.
2. Another perk is the cash value component that comes with the policy, allowing you to have some control over your investment decisions, which is great if you like to have a say in how your money is managed.
Disadvantages:
1. The returns on universal life insurance may not be as stable as those offered by whole life policies, and there are no guarantees on return.

Choosing Between Whole Life and Universal Life:
Now, when it comes to choosing between whole life and universal life insurance, it really depends on your preference. If you're someone who prefers a no-fuss option, whole life insurance might be the better fit for you—it's straightforward and doesn't require much involvement on your part. But if you like to have more control over where your money goes and how it's invested, then universal life insurance could be right up your alley. Additionally, it's essential to weigh the cost against the benefits. It's not just about what you pay today but what you get in return over the years.

What type of life insurance do you need?

Now that we have a clear understanding of the different types of life insurance, let's revisit our original question: What type of life insurance do you need? The choice between term life insurance and permanent life insurance ultimately depends on your specific needs and financial situation.

Term life insurance is ideal if you're looking for affordable coverage for a specific period, such as during your working years or while raising a family. It provides a straightforward, no-frills safety net that pays out if you pass away during the policy term. However, once the term ends, so does the coverage, unless you renew it—often at a higher cost.

Permanent life insurance, on the other hand, offers lifelong coverage and includes a cash value component that grows over time. This type of insurance is more expensive, but it can be a good option if you want to ensure your loved ones are taken care of no matter when you pass away or if you're interested in using the policy as an investment tool.

When deciding between these two types of insurance, consider your long-term financial goals, your budget, and how long you need coverage. If affordability and temporary protection are your primary concerns, term life insurance might be the way to go. But if you're looking for lifelong coverage with added financial benefits, permanent life insurance could be a better fit. Ultimately, it's about finding the balance that aligns with your financial needs and the protection you want for your family.

4. How Much Will You Pay for Premiums?

Premiums vary based on factors like age, gender, smoking status, health, lifestyle, and family medical history. For example, for $1,000,000 coverage amount, a 45-year-old female non-smoker might pay:

- **Term 20:** $1,200 annually
- **Whole Life:** $20,500 annually

- **Universal Life:** $9,500 - $38,000 annually (depending on investment performance and payment choices)

There's a significant price difference between term and permanent life policies. Term life is cheaper because there's a chance the insurance company won't have to pay out if you outlive the term. Permanent life insurance, however, guarantees a payout—it's just a matter of when.

Factors Affecting Your Premiums:

- **Age:** Younger individuals pay less.
- **Gender:** Women generally pay less than men.
- **Smoking:** Smokers face higher premiums.
- **Health:** Poor health leads to higher premiums.
- **Lifestyle:** Risky hobbies can increase costs.
- **Family Medical History:** Chronic illnesses in your family can lead to higher premiums.

How Long Do You Need to Pay?

1. **Term Life Insurance:** You pay annually or monthly for the duration of the term. If you renew after it expires, you continue paying for as long as you want coverage until you reach certain age limit, generally around age 75.
2. **Whole Life Insurance:** You don't have to pay forever. Options include 10 Pay (pay it off within 10 years), 20 Pay (pay it off within 20 years), Pay to Age 90 (make payments till 90 years old), or Life Pay. Shorter terms mean higher annual premiums. But why choose 10 or 20 pay? This could be an option when you're earning well now or planning to retire soon. This way, you control your cash flow.
3. **Universal Life Insurance:** Similar options to whole life, but with the added flexibility of adjusting the premium amounts within a certain range.

The "Paid Up" Status

Ever heard someone say they have a "paid up" policy? That means their

Whole Life policy has enough cash value to cover future premiums on its own. No more payments required!

What Happens When You Can't Make Premium Payments?
First of all, NEVER sign up for a policy you can't afford! Make sure you either have enough savings or consistent cash flow coming in to pay for it. However, if your financial situation changes and you cannot make payment anymore, the following would apply:

1. For **term life insurance**, if you miss a payment, you get a 30-day grace period. After that, your policy lapses and you lose coverage. Reinstatement might be possible if you pay missed premiums with interest.

2. For **Whole Life** and **Universal Life** policy, after the 30-day grace period, an automatic premium loan might cover the payment if you've consented. If your policy is new and has little cash value, it will eventually lapse. Reinstatement might still be possible under certain conditions.

5. Which Riders Should You Consider?
Riders are additional features you can add to your life insurance policy for extra coverage. Common riders include:

Accidental Death Benefit: Provides extra coverage if death is accidental.
Waiver of Premium: Stops premium payments if the insured becomes disabled.
Disability Income: Pays a monthly income if the policyholder can't work due to illness or injury.
Accelerated Death Benefit: Allows access to a portion of the death benefit if diagnosed with a terminal illness.
Long-Term Care: Provides funds for nursing-home or in-home care.
Guaranteed Insurability: This allows you buy additional insurance later without a medical review.

We have to remember, extra riders cost extra fuel (premium). However, some riders may be included in the base premium in certain cases. This is important to consider when choosing between different polces from different insurance companies. With the same premium amount, obviously you should choose the one with additional riders included.

6. Who Should You Designate as Beneficiaries?

The primary reason for life insurance is to protect your loved ones, so it's essential to designate beneficiaries who will receive the death benefit. Beneficiaries can include:

- Spouse
- Parents
- Siblings
- Adult Children
- A Trust for Minor Children
- Business Partners
- Charitable Organizations

You have the option to name a primary beneficiary and, additionally, one or more contingent beneficiaries. Contingent beneficiaries are designated to receive the death benefits if the primary beneficiary is deceased at the time of the claim. It is common to designate your spouse as the primary beneficiary and children as contingent beneficiaries.

7. What to Consider When Applying for Life Insurance? Are There Alternatives?

Before applying for life insurance, you should consider the following:

a. Affordability: Funding a life insurance policy is a long-term capital commitment. Can you afford the annual premium for as long as it takes without impacting your lifestyle? This involves reviewing your monthly budget, figuring out your cash flow.

b. Priority: We all wish we have more money than we ever need. But the reality is, it is a limited resource and we need to use it efficiently. If we allocate the money to insurance premium, then we cannot use it to invest, or save it towards your retirement goal. Bear in mind yourself will not really benefit from the death benefit directly, but your beneficiaries will. Consider whether life insurance is a priority for you now.

c. Are there alternatives to life insurance policies?

Alternatives to Term Life Insurance: Wondering if there's a solid alternative to term life insurance? Not really. The only other option is self-insurance, which is fancy talk for stashing away the cash you'd spend on premiums. But unless you've got a few decades and a magical savings account, matching that death benefit on a term life policy is a tall order. If you live through the term, congrats — you're rolling in your own money! If not, your family might be in a bit of a financial pickle if something happens to you prematurely.

Alternatives to Permanent Life Insurance: Are there good alternatives to permanent life insurance? The answer is: Maybe.

One alternative is, you opt for term life insurance during your working years and invest the extra money you would have spent on permanent life insurance premiums. This could potentially work out well.

Whole life insurance typically achieves return between 3% to 8% in the long run, depending on various factors, age, health and insurance company etc. Remember, the cash value grows tax-free in a whole life policy. You would need to invest in a portfolio with an after- tax return higher than that 3%-8% in a whole life to come out ahead.

If you prefer guaranteed returns and are risk-averse, whole life might be better for you. But if you're willing to take on certain risk for potentially higher returns, investing those premium difference could be the way to go. Knowing what you want is crucial, but sometimes it's not an easy thing to do, is it? If you have maxed out all your registered accounts room and would like to diversify partial of your non-registered investments, then funding a whole life insurance could be a good alternative. It offers guaranteed return regardless of the market performance, and it's growing tax free.

8. Can You Cancel Your Life Insurance If Not Needed Anymore?

Sometimes, you might take out a life insurance policy but later find you no longer need it, perhaps due to receiving an inheritance or paying off all your debts. You can cancel your life insurance at any time:

a. Term Life Insurance: If you cancel after paying the annual premium, you may receive a partial refund prorated for the year.

b. Whole Life or Universal Life Insurance: You have the following options:

Cash Out the Life Insurance: You have the option to terminate your life insurance policy and receive the accumulated cash value — this process is known as cashing out your life insurance. In this case, you would receive the payout, which is the cash value minus any cancellation fees. However, it's important to note that taxes may be triggered, as the cash value has been growing tax-free while it was part of your tax-exempt life insurance policy.

Keep the Paid-Up Value in Place as Coverage: Instead of taking the cash value, you could stop paying premiums and keep the paid-up value as coverage. Paid-up value is the value of insurance coverage has been paid up till the cancelation date. It is a prorated value of the face amount based on how many years of premium has been paid.

For example: you had taken out a 20-pay whole life insurance for the face amount of $1,000,000. 10 years paying into it and you would like to stop paying, but keep the paid-up value in place as coverage, you would have $500,000 Paid Up Value at this stage. This value is paid out to your beneficiary upon your passing. One thing to note that a policy needs to be in place for at least 3 years to have a paid-up value.

Word of caution

When it comes to life insurance, your policy is only as solid as the company behind it. Choose a financially robust insurance provider that will be around for the long haul — ideally, longer than you! Sure, there are industry guarantees like Assuris to back you up if your insurer goes under, but there are limits to how much you can recover and large policies are not likely made whole. Some major life insurance companies in Canada include Manulife Financial Corporation, Great-West Lifeco, Desjardins, Sun Life Financial, Industrial Alliance Insurance and Financial Services (iA Financial Group), and Empire Life etc. These companies offer a wide array of products and services with a strong market presence. Take your time, do your research, and pick an insurance provider that suits your needs. Alternatively, you can work with an insurance agent who has access to multiple insurers, giving you more coverage options and competitive pricing. Let them assess your needs and recommend the best policy for your situation.

Conclusion

In this chapter, we've unraveled the complexities surrounding life insurance, breaking down the key differences between term and permanent policies, and helping you understand how to choose the right type of coverage for your unique needs. We've explored the crucial questions to ask when considering life insurance, including how much coverage you need, the types of insurance available, and what factors influence your premiums. We've also discussed the importance of riders, the significance of designating beneficiaries, and the options available if you ever need to cancel your policy.

Life insurance is more than just a safety net — it's a strategic financial tool that, when chosen wisely, can provide peace of mind, financial security for your loved ones, and even serve as an investment vehicle.

Whether you're leaning toward the affordability and straightforwardness of term life insurance or the lifelong coverage and potential cash value growth of permanent life insurance, the key is to align your choice with your long-term financial goals and current life stage.

But the conversation doesn't end here. In the next chapter, we'll delve into the more creative and advanced uses of permanent life insurance. We'll explore how you can leverage the cash value as a living benefit, the intricacies of immediate financing arrangements, and the concept of infinite banking. These strategies can offer powerful financial benefits, but they also come with risks and complexities that need to be carefully considered. Stick around—you won't want to miss the insights that could take your financial planning to the next level!

(32)

CREATIVE STRATEGIES WITH WHOLE LIFE INSURANCE

How to Use Permanent Life Insurance Like a Pro: IFA and Infinite Banking Explained

Reading Guide Reminder: This chapter is especially helpful if you're considering applying for permanent life insurance or already have one. If these situations don't apply to you right now, feel free to skip ahead — you can always revisit this chapter when it becomes more relevant to your needs.

Introduction:

Are You Making the Most of Your Life Insurance? Have you ever wondered if there's more to your permanent life insurance than just a death benefit for your loved ones? With the right strategy, your permanent life insurance policy can be a versatile financial tool while you're still alive. Terms like "Immediate Financing Arrangement (IFA)" and "Infinite Banking" might sound like complicated financial jargon, but they're essentially ways to access the cash value in your life insurance policy to enhance your financial flexibility. But before you jump on the trendy bandwagon, it's crucial to understand what these strategies entail, their benefits, and their risks.

In this chapter, we'll explore creative ways to leverage your permanent life insurance policy, focusing on how you can use the cash value as a living benefit rather than just a death benefit. We'll also take a closer look at Immediate Financing Arrangements (IFA) and Infinite Banking, demystifying these concepts so you can make informed decisions.

Borrowing Against Your Permanent Life Insurance: Using Cash Value as Your Living Benefit

Cash value is also sometimes referred to as "Living Benefit", as oppose to "Death Benefit". The cash value is a financial resource you can tap into during your lifetime. Here are some common scenarios where you might use this living benefit:

Supplement Your Income: If you find yourself unable to work, you could borrow against your policy's cash value instead of relying solely on disability insurance.

Cover Medical Expenses: Should you face a critical illness, a cash value loan might help cover medical expenses, potentially reducing the need for a separate Critical Illness Insurance policy.

Estate Planning: Borrowing against the cash value can be a tax-efficient way to transfer the accumulated cash in your corporation to your beneficiaries, which we'll discuss in detail in a later chapter on estate planning.

Immediate Financing Arrangement (IFA)

If you have spent any time around insurance agents, you've probably heard the term "Immediate Financing Arrangement," or IFA. It has become a bit of a buzzword on social media, but what exactly is it, and is it as good as it sounds?

What is IFA?

An Immediate Financing Arrangement (IFA) is a strategy that allows you to borrow money to pay for the premiums on a permanent life insurance policy, rather than using your own cash. This can be particularly appealing if you have a certain level of income and don't want to sell your investments to cover the cost of insurance. To qualify for an IFA, you typically need to secure the loan with the cash value of your policy and an additional investment portfolio, since the initial cash value of a permanent life insurance policy may not be sufficient. These insurance premium loans are usually provided by banks.

Why Do People Choose IFA?

There are several reasons why someone might opt for an IFA. For starters, it allows you to avoid selling off your investment portfolio. If you have investments that you want to hold onto but also want to purchase whole life insurance, an IFA lets you do both. Instead of liquidating your assets, you borrow against them, which means you can keep your investments intact while securing the insurance coverage you need.

Another big draw of an IFA is the potential tax advantages. The money you borrow isn't considered taxable income, making it a tax-efficient way to access cash. Additionally, if the borrowed funds are used to generate income, the interest on the loan could be tax-deductible, adding another layer of tax efficiency to the strategy.

IFAs also offer flexibility that traditional loans don't. There's no fixed repayment schedule, so you can repay the loan on your own terms, although it's important to keep in mind that interest will accrue over time. This flexibility can be a significant advantage if you need to manage your cash flow carefully. Plus, by using the IFA structure, you might be able to secure a higher benefit amount than you otherwise could have, thanks to the immediate access to credit.

What Are the Risks?

While an IFA can sound like a great deal, it's not without its risks. For one, the interest charges on the loan can accumulate significantly over time, especially if you don't have a clear plan for repayment. This could end up costing you more in the long run than you initially anticipated.

There's also the risk of your policy lapsing. If you borrow too much or if interest rates rise unexpectedly — like they did in 2022 — there's a chance that your policy could lapse. This would not only leave you without coverage but could also disrupt your overall financial plan.

Summary of IFA

In summary, an Immediate Financing Arrangement (IFA) offers a way to access cash while maintaining the benefits of a life insurance policy. It's particularly appealing if you want to keep your investment portfolio intact while securing permanent life insurance coverage. The potential tax advantages and flexible repayment terms can make IFAs an attractive option for some people.

However, it's crucial to weigh these benefits against the risks. Interest charges can accumulate over time, and the possibility of your policy lapsing is something to consider seriously. If an IFA aligns with your financial goals, it could be a valuable tool in your financial strategy. But as with any financial decision, it's essential to consult with a financial advisor who can help you navigate the complexities and determine if an IFA is the right fit for you.

Infinite Banking

You may have heard the term "Infinite Banking" circulating on social media, often touted as a financial game-changer. But what is it really, and how does it compare to an IFA?

What is Infinite Banking?

Infinite Banking is a strategy, not a specific product. It leverages the cash value of a whole life insurance policy as a personal line of credit. The idea is to become your own banker, borrowing against the cash value in your policy rather than turning to traditional banks.

The cash value in a whole life policy grows at a guaranteed rate determined by the insurer. Once you've accumulated enough cash value, you can request a loan against it. Unlike traditional loans, there's no need for credit checks, and the loan terms are flexible since the policy itself serves as collateral. However, borrowing too much can jeopardize your coverage. While you aren't obligated to repay the loan, any outstanding balance will reduce the death benefit paid to your beneficiaries.

Why do People Consider Infinite Banking?

One of the key reasons people consider it is the easy access to loans. Once your policy's cash value has grown, you can borrow against it without having to jump through the usual hoops like credit checks or strict repayment deadlines. This can be incredibly useful when you need quick liquidity for unexpected expenses, such as medical bills or emergency repairs.

Another appealing aspect of Infinite Banking is the flexibility it offers in repayment. There's no fixed repayment schedule, which means you can repay the loan at your own pace — or not at all if you choose. However, it's important to remember that if you don't repay the loan, it could reduce the death benefit payout, so it's something to consider carefully.

What Are the Risks?

Infinite Banking isn't without its downsides. One of the main drawbacks is the slow growth of your policy's cash value. It can take at least 10 years of consistent premium payments to build up enough cash value to borrow against. This approach isn't a quick route to wealth; it's more about providing a death benefit, with the cash value serving as a secondary, long-term benefit.

Another challenge is the need for overfunding your policy to make Infinite Banking work. This means contributing more than the required premiums, which can put a strain on your budget. You might find yourself needing to allocate around 10% of your income to the policy each month, which isn't feasible for everyone.

Lastly, there's the complexity involved in managing an Infinite Banking strategy. It requires careful monitoring of your policy's cash value and a solid understanding of how it functions as both an investment and a source of liquidity. In Canada, for instance, taking out a cash value loan through your insurance company and not repaying it within a certain period could lead to tax liabilities, adding another layer of complexity to the strategy.

Summary of Infinite Banking

Infinite Banking offers a way to access your policy's cash value, providing financial flexibility without relying on traditional lenders. However, it's important to fully understand the strategy and its implications before diving in.

Conclusion: Are These Strategies Right for You?

Now that we've explored the ins and outs of borrowing against your permanent life insurance, whether through an Immediate Financing Arrangement or Infinite Banking, it's time to ask: Are these strategies right for you?

While both approaches offer unique benefits, they also come with significant risks. The key is to thoroughly understand these strategies and consider how they align with your overall financial goals. It's easy to get caught up in the excitement of trendy financial products or concepts, but it's crucial to make informed decisions rather than jumping on the bandwagon. Before moving forward with either strategy, consult with a financial advisor to ensure it fits your long-term plan.

As we transition to the next chapter, we'll shift our focus to another important topic: Creditor Insurance. This type of insurance can protect your financial obligations, but like everything else, it comes with its own set of pros and cons. Stick around to learn more and keep building your financial knowledge!

33

PROTECTING YOUR LOAN OBLIGATIONS

Understanding Creditor Insurance and Its Role in Financial Planning

Introduction:

Have you ever been offered creditor insurance? Picture this: You're at the bank, finalizing the paperwork for your mortgage, and everything's going smoothly. Then, just as you're about to sign on the dotted line, the credit manager casually asks, "Would you like to add disability and life insurance to your mortgage?" You hesitate. Is this something you really need? How is it different from the other insurance policies you might already have? If this scenario sounds familiar, you're not alone. Many people are unsure about what creditor insurance actually covers and how it fits into their overall financial picture.

In this chapter, we're going to demystify creditor insurance. We'll explore what it is, how it works, and whether it's something you should consider. By the end, you'll be equipped to make an informed decision the next time an insurance offer is slid across the table at your bank.

What Is Creditor Insurance?

When it comes to creditor insurance, it's important to understand exactly what you're signing up for and how it fits into your overall financial plan. Creditor insurance is always linked directly to a specific loan or credit product, such as a mortgage or personal loan, and is typically offered at the time you're applying for that loan. The primary purpose of this insurance is to protect both you and the lender by covering your loan obligations in the unfortunate event of disability, critical illness, or death. If something unexpected happens, the insurance steps in to either pay off the remaining balance or make payments on your behalf, providing a safety net during challenging times. However, there are several key aspects of creditor insurance that you should keep in mind:

1. Beneficiary: The beneficiary of creditor insurance is always the lender, not you or your family. This means that any payout goes directly to the financial institution that issued the loan, not to your loved ones.

2. Coverage Amount: The coverage amount is tied directly to your loan balance. Unlike traditional insurance policies where you can choose the coverage level, creditor insurance only covers what you owe at the time of the claim.

3. Payment: If a claim is made, the payment goes directly to the lender, not to you. This ensures that the loan is repaid, but it doesn't leave any additional funds for other needs your family might have.

Advantages of Creditor Insurance

At first glance, creditor insurance can seem like a convenient option, especially when offered during the loan application process. Here are some of its key benefits:

1. Easy Application: The process to apply is generally quick and straightforward. Typically, you'll only need to answer a few basic questions, and most young borrowers won't need to undergo a medical exam.

2. Automatic Payments: Once a claim is approved, the insurance takes care of the loan payments automatically. This can be a huge relief in stressful situations, providing peace of mind that your financial obligations are being met even when you're unable to manage them yourself.

Disadvantages of Creditor Insurance

Despite its convenience, creditor insurance comes with several drawbacks that are important to consider:

1. Limited to Loan Repayment: Creditor insurance is like a one-trick pony — it only covers your loan. Unlike traditional life or disability insurance, it doesn't offer any benefits beyond paying off the debt. This limitation might not fully protect your overall financial situation or your family's future needs.

2. Potentially Higher Premiums: Since the insurance is tied to the lender, you don't have the flexibility to shop around for the best rates. This lack of competition can lead to higher premiums than you might pay for a standalone policy.

3. Declining Benefit: With loans like mortgages, as you pay down the principal, the insurance coverage decreases, which might not align with your needs.

4. Risk of Claim Denial: Creditor insurance policies often don't require a medical exam upfront. While this simplifies the application process, it can also increase the chances of a claim being denied later, especially if you have pre-existing conditions or if there are other exclusions in the fine print.

Is Creditor Insurance Right for You?

Choosing whether to go with creditor insurance is a decision that requires careful thought and consideration of your unique financial situation. If you already have comprehensive insurance coverage, creditor insurance might be unnecessary. However, if you're someone who values convenience and might otherwise delay setting up a separate insurance plan, creditor insurance could be a quick and easy way to ensure you're protected.

Ultimately, the right choice depends on balancing your need for convenience, cost-effectiveness, and the level of protection you want for yourself and your loved ones.

Choosing the Right Insurance Agent

Insurance can feel as complicated as putting together a piece of flat-pack furniture without instructions. Consulting a financial professional can make a significant difference. When selecting an insurance agent, look for someone who has access to a variety of insurance products from multiple companies. This increases your chances of finding the best coverage at the best price. Ask your agent to evaluate your specific needs and recommend policies that are both suitable and cost-effective. And remember, anyone who tries to sell you insurance without first taking the time to understand your circumstances is more of a salesperson than a trusted advisor.

Conclusion: Weighing the Pros and Cons

Insurance might not be the most thrilling aspect of your financial plan, but it's a crucial safety net that can protect you from life's unexpected challenges. Creditor insurance, while convenient, is not without its limitations. It's essential to weigh the pros and cons carefully and consider whether traditional standalone insurance policies might offer more comprehensive and flexible protection.

Think of insurance like an umbrella — a good insurance plan should shield you from the rain without weighing you down. Whether it's your car, home, health, or family that you're protecting, make sure you're covered where it counts.

As we wrap up this chapter, we'll transition to a topic often associated with the wealthy: Trusts: The Secret Weapon for Asset Protection. Trusts are a powerful tool for families looking to safeguard their assets and ensure their financial legacy. Stay tuned to learn more!

(34)

TRUSTS – THE SAFETY NET

The Secret Weapon for Asset Protection: Keeping Your Legacy Intact

Reading Guide Reminder: This chapter is particularly useful if you're focused on preserving your legacy or planning to leave assets to minor children or children with special needs. Given the costs associated with setting up and maintaining a trust, it typically makes financial sense if you have assets valued at a million dollars or more. If these situations don't apply to you at the moment, feel free to skip ahead — you can always come back to this chapter when it becomes more relevant to your circumstances.

Introduction:

Is there someone in your family that spends a bit too much? How do you ensure that your hard-earned legacy isn't depleted like a house caught in a tornado? Enter the world of trusts, a tool that has been used for centuries to safeguard assets and provide for families.

In the glamorous world of media moguls and high-stakes business, Mr. Rupert Murdoch stands out—not just for his immense influence, but also for his colourful personal life. With four divorces and six children from three different marriages under his belt, you can imagine the complexities of his estate situation. It's safe to say his family gatherings could use a seating chart worthy of a royal wedding.

But beyond the headlines and tabloid fodder, there's an important lesson to be learned from Murdoch's intricate family dynamics. The Murdoch family has long utilized trust structures to protect and pass down their wealth across generations. And while trusts often seem like the playthings of the ultra-wealthy, they're actually practical to ensure the financial well-being of your loved ones — especially minor children. As previously mentioned, you could designate a Trust as your life insurance's beneficiary to provide financial support for your minor children.

Trusts are designed to protect your wealth, control how and when your assets are distributed, and ensure that your legacy is preserved for generations to come. Whether you're worried about spendthrift relatives, potential creditors, or just want to maintain control over your assets after you're gone, trusts offer a versatile and powerful solution. In this chapter, we will dive into the world of trusts and see how they may help you protect what matters most.

What Is a Trust?

At its core, a trust is a legal arrangement where one person, the "grantor" or "settlor," transfers assets to another person or entity, the "trustee," to manage for the benefit of someone else, the "beneficiary." Think of it as a financial safety deposit box: the grantor puts assets into it, the trustee holds the key, and the beneficiary enjoys the contents.

But trusts aren't just about stashing away money — they're about creating a clear, legally binding plan for how your assets should be managed and distributed. Whether it's protecting your wealth, ensuring your kids are taken care of, or even managing your assets in case you're no longer able to do so, trusts can be incredibly versatile.

A Brief History of Trusts

The concept of trusts dates back to ancient Rome.

Imagine this scenario: Roman soldiers, many of whom were wealthy landowners, had to leave for battle. Since they might be away for a long time, or worse, never be able to make it back, they have to find someone to look after their property and family. You might think, wouldn't their wife be the best person to look after their properties. Here is where it gets tricky: Back then, Roman law dictated that, unless the soldier's wife was a Roman citizen, she could not inherit the property. So, the soldiers, faced with these challenges, turned to their trusted buddies to safeguard their interests. Unfortunately, not all "trusted" friends lived up to their titles, leading to some rather sticky situations where properties mysteriously changed hands, sometimes, along with the wives. In a stroke of bureaucratic genius (or necessity), to reassure the soldiers that their families and estates would be safe while they gallivanted off to battle, the government established laws using a legal structure, **_Fiducia,_** to protect the soldiers' rights. Thus, the concept of trusts was born—an ingenious solution to safeguard assets from the clutches of untrustworthy buddies.

This ancient solution to a very practical problem has evolved into the modern-day trust, a tool that allows you to ensure your assets are managed according to your wishes, even when you're not around.

How Does a Trust Work?
A trust involves three main parties:

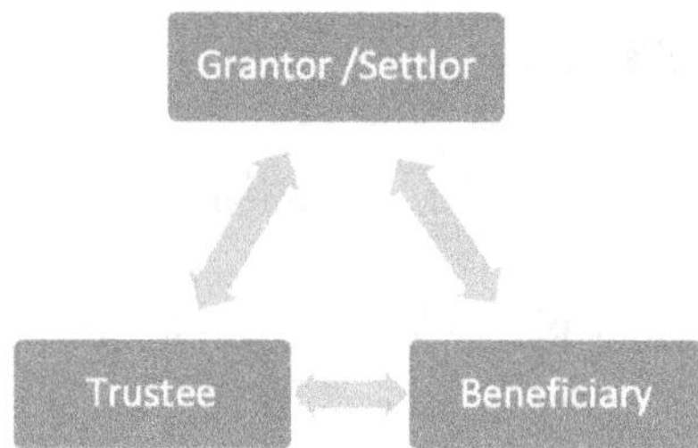

Grantor/Settlor: The person who sets up the trust and transfers assets into it.

Trustee: The person or entity responsible for managing the trust's assets according to the terms set out in the trust agreement.

Beneficiary: The person or group who benefits from the trust.

These roles are crucial to ensure that a trust functions smoothly. The grantor decides who will benefit from the trust and under what conditions. The trustee takes on the responsibility of managing the trust's assets — this could include anything from real estate, business ownership, to stocks and cash. The beneficiary, in turn, receives the benefits as laid out in the trust agreement, which might include income from the trust's investments, access to funds for education, or even the ownership of assets when they reach a certain age.

Trusts are highly customizable, which is why they're such powerful tools in estate planning. The grantor can also be the trustee or a beneficiary, but this can have tax and legal implications. A trust agreement, or trust deed, outlines all the details—who the beneficiaries are, what assets are in the trust, how those assets should be managed, and when and how they should be distributed.

What Are Trusts Used For?

Trusts aren't just about passing on wealth — they serve a variety of purposes, each tailored to different needs:

- **Supporting Family Members**: A trust can be set up to provide ongoing financial support for a disabled child or elderly parent, ensuring they're taken care of even when you're not around. In the case of a spendthrift offspring, you can limit how much they can receive from the trust every month so they don't blow through their inheritance like a kid in a candy store.
- **Maintaining Privacy**: Unlike wills, which can become public record during the probate process, trusts remain private. If you prefer to keep your financial matters out of the public eye, a trust is a good way to go.
- **Estate Planning**: Trusts are often used in estate planning to "freeze" the value of an asset, such as a business, and pass on any future growth to your heirs. This can be a savvy way to manage taxes and protect your estate.
- **Asset Protection**: An irrevocable trust can protect your assets from creditors and lawsuits. It's like putting your assets in a financial fortress.
- **Avoiding Probate**: Assets held in a trust aren't subject to probate, which means they can be transferred to beneficiaries without the delays and costs associated with the probate process.
- **Asset Management**: Trusts can help manage and preserve your wealth, especially if your family relies on you to manage finances. By appointing a capable trustee, you ensure that your assets are managed professionally, safeguarding your family's future.

Tax Implications of Trusts: Navigating the Maze

Before you get too excited about the benefits you can reap from a trust, it's crucial to understand the tax implications that come along with it. With changes in tax rules over the years, the tax benefits of trusts are diminishing:

- **Living Trusts**: Trusts are considered separate taxpayers and must file tax returns if they meet certain criteria. When assets are transferred to a living trust, they're treated as if they've been sold at fair market value, which can result in tax liabilities. However, with proper management, the income and capital gains earned within the trust can be taxed to the beneficiaries, offering some income-splitting benefit.
- **The 21-Year Rule**: In Canada, trusts are required to undergo what is called a "deemed disposition" every 21 years. This means that every 21 years, the trust is considered to have sold and repurchased its assets at fair market value, triggering potential capital gains taxes. There are exceptions, such as spousal trusts, but careful planning is required to manage this tax burden.

Who Should Consider a Trust?

Trusts are beneficial for individuals and families with specific financial goals and circumstances, including:

- **High Net Worth Individuals**: Trusts can help preserve wealth and provide effective estate planning solutions.
- **Business Owners**: Trusts can protect personal and business assets, plan for succession, and manage tax implications.
- **Families with Minor Children or Special Needs**: Trusts can ensure that assets are managed responsibly and used to provide for loved ones' future needs.
- **Philanthropists**: Trusts can support charitable causes while also providing tax benefits.

The Costs Associated with Trusts

Setting up and maintaining a trust involves costs, which can vary depending on the complexity of the trust:

- **Legal Fees**: Establishing a trust requires legal expertise, with costs ranging from $2,000 to $5,000, depending on the complexity.
- **Annual Tax Filing**: Trusts must file annual tax returns, which can cost between $500 and $1,000, depending on the complexity.
- **Trustee Fees**: If you appoint a professional trustee, expect to pay fees based on a percentage of the trust's assets or an hourly rate, often starting at $1,000 annually.
- **Winding Down**: When a trust is terminated, there are costs associated with distributing the assets, filing final tax returns, and closing the trust, which can range from $2,000 to $5,000.

It's important to weigh these costs against the benefits to ensure that a trust makes financial sense for your situation.

Finding Trust Service Providers in Canada

If the idea of managing a trust sounds overwhelming, no need to worry. Fortunately, there are professionals who specialize in trust management. In Canada, trust services are offered by corporate trustees such as RBC Royal Trust, BMO Trust Company, CIBC Trust Corporation, Scotiatrust etc. These institutions can help you set up and manage your trust, ensuring that it meets your financial goals.

Conclusion

Trusts are powerful tools for families to protect their assets, provide for their loved ones, and ensure their financial legacy. Whether you're a business owner planning for the future, a parent looking to safeguard your children's inheritance, or someone wanting to support a charitable cause, a trust can be a powerful part of your financial plan.

As we wrap up this chapter, let's transition to our next topic: How Do You Protect Yourself from Fraud and Financial Exploitation? With your assets protected by a well-structured trust, it's just as important to safeguard yourself against those who might try to take advantage of your hard-earned wealth. Stay tuned to learn more about protecting yourself in today's digital age.

35

FRAUD FIGHTING 101

Protecting Yourself from Fraud and Financial Exploitation: Staying Safe in a Digital World

Introduction

Have you ever heard of the name, Bernie Madoff?

Madoff's Ponzi scheme was one of the largest and most infamous financial frauds in history. Operating through his investment firm, Madoff Securities, Bernie promised **high, and stable returns** to investors through a strategy that seemed too good to be true. 12% annual returns to be exact, regardless of market conditions. Instead of investing the funds as promised, Madoff used new investors' money to pay returns to existing investors, creating the illusion of legitimate profits.

The scheme unraveled in 2008 during the global financial crisis when investors attempted to withdraw their funds en masse, exposing Madoff's fraudulent activities. It was later revealed that Madoff had defrauded investors out of 65 billions of dollars over several decades, devastating countless individuals, charities, and financial institutions.

Bernie Madoff's ascent to prominence as the chairman of the NASDAQ stock exchange and his potential candidacy for the chairman of the U.S. Securities and Exchange Commission (SEC), one of the most powerful financial agencies in the U.S., underscored his influence and credibility in the financial world. When reports surfaced alleging fraudulent activities at Madoff Securities, the SEC initiated an onsite audit. However, Madoff's charm and authoritative demeanour swiftly dissuaded the inexperienced investigative agents, leading the SEC to conclude their investigation without uncovering any abnormalities.

For average investors, discerning the legitimacy of Madoff's investment scheme proved challenging. Despite suspicions surrounding the opaque investment process, Madoff employed emotional manipulation tactics, urging investors to trust him implicitly or not invest at all. Fuelled by the fear of missing out on the seemingly consistent 12% annual returns, many brushed aside their doubts and entrusted their life savings to his Ponzi scheme.

What can we do to protect ourselves from malicious fraud schemes like this? The unsettling truth is that even the savviest among us can fall victim to financial fraud. The tactics used by scammers are increasingly sophisticated, playing on our emotions, trust, and sometimes even our desperation. But while the threat of fraud is real, being aware of common schemes and knowing how to protect yourself can make all the difference. In this chapter, we will explore how you can safeguard your finances from scams and exploitation.

What Are the Typical Financial Fraud Schemes Lately?

The first step to protecting yourself is staying informed about the latest financial fraud schemes. Here are some of the more common ones that have been making the rounds:

Phishing Scams

These scams involve cybercriminals pretending to be legitimate organizations — like the CRA, a bank, or even a popular online store — trying to trick you into revealing personal information. They'll send you emails, texts, or make phone calls that look and sound official, asking you to click on a link or provide sensitive details like your passwords or credit card numbers. Once they have this information, they can drain your bank account, steal your identity, or commit other fraudulent activities in your name.

Identity Theft

In this scenario, someone steals your personal information to impersonate you. They might open credit accounts, make purchases, or even take out loans in your name, leaving you with the financial mess to clean up. Identity theft can have long-lasting effects on your credit score and financial stability, and it can take years to fully recover.

Romance Scams

This particularly heartbreaking scam preys on people seeking companionship. Scammers create fake online profiles to lure victims into romantic relationships, building trust over time. Once they've gained their victim's confidence, they start asking for money, often citing emergencies or travel expenses. These scams can go on for months or even years, and victims can lose substantial amounts of money. A notable case involved an Ontario senior who lost over $732,000 to a scammer pretending to be stranded in Malaysia.

Investment Scams

Fraudsters may promote fraudulent investment opportunities promising high returns with little risk. These schemes often target unsuspecting individuals seeking lucrative investment opportunities, ultimately resulting in financial losses.

A rising threat in English-speaking countries, the "pig butchering" scam originating in East Asia relies on long-term emotional manipulation to defraud victims, often involving cryptocurrency investments. The term "pig butchering" draws a parallel to the method of fattening pigs before slaughter, symbolizing how victims are meticulously drawn into a seemingly genuine relationship. Once trust is established, they are ensnared in fraudulent investment schemes, mirroring the unsuspecting pigs led to their demise.

Scammers create attractive online personas to build trust with victims before luring them into fraudulent investment schemes. Here's how the scam unfolds:

1. Victims are enticed into trusting relationships with scammers mostly through emails, WhatsApp, Telegram or dating sites
2. The relationship evolves into a money-making phase, with victims persuaded to invest in fake cryptocurrency platforms. Those fake platforms often impressively crafted to appear legitimate. These platforms allow users to create personal accounts with **your own login and password**, fostering a false sense of security as funds are seemingly transferred to your own accounts with exclusive access. However, unbeknownst to them, the money ultimately ends up in the hands of criminals, cleverly disguised within the facade of the victims' own accounts.
3. Scammers reward investments with **fabricated balance increases** and permit **small withdrawals** to gain victims' trust.
4. When victims refuse or are unable to invest more money, the scam abruptly ends, and the account will be frozen, leaving them with substantial financial losses.

Cybersecurity experts have identified 55 web domains hosting fake investment platforms used by scammers.

How Can You Protect Yourself from Fraud?

Awareness is your first line of defence against fraud, but here are some specific steps you can take to protect yourself:

Use Call Control Features

Ever get those annoying automated spam calls? They're not just a nuisance — they can also be the start of a scam. What happens if you answer auto spam call? Scammers then know your number is connected to a real person and can target you with real people spam calls. How can you stop those calls?

You might have experienced this, you dialled a number and hear: "this number has call control, to get through, please press 2". Once you press the number, the call will connect. This is the call control feature, intending to block all automated scam calls.

Many carriers in Canada, like Bell, Rogers, Telus, and Freedom Mobile, offer call control features that block automated calls. Enable this feature on your phone so only human dials come through, making it harder for scammers to reach you.

Protect Your Information: do not click on unknown links

Always be cautious about sharing personal or financial information, especially if you didn't initiate the contact. If you receive an unsolicited request for sensitive data, verify the sender's identity before you respond. Never click on links in unexpected emails or texts — these could lead you to fake websites designed to steal your information.

Strengthen Your Security Measures

Implement multi-factor authentication on your online accounts. This extra layer of security makes it harder for scammers to access your accounts, even if they get hold of your password. Also use long passwords with a mix of letters, numbers, and symbols to make them more secure.

Stay Informed

Keep yourself up to date on the latest scams. The Canadian Anti-

Fraud Centre is a great resource for information on current fraud schemes and how to avoid them. The more you know, the better prepared you'll be to spot a scam.

Monitor Your Financial Accounts

Check your bank and credit card statements regularly for any unauthorized transactions. If you notice anything suspicious, report it to your financial institution immediately. Early detection can prevent small issues from becoming big problems.

Educate Yourself

Educate yourself about financial matters and develop a thorough understanding of your rights and responsibilities. Take an active role in managing your finances, and don't be afraid to ask questions or seek advice from trusted sources.

Stay Connected

Maintain open communication with trusted family members, friends, or advisors about your financial affairs. Discussing financial matters openly can help deter potential exploitation and ensure your financial interests are safeguarded. Scammers often target people who are isolated, so keeping your loved ones in the loop can provide an extra layer of protection.

Be Skeptical of Unrealistic Returns

Be cautious of investment opportunities that promise consistently high returns with little to no risk. Remember the age-old adage: if it sounds too good to be true, it probably is. Familiarize yourself with investment principles and strategies to make informed decisions. High returns with little risk should raise red flags. Always do your research, and if you're unsure, seek professional advice before investing.

What to Do If You Think You're Falling into a Fraud Scheme

If you suspect you're being scammed, taking immediate action is crucial to protect yourself and your finances. Here are some steps you can take:

Stay Calm

It's natural to feel panicked or stressed, but staying calm will help you think clearly and take effective action.

Stop All Communication

Cease all contact with the suspected scammer immediately. Don't respond to any further emails, texts, or calls.

Document Everything

Keep a record of all communications, including emails, text messages, and phone call details. This documentation could be valuable if you need to report the scam to authorities or take legal action.

Contact Your Financial Institution

If you've provided any personal or financial information, contact your bank or credit card company immediately to report the potential fraud. They can help monitor your accounts for suspicious activity and take steps to protect your assets.

Report the Scam

Report the scam to the relevant authorities, such as the police and the Canadian Anti-Fraud Centre. Provide as much detail as possible about the scam and any losses you may have incurred. You might feel there is not much the authorities can do, and the truth is not far off sadly. However, reporting it gives you a slim chance of getting your money back. Your report will also provide a source of information for related investigations, and potentially protect others from falling victim to the same scheme.

Protect Your Identity

Monitor your credit report for any unauthorized activity, and consider placing a fraud alert on your accounts. This can help prevent further unauthorized access.

Seek Support

If you're feeling overwhelmed or uncertain about what to do, don't hesitate to seek support from trusted friends, family members, or professionals. They can provide guidance and assistance as you navigate the situation.

How to Support a Loved One Who Experienced Fraud

Supporting a loved one who has experienced fraud requires both empathy and practical assistance. Victims often feel embarrassed or ashamed, which can make them hesitant to report the crime or even discuss it. It's important to reassure them that they didn't lose their money due to being foolish, but because they were targeted by a sophisticated scam.

When offering support, acknowledge the range of emotions they may be experiencing — guilt, denial, and self-blame are common. Scammers use psychological tactics to manipulate their victims, which can make it difficult for them to accept what happened.

Start by reassuring them that they're not alone and that many people fall victim to scams. Encourage them to report the fraud to authorities, offering your support through the process. Remind them that taking action is important for recovering their losses and preventing others from being targeted. Provide emotional support by listening without judgment and validating their feelings. If necessary, help them connect with financial professionals who can guide them on protecting their remaining assets and avoiding future scams. Finally, remind them that recovery — both financial and emotional — takes time, but with the right support, they can rebuild and move forward.

Conclusion: Knowledge Is Your Best Defence

Fraud and financial exploitation are growing threats in today's world, but knowledge is your best defence. By staying informed, protecting your information, and trusting your instincts, you can safeguard your finances and avoid falling victim to scams. Remember, it's not about being paranoid — it's about being prepared.

As we wrap up this chapter, we'll transition to the last part of the book — Estate Planning. Now that you're equipped with the tools to protect yourself from fraud, it's time to think about protecting your assets for the future. Estate planning is all about making sure your hard-earned wealth is passed on according to your wishes, and we'll explore how to do just that in the next chapter.

Part Six

LEAVING A LEGACY

Planning for the Inevitable: Estate Planning and Beyond

The final part of the book, Part 6, focuses on estate planning and ensuring your legacy is preserved. We guide you through what happens when someone passes away, the steps you can take to prepare, and the intricacies of estate and succession planning, particularly for business owners. This section concludes with a call to action, encouraging you to take the necessary steps today to secure your financial future and protect your loved ones. The goal of this part is to help you plan for the inevitable, ensuring your wishes are respected and your legacy endures.

36

WHEN THE TIME COMES

What Happens When Someone Passes Away: A Practical Guide

Introduction:

Have You Thought About What Happens When You're Gone? What would happen if you were to pass away today? It's a question most of us prefer not to dwell on, but it's an important one. What will happen to your spouse, kids, pets, and all the assets you've worked so hard to accumulate — like your investments, businesses, house, and personal belongings? Without clear instructions and proper planning, your loved ones could face a complicated, painful process that could have been avoided.

Consider the story of Bob Ross, the gentle-voiced artist known for his "happy little trees." Despite bringing joy and peace to millions, Bob faced a bitter struggle with his business partners even as he battled cancer. After his death, his family was left in turmoil. His former business partners took control of his share of the company against his will, leading to a prolonged legal fight with Bob's family that added stress during a time of grief. The documentary "Bob Ross: Happy Accidents, Betrayal & Greed" on Netflix tells this heartbreaking tale. Till today, Bob Ross Inc. continues to thrive as a $15-million business, offering art supplies and painting classes, but all the benefits go solely to Bob's

265

former business partner. Despite the enduring popularity of Bob Ross's creations and teachings, his family has been left out of the equation entirely.

This story illustrates why estate planning is so crucial. It's about more than just dividing up your belongings—it's about protecting your loved ones from unnecessary stress and ensuring your legacy is honoured in the way you intend. Think of it as leaving a well-organized instruction manual for your life's final chapter. So, let's walk through what actually happens when someone passes away and why planning ahead can save your family from unnecessary pain and turmoil.

1. What Happens When There's a Will

If you've taken the time to create a will, you've already done your loved ones a great service. A will names an executor (or "liquidator" in Quebec) who is responsible for handling the affairs of your estate. When you pass away, the executor will perform the onus duty, notifying all of the key parties:

- **Service Canada:** To inform them of your death and stop any benefits you were receiving.
- **Canada Revenue Agency (CRA):** They'll need your Social Insurance Number (SIN) to process your final tax return.
- **Any foreign pension agencies:** If you were receiving a pension from another country, they'll need to be notified.
- **Financial institutions:** Banks, investment firms, and any other institutions where you held accounts.
- **Life insurance companies or agents:** If you had life insurance, your executor will need to contact the insurance company to start the claims process.

To do all this, the executor will need to jump though many bureaucratic hoops, gathering all three key documents: the original will or a certified copy, the death certificate, which is usually provided by the funeral home, and proof of their own identification.

Insurance Payouts

If you named beneficiaries for your life insurance policy, they would receive the death benefit within about 30 days after the claim is approved. This can provide much-needed financial support during a difficult time.

What happens to your Financial Assets

Here's how different types of assets are handled:

- **Registered accounts with designated beneficiaries (like RRSPs or TFSAs):** These are paid out directly to the beneficiaries.
- **Registered accounts with no designated beneficiaries (like RRSPs or TFSAs):** These assets are temporarily frozen and become part of the estate. The executor will distribute them according to the will after probate is granted by the court (more on probate later).
- **Joint non-registered investment or bank accounts:** The surviving account owner(s) will automatically take over the account under the Right of Survivorship provision (though Quebec has different rules).
- **Joint real estate properties:** Ownership will be transferred to the surviving owner(s) under the Right of Survivorship provision, except in Quebec where different rules may apply.
- **Solely owned accounts and real estate properties:** These assets are temporarily frozen and become part of the estate. The executor will distribute them according to the will after probate is granted by the court.

Custody of Underage Children

If the deceased had minor children and their spouse is also deceased, the executor will coordinate with the legal guardian named in the will. However, just naming someone as a guardian doesn't automatically give them the job. The court will review the nomination to ensure that the person is suitable and that this arrangement is in the best interest of the child. The nominated guardian might need to provide documentation and demonstrate their ability to care for the child.

2. What Happens When There's No Will

If someone passes away without a will, things can become more complicated. Without a named executor, the responsibility of notifying institutions and managing the estate typically falls to the next of kin, usually the closest living relative. It's important to note that many people assume common-law partners are treated the same as married spouses in such situations. While this is true in many cases, estate distribution is an exception — common-law partners often don't receive the same legal recognition. If you're in a common-law relationship, it's crucial to set up a will to ensure your partner is taken care of according to your wishes, rather than leaving it up to estate law.

What happens to your Financial Assets?

Here's how the assets are handled in the absence of a will:

- **Registered accounts with designated beneficiaries:** These still get paid out directly to the beneficiaries.
- **Registered accounts with no designated beneficiaries:** These assets are temporarily frozen and become part of the estate asset.
- **Joint assets:** These will still be transferred to the surviving owners.
- **Solely owned assets with no beneficiaries:** These

assets are temporarily frozen and become part of the estate asset.

If the estate contains significant assets, the family will need to apply to the court to have an executor appointed. This can be a burdensome process, adding stress to an already difficult time. After an executor is appointed, then the estate assets will be distributed according to the estate law, which may or may not be what the deceased wanted.

Custody of Underaged Children

Without a will, the court will decide who becomes the legal guardian of the deceased's children. If a family member wishes to take on this role, they'll need to apply to the court, which will assess their suitability.

Commonly Asked Questions About Estate Handling

What Assets Form Part of the Estate?
Assets that typically form part of the estate include:

- Registered investment accounts with no beneficiary designations
- Solely owned investments or bank accounts
- Life insurance payouts where the estate is named as the beneficiary
- Solely owned real estate properties
- Business shares

What Happens to Debts and Liabilities?

The estate is responsible for paying any outstanding debts, including credit card balances, loans, and taxes owed to the CRA. If there aren't enough assets in the estate to cover these debts, creditors can auction off collateral assets like houses, cars, or investments. Family members or executors are not responsible for paying off the deceased's debts in Canada. Additionally, assets in registered accounts with designated beneficiaries (like RRSPs or TFSAs) are generally protected from creditor claims.

Tax Consequences: The Final Sale

At this point, you should not be surprised to learn that there would be tax consequences when someone passes away. Death means different things to different people. However, to CRA, death means a big final sale. It means it's time for them to collect your unpaid taxes. Upon passing, any assets owned would be deemed disposed of, meaning in the eyes of CRA, you have sold everything you own right before passing, which can have significant tax implications:

- **RRSP/RIF accounts:** The entire balance is included as income in the year of death, potentially resulting in a large tax bill, cutting the account balance in half.
- **Investment properties and portfolios:** Any unrealized capital gains are considered realized, meaning there could be substantial capital gains tax owing.
- **Business assets:** If you owned a business, the CRA will determine the business's value, and the resulting capital gains could lead to a hefty tax bill.

It's not uncommon for an estate valued at over $2 million to shrink to just $1 million due to tax liabilities. To help minimize this impact, we'll explore some key planning strategies in the next two chapters that can help reduce the tax burden on your estate and preserve more of your wealth for your family.

Spousal Rollover: A Tax Break for Lovebirds

If assets are transferred directly to a surviving spouse, they can be transferred tax-free under what's known as a spousal rollover. This thoughtful provision includes assets like investments, real estate, and certain registered accounts such as RRSPs and RRIFs. The taxes on these assets are deferred until the surviving spouse either disposes of them or passes away, giving them a financial breather during a difficult time.

All about Probate

What Is Probate?

Now, the infamous Probate. Probate refers to the legal process the court audit the deceased's Will and assets, deciding if the Will is valid, and confirming the executor's authority to handle the estate. It's like a stamp of approval from the court that allows the executor to distribute the deceased person's assets according to their will.

If there's no will, the court decides who gets what based on provincial laws.

During probate, the deceased's Will and assets become public record as the court includes the probated Will in a public registry. Within 180 days after Probate is granted, anyone who believes they are entitled to the estate assets can potentially challenge the will.

Once probate is granted, the executor can carry out the instructions in the will.

How Long Does Probate Take?

The length of the probate process varies depending on the complexity of the estate and the court's workload. It can take anywhere from a few months to several years. In one case I've witnessed, it took over nine years due to a complex executor situation, followed by the executor's passing, and the alternate executor taking over. This highlights the importance of thorough estate planning to avoid delays and complications.

Are There Probate Fees?

Yes, there are fees associated with probate like any other legal procedures, and they can vary significantly depending on the province. Some provinces charge a flat fee, while others charge a percentage of the estate's value. In provinces like British Columbia, Ontario, and Nova Scotia, these fees can be quite high. Probate fees are only charged on assets form part of the estate, which do not include joint assets or registered accounts with beneficiaries. You can refer back to our conversation regarding what assets form part of the estate to gauge the potential fees. Planning strategies like joint ownership, trusts, or gifting assets during your lifetime can help reduce probate fees, but each approach has its own pros and cons.

Conclusion: Estate Planning Is a Gift to Your Loved Ones

Thinking about what happens after you pass away isn't exactly fun, but it's one of the most important things you can do for your loved ones. By planning ahead, you can protect them from unnecessary stress and ensure that your wishes are honoured. Whether it's through a carefully crafted will, thoughtful beneficiary designations, or strategic tax planning, the steps you take now will make a world of difference later.

In the next chapter, we'll dive into the nuts and bolts of planning — wills, powers of attorney, and everything you need to prepare. It's not just about making life easier for your loved ones; it's about giving yourself peace of mind, knowing that everything will be taken care of when you're no longer able to. So, let's continue this journey and make sure you're fully prepared for whatever the future holds.

37

LEGACY PLANNING

Preparing for the Future: Steps to Protect Your Estate

Introduction:

Have You Prepared for the Inevitable? Now that you have a general understanding of what happens when someone passes away, let's explore the steps you can take to protect your family and to minimize the impact of taxes and fees on your estate, ensuring that more of your wealth goes to your loved ones. This process also involves putting the right documents and agreements in place to make sure your wishes are respected and carried out as you intend. Let's dive into the strategies that will help protect your legacy and ensure your loved ones are well taken care of.

1. Create a Will

Talking about wills might feel a bit like planning your own demise, but think of it as creating a roadmap for your loved ones to follow when you're no longer around. A will is your opportunity to clearly outline how you want your assets and belongings distributed, ensuring your wishes are respected and preventing any unnecessary disputes. And remember, everyone needs their own will. That means both you and your spouse need separate wills to cover your individual wishes and assets. When setting up a will, there are a few key considerations:

Choosing an Executor:

Your executor is the person or entity responsible for carrying out your final wishes. This role can be quite demanding, as it involves dealing with various institutions, navigating bureaucratic processes, paying off debts, and distributing assets. Choose someone who is trustworthy, capable, impartial and preferably resides in Canada to avoid any potential tax complications.

If you're struggling to find the right person, you could hire a licensed trust company to act as your executor. You might have seen the classic movie scene where a rich person passes away, and a group of people in black suits with briefcases swoops in to take charge. Those are corporate executors in action, though real-life scenarios are usually less dramatic. There are some benefits of hiring a corporate executor:

- **Expertise**: They have extensive experience dealing with estate affairs such as selling off assets, filing taxes, and communicating with beneficiaries.
- **Impartiality**: They act impartially towards beneficiaries, helping to reduce family stress, especially during the grief period.
- **Continuity**: Unlike an individual executor, a trust company doesn't pass away. If they are acquired by another company, the new company will assume the executor responsibilities.

However, corporate executor services do come at a cost and they are typically only available for larger estates, usually those with assets over one million dollars.

Naming an Alternative Executor

It's not uncommon for siblings to be appointed as executors without their prior knowledge, only to find that they are unwilling or unable to fulfill the role due to advanced age or other reasons. That's why it's crucial to have a backup plan. Always appoint an alternative executor in case the primary one can't or won't act. Make sure you discuss the responsibilities with your chosen executor(s) ahead of time to ensure they are both willing and able to take on the role. This way, you can be confident that your estate will be managed according to your wishes.

Compensation for Executors

Executors typically receive up to 5% of the estate assets as compensation, or as specified in the will. Trust companies usually charge fees between 3% and 4% of the estate assets. Executors also have the option to hire agents (typically trust companies) to handle specific tasks if needed.

Identifying Beneficiaries:

Clearly specify who will inherit your assets and in what proportions. This is essentially your final gift list, and it's crucial to be as clear and detailed as possible to avoid any confusion or disputes.

Guardianship for Minor Children:

If you have minor children, you need to designate a guardian in your will. This is an important decision, and it's vital to discuss it with the potential guardian beforehand to ensure they're willing and able to take on the responsibility.

Witnesses:

Your will needs to be signed and witnessed by at least two people who are not beneficiaries. This step is crucial to ensure the will is legally valid and to prevent any future disputes.

Regular Updates:

Your will isn't a set-it-and-forget-it document. Life changes, and so should your will. Whether it's marriage, divorce, the birth of children, or the acquisition of new assets, it's essential to update your will regularly to reflect your current circumstances and wishes.

> Did you know that getting married can actually revoke your will in some provinces? However, due to the rise in predatory marriages — where unscrupulous individuals marry elderly people for financial gain — many provinces are changing this rule.

What services you can use to set up a Will?

You could set up a will through lawyers or online will kit depending on the complexity of your situation:

a. Lawyers: One of the most common and traditional methods of setting up a Will is by working with an Estate Lawyer. A Public Notary can also help draft your Will in BC. This ensures that your Will is legally valid and properly drafted according to the laws of your jurisdiction. Additionally, legal professionals can provide valuable guidance and advice to ensure that your Will accurately reflects your wishes and addresses any potential complexities or concerns. Costs can vary depending on the complexity of the Will and the Lawyer. The fee can range from $500 - $4,000. It's essential to ask for the cost before engaging any service.

b. Online Will Kits: If your will is straightforward, online services like Willful, Canadian Legal Wills, or Epilogue Wills offer a more affordable and quicker alternative. Just be sure the service is recognized in your province and allows you to update your will in the future as needed. Costs can vary, ranging from $80 - $800 depending on the provider

Creating a will might feel like a chore, but it's one of the most important things you can do to protect your loved ones.

I know I sound very persuasive here, convincing you all to get a will. Ironically, I couldn't even convince my own parents. They're nearing their 60s and still don't have wills set up. I truly understand how tough it is to have conversations with family about money and estate planning.

Here's a tip: just show them this book and they might come around. For my parents, I'll need to translate this book into Mandarin first. I'll keep you posted on whether I succeed. If I can get my stubborn parents on board, then there's hope for everyone!

2. Designate Beneficiaries

Now that we've covered the essentials of setting up a will, let's explore other steps to simplify the estate process. One key action is designating beneficiaries for all your registered accounts and life insurance policies. This ensures those assets pass directly to your loved ones without going through probate, which can be both costly and time-consuming. It's also important to regularly review and update your beneficiary designations to make sure they align with your current wishes and overall estate plan.

3. Establish Trusts

We've discussed trusts before, and they can be an incredibly effective tool for managing your estate, especially if you have minor children, beneficiaries with special needs, or significant assets. Trusts can also potentially reduce estate taxes and probate fees, depending on how they are structured.

4. Plan for Incapacity

As life expectancy rises well into 80s, the likelihood of experiencing mental incapacity before needing a will increases. It's uncomfortable to think about, but failing to plan for such scenarios leave you vulnerable to financial exploitation. To mitigate these risks, it's crucial to put legal documents in place beforehand.

a. Power of Attorney (POA) for Financial Affairs:
This document allows you to appoint someone you trust to manage your financial affairs if you're unable to do so. Despite the name, it doesn't need to be a lawyer. It can be anyone you trust with your money, like your spouse, child, parent, a lawyer, or a trust company. It's like handing over the keys to your financial kingdom, so choose someone who will handle your affairs with care and responsibility.

b. Power of Attorney for Personal Care:
Also known as a Representation Agreement in some provinces, this document allows you to appoint someone to make medical decisions on your behalf if you're unable to. This ensures that your healthcare wishes are respected, even when you can't voice them yourself.

> For example, when my friend's grandmother suffered from dementia and could not live by herself, her son, the appointed Power of Attorney for personal care made the decision that it is best for the grandmother to live in a senior home with readily accessible medical care.

Just like with a will, Power of Attorney documents must be set up while you're still mentally capable—otherwise, they won't be valid. It's like trying to buy insurance after the accident—too late! By proactively establishing these documents, you can ensure your wishes are respected and protect yourself from potential exploitation during times of vulnerability. It's not just about preventing future headaches— it's about ensuring your story unfolds exactly as you want, even if you're not able to turn the pages yourself.

5. Saving on Estate Taxes and Probate Fees
Estate taxes and probate fees can significantly reduce the value of your estate, but there are strategies to minimize these costs:

- **Joint Ownership:** Holding assets jointly with a spouse or child allows them to pass directly to the survivor without going through probate. However, be mindful of the potential risks, such as spousal or divorce claims.

- **Beneficiary Designations:** Naming your spouse as the beneficiary or successor holder for your registered accounts (like RRSPs, RRIFs or TFSAs) allows these accounts to roll over to your spouse tax-free, deferring estate taxes.
- **Leverage Annuities and Segregated Funds**: Since annuities and segregated funds have an insurance component, beneficiaries can be designated. By utilizing these types of investments, assets can be efficiently transferred to heirs, thereby bypassing the probate process.
- **Gifts and Trusts:** Gifting assets before death or setting up trusts can reduce the value of your estate subject to probate and taxes. But be cautious—gifting too early could leave you without enough resources later in life, and once assets are gifted, you lose control over them.
- **Seek Professional Advice:** Consulting with an estate planning lawyer or financial advisor can help you navigate these strategies effectively, balancing the benefits with potential risks.

6. Consolidate Your Assets and Organize Important Documents

To enable your executor or power of attorney to carry out your wishes more effectively as you approach your later years, it is advisable to consolidate your assets into one bank. This can significantly reduce the workload for the executor, who will no longer have to deal with multiple banks, provide documents, and handle the cumbersome estate procedures. By consolidating all your assets into one financial institution, it simplifies the process of distributing the estate to the beneficiaries. Additionally, make sure to organize all important documents and store them in a safe place. These documents include:

- Your will
- Power of Attorney documents
- Trust agreements
- Insurance policies

- Property deeds
- A list of your accounts, including bank accounts and investment accounts.

Consider storing these documents in a safety deposit box at your local bank, with joint ownership given to your spouse or executor. This ensures they can access the documents when needed. To ensure a smooth process, consider having your lawyer prepare 3 copies (1 original and 2 certified copies) of your Will and Power of Attorney. Retain the original with your lawyer, keep one copy for yourself, and provide the other copy to your Executor/Power of Attorney.

7. Communicate Your Intentions

Having a plan is great, but if no one knows about it, it's not very helpful. Open and honest communication with your loved ones about your estate plan is crucial. Discuss your intentions and decisions to minimize potential conflicts and ensure that your wishes are understood and respected.

However, be careful and trust your gut when deciding to start these conversations. Make sure your beneficiaries are ready to handle them emotionally. Sometimes, this may only jump start the potential conflicts early if not handled properly. If you're worried about stirring up conflicts, consider bringing in specialists who can help navigate these tricky discussions.

8. Plan for Digital Assets

In our increasingly digital world, assets like cryptocurrencies and NFTs are forming part of people's assets. If you own any digital assets, it's important to include them in your estate plan. If your digital assets were held in regulated centralized exchanges, the standard estate procedure applies, and it can be dealt together in the Will. If they were held in an online or Cold Wallet, or decentralized exchange, make sure you keep a record of the passwords, seed phrases and instructions on how to access and liquidate the assets, and keep the record in a safe place for your executor to access.

9. Seek Professional Guidance

Estate planning can be complex, and estate laws change over time. Working with an experienced estate planning attorney and a financial advisor can help you navigate the legal and financial aspects, ensuring your plan is comprehensive and up-to-date.

Conclusion: Preparing for Peace of Mind

Estate planning is more than just a responsible step - it's a thoughtful gift to your loved ones. By taking the time to prepare, you're ensuring that your wishes are respected, your legacy is protected, and your family is spared unnecessary stress during a difficult time.

In the next chapter, we'll delve into estate and succession planning for business owners. If you've worked hard to build a business, you'll want to make sure it's in good hands when you're no longer around. So, let's continue this journey and make sure your plans are as solid as your hard-earned success.

THE BUSINESS OWNER'S BLUEPRINT

Estate and Succession Planning for Business Owners: Keeping the Dream Alive

Reading Guide Reminder: This chapter is particularly valuable if you're a business owner planning for the future, both for yourself and your business. If these situations don't apply to you at the moment, feel free to skip ahead — you can always come back to this chapter when it becomes more relevant to your needs.

Introduction:

Have You Considered the Future of Your Business? Planning for personal assets is complex enough. For business owners, it's just that much more complicated. If you've built a successful business, it means you took significant risks, poured your heart and soul into it, and invested countless hours to make it thrive. In return, you've been rewarded for your hard work and the leap of faith you took to grow your business. But as you look toward the future, have you considered what will happen to your business when you're no longer at the helm? Business succession planning is more than just a smart move; it's essential. Without a solid plan, the value of your business could plummet, disputes among family members or business partners might arise, and your hard-earned legacy could be at risk. Let's dive into how you can ensure your business transitions smoothly, whether you're planning for retirement, facing disability, or simply preparing for the inevitable.

The Importance of Business Succession Planning

Succession planning is not just about figuring out who takes over the family business; it's about ensuring the continuation and growth of what you've built. Whether you plan to sell the business, pass it down to your children, or wind it down upon your passing, having a strategy in place is crucial.

No matter what your business succession plan is, keeping a solid record of its financial statements is essential. These statements — income statement, cash flow statement, and balance sheet — are your business's report cards. They show how much money is coming in, going out, and what's left over. Yes, maintaining these records can increase your accounting costs, but it would come in handy in many situations. When you plan to sell your business, having these statements can attract more buyers and potentially fetch a higher price because they simplify business valuation and due diligence checks. Plus, they would help a lot when applying for a loan from the bank.

What's Your Goal?

When it comes to business succession planning, it's essential to think about what the future holds for your business. What are your goals for its future? What aspects are most important to you? Is it keeping the business in the family, ensuring the right leadership is in place, or securing a financial legacy for your loved ones? Having a clear plan helps you outline the necessary steps to achieve these goals. Below are the four most common succession plans for business owners:

1. Selling the Business for Retirement:

If your goal is to sell the business and use the proceeds for retirement, you'll want to implement strategies to minimize capital gains taxes on the sale. This way, more of your hard-earned money goes into your retirement. Potential strategies include preparing your business to be eligible for the Lifetime Capital Gains Exemption (LCGE) or claiming the Capital Gain Reserve. The Capital Gains Reserve allows individuals or corporations to defer paying the full amount of capital gains tax on the sale of an asset when the payment is received over several years, instead of all at once. Essentially, it spreads out the capital gains tax liability over time, based on how the proceeds from the sale are received.

However, these strategies require careful planning, so it's essential to consult with a tax or financial professional. Also, since LCGE eligibility comes with specific rules, it's best to start planning at least two years before selling the business to take full advantage of the tax exemption.

2. Selling Your Share to a Business Partner:

Sometimes, the best option is to have your business partner buy out your share if anything happens to you. But what if they can't afford it? Setting up a Buy-Sell Agreement can provide clarity and security for both parties, ensuring a smooth transition and protecting the future of the business.

What is a Buy-Sell Agreement?

Think of a Buy-Sell Agreement as a roadmap for what happens if a business owner needs to exit the business due to retirement, illness, or even death. It outlines how shares will be bought and sold, ensuring that the shares stay within the business or go to known parties. For small businesses, it provides a way to turn shares into cash when needed, preventing potential disputes among remaining partners.

Funding Options for a Buy-Sell Agreement:

- **Establishing a Sinking Fund:** This involves setting aside retained earnings within the corporation to buy out a departing shareholder. While practical, it may not always be adequate, especially for significant buyouts.

- **Financial Institution Loan:** This option allows shareholders or the corporation to borrow funds to buy out a shareholder. However, this may require collateral and impose restrictions on the business.
- **Instalment Payments:** This option spreads out the cost over time, reducing immediate liquidity needs but posing risks if future earnings can't cover the payments.
- **Life Insurance:** Using life insurance to fund a Buy-Sell Agreement is a popular option. It provides immediate cash upon a shareholder's death, with the added benefit of potential tax advantages. However, this requires on-going premium payment to keep the insurance in place

It's important to carefully weigh the pros and cons of each option and choose the solution that best fits your situation.

3. Passing the Business to Your Children:

If your plan is to pass the business down to your children, and the business has grown significantly, you may want to consider implementing an Estate Freeze. This strategy helps reduce tax liability on the future growth of your business, ensuring that your children can inherit it without facing a massive tax burden.

What is an Estate Freeze?

An Estate Freeze is a way to lock in the current value of your assets, effectively pausing their growth for tax purposes. The idea is to transfer the future growth and the associated tax burden to your chosen beneficiaries, often your children. By doing this, you can limit the capital gains tax now, while planning ahead for any taxes due when the property is eventually sold or passed on.

4. Winding Down the Business upon passing:

For business owners, one of the biggest challenges you face is how to pay out cash assets within the corporation to yourself and your family members without getting hit hard by taxes. Here's the problem: If you decide to close up shop upon passing and dish out all the money your business has saved up as dividends, you could end up handing over a whopping 60% to 75% of your business assets in taxes. That's because of the double whammy of taxes:

- First layer of Capital gain taxes upon passing as everything you own is deemed disposed of in the eyes of CRA
- Second layer of Dividend tax to payout corporate assets to personal level

However, there are potential strategies to handle this sticky situation:

- Leverage whole life insurance to cover the estate tax
- Post-mortem pipeline strategy

a. Leverage Whole Life Insurance:

One effective strategy to preserve your assets is using whole life insurance to cover estate taxes. Here's why it works well for business owners:

- **Pre-Personal Tax Payment:** Business owners can pay insurance premiums with pre personal tax money, which is much more advantageous than paying with after personal tax income.
- **Capital Dividend Account (CDA):** A significant portion of the insurance payout (70% to 90%) goes into the Capital Dividend Account (CDA) of the business, allowing the balance to be paid out to shareholders tax-free.
- **Immediate Financing Agreement (IFA):** If combined with an IFA, when the life insured passes away, the business

can use cash within the business to pay off the IFA loan under the same business, and still have the majority of the insurance payout amount available for distribution to the estate through CDA account tax-free. In essence, by utilizing the IFA loan, the business effectively converts its cash reserves into a tax-efficient payout via the CDA.

Examples:

Let's explore an example to illustrate how whole life insurance can be a powerful tool in business tax planning:

Meet Mary, who lives in Vancouver, BC, and owns her company, Mary Co., 100%. Her company isn't eligible for the Lifetime Capital Gains Exemption, and it currently has $3,005,000 in retained earnings. Mary initially invested $5,000 as the start-up capital when she founded the company.

Scenario 1: No Life Insurance

In this scenario, Mary doesn't have any life insurance in place. When she passes away at age 85, her estate will face two significant layers of tax.

First, there's the capital gains tax: Upon her passing, the company is deemed sold, triggering a capital gain of $3,000,000 ($3,005,000 - $5,000). This gain is taxed on Mary's estate. With a marginal tax rate of 53.5%, the tax owed would be approximately $1,047,757.

Next comes the dividend payout tax: Mary's wish is to wind down the business and pay out the entire $3,005,000 in retained earnings as dividends to her estate, which will eventually be distributed to her family. Assuming these are eligible dividends, the tax payable based on BC's income tax rates would be about $1,049,397.

Total taxes in this scenario would amount to $2,097,154. After all taxes are paid, out of the $3,005,000 in business assets, only $907,846 would be left for Mary's heirs. That means nearly 70% of the business's value is lost to taxes.

Scenario 2: With Whole Life Insurance

Now, let's see what happens if Mary had planned ahead and purchased a whole life insurance policy 30 years ago at age 55. In this scenario, both the owner and beneficiary of the policy is her corporation, Mary Co. Instead of drawing money from her business to pay premiums, Mary uses an Immediate Financing Arrangement (IFA) to borrow money under the business name every year to cover the premium. In addition, as the cash value of the policy builds up, she also borrows up to 90% of the cash value to invest.

Here are the key details of the policy:

The face amount is $2,000,000, with an annual premium of $55,391 and a dividend rate of 6.5%. By the time Mary passes away at age 85, the policy's cash value has grown to $2,808,330, and the IFA loan amount stands at $2,527,497. Over 30 years, Mary paid $1,661,730 in premiums, and the interest on the IFA loan, which is tax-deductible, amounted to $1,706,060. The difference between the loan value and the premiums paid, $865,767, was invested to generate additional income. The total death benefit from the policy is $3,691,749, with $3,147,928 credited to the Capital Dividend Account (CDA).

Now, let's look at the tax implications in this scenario:

First, the value of Mary's business at the time of her passing is calculated. The business value is reduced by the IFA loan amount ($2,527,497) and its interest cost ($1,706,060), as these two are considered business loans. Business loans reduce the value of the business. Then, the business value is increased by the difference between the loan value and the premiums paid, ($865,767). This results in a negative business value of -$362,790, meaning there is no capital gain to tax. The first layer of capital gains tax is completely eliminated.

Next, let's consider the cash left in Mary's business. After accounting for the IFA loan and interest, and adding the insurance payout, the business has $3,328,959 remaining. Normally, this amount would be subject to dividend tax. However, since the insurance payout generated a CDA credit of $3,147,928, this amount can be paid out to Mary's estate tax-free. The remaining $181,031 would be taxed as a dividend, with the tax amounting to just $19,697.

In this scenario, the total tax owed is only **$19,697.** After taxes, the total amount distributed from the business to Mary's estate is $3,309,262, leaving Mary's heirs with significantly more than in the first scenario.

The tax savings in this scenario are substantial, totalling **$2,401,416.** Compared to the first scenario, where only $907,846 was left after taxes, Mary's estate would save over $2.4 million, greatly benefiting her children and grandchildren. This example highlights the significant advantage of using whole life insurance as part of a smart tax-planning strategy.

> **Note:** Some calculations used approximations. Actual results may vary based on factors such as interest rates, the specific insurer, and the life insured's health and age.

b. Post-Mortem Pipeline Strategy:

Another solution to avoid double taxation is the post-mortem pipeline strategy, which is now recognized as a legitimate tax tool.

Pipeline Road Map

1. Upon the Mary's passing, Mary Co. shares are considered sold at a fair market value, say $3 million.
2. The estate forms PipelineCo and transfers Mary Co. shares to it for a $3 million promissory note.
3. If the note doesn't exceed the shares' cost base, no tax issues arise. Both companies run for a year.

4. After a year, they can merge, or Mary Co can merge into PipelineCo, .
5. Merging can prevent tax problems.
6. PipelineCo can then "pipeline" funds to the estate as tax-free repayments on the outstanding promissory note. The post-mortem pipeline allows the $3 million to flow to the estate while avoiding dividend tax.
7. Once all funds are transferred, PipelineCo is wound up.

This strategy allows the estate to transfer funds tax-free, reducing the impact of double taxation by eliminating the second layer of dividend tax, saving $1,049,397 in tax. However, it requires careful planning and may involve setting up a separate corporation, and keeping both businesses for a year. Additionally, there would be accounting and legal fees involved.

Setting Up a Separate Will

Another strategy business owners can consider is setting up a separate will specifically for your business. In provinces like Ontario and British Columbia, a separate will can help you bypass probate for business assets, saving on probate fees and ensuring a smoother transition. This separate will allows you to clearly outline your wishes regarding the management and ownership of your business after you're no longer able to lead it, providing clarity and direction for those left in charge.

Conclusion: The Importance of Planning

As a business owner, you have a range of tax-saving strategies at your disposal to protect your business and ensure that your legacy is preserved. However, these strategies often involve complex planning and legal mechanisms. Consulting with legal and financial advisors who specialize in business succession can help navigate these complexities and ensure a seamless transition for both personal and business assets.

Remember, the ultimate goal is to protect what you've built, ensure the continuation of your business, and provide for your loved ones. By taking the time to plan, you're setting the stage for a smoother, more secure future.

In the next and final chapter, we'll pull it all together with a call to action, urging you to take the necessary steps to protect your assets, plan for the future, and ensure peace of mind for you and your family. Let's wrap up this journey and get started on securing your legacy.

(39)

THE CALL TO ACTION

Taking the Next Steps: What You Can Do Today to Secure Your Future

What can you do today to help yourself?

Now that you've equipped yourself with a wealth of knowledge, it's time to put it into action. Understanding the principles of personal finance is just the first step; the real progress comes from applying these concepts to your everyday life. It might feel overwhelming at first, but remember that even small, consistent steps can lead to significant financial improvements over time. So, what can you do today to set yourself on the path to financial security?

Calculate Your Net Worth

Understanding your financial position is crucial for making informed decisions. Begin by calculating your net worth. Add up all your assets — such as savings, investments, and property — then subtract your liabilities, including mortgages, loans, and credit card debt. This snapshot of your financial health gives you a baseline to track your progress over time. Regularly reviewing your net worth will help you see how well you're moving toward your financial goals and where you might need to make adjustments.

Set Financial Goals

Now is the time to get specific about what you want to achieve financially. Start by asking yourself: What truly matters to you in life? Who are the important people you want to support? Reflect on the key financial areas we've discussed throughout this book, and set goals that align with your personal and financial priorities. For example:

• **Saving for Retirement**: Determine how much you need to retire comfortably and set a target for your retirement savings. Use the calculation method discussed in chapter 24 to estimate how much you should be saving each month to reach your goal by your desired retirement age.

• **Investment Strategy**: Decide on an investment strategy that aligns with your risk tolerance and financial objectives. Whether it's a mix of stocks, bonds, and mutual funds, or a more aggressive growth-focused portfolio, make sure it's a strategy you understand and are comfortable with.

• **Cash Flow Management**: Figure out your cash flow by comparing your income and expenses. Identify any surplus and decide how to allocate it toward your savings goals, such as an emergency fund, retirement, or investing in education for your children.

• **Insurance Needs**: Review your current insurance coverage. Do you have adequate life, health, and disability insurance? If not, consider what policies you need to protect yourself and your family from unexpected events.

• **Estate Planning**: If it's relevant to your stage in life, start thinking about your estate plan. This includes writing a will, designating beneficiaries, and possibly setting up trusts to ensure your assets are distributed according to your wishes and with minimal tax implications.

Craft Your Financial Plan

Goals are only dreams until you put a plan in place to achieve them. Here's how you can turn your goals into reality:

1. Break Down Your Goals: Take each financial goal and break it into smaller, actionable steps. For instance, if your goal is to save for retirement, your steps might include opening an RRSP or TFSA, setting up automatic contributions, and regularly reviewing your investment portfolio.

2. Set Deadlines: Assign realistic deadlines to each task. For example, you might set a goal to fully fund your emergency savings within 12 months, or to review and update your insurance coverage within the next three months.

3. Allocate Resources: Determine how much of your monthly income you can allocate toward each goal. For example, decide what percentage of your income will go to retirement savings, how much to invest, and how much to keep in your emergency fund.

4. Seek Professional Guidance: If you're unsure about any aspect of your financial plan, don't hesitate to seek advice from a financial planner or advisor. They can provide personalized recommendations and help you stay on track.

5. Review and Adjust: Your financial plan isn't set in stone. Regularly review your progress and adjust your plan as needed to reflect changes in your life circumstances or financial situation.

Solidify Your Commitment

Cognitive dissonance is a psychological phenomenon that suggests you're more likely to do things if you've said you will do them. So, saying your intentions out loud can help cement your commitment to them. Here's a little exercise: read the following statements to yourself, and feel the commitment grow as you do:

- I will set up a budget this weekend.
- I will set up regular savings to my investments.
- I will find out if I have a pension through work and how it works.
- I will review my insurance coverage to ensure it meets my needs.
- I will set up a will to protect my loved ones.
- I will seek professional advice if I need help with any of these steps.

It might feel a bit silly, but speaking these statements out loud can make them feel more real and achievable. It's a fun way to keep yourself on track!

What Can You Do to Help the People You Care About?

Financial knowledge is a powerful tool, not just for yourself but also for those around you. Here's how you can spread the wealth of knowledge:

Share Your Wisdom:

According to a 2022 Financial Literacy Survey by MYDOH, 68% of parents wish their own parents had taught them more about managing finances. Don't let history repeat itself! Spread the wealth of knowledge by sharing what you've learned with your parents, children, and close friends. Open dialogue about finance can foster understanding and inspire positive financial habits within your inner circle. Better yet, share this book with them. It's like giving them a treasure map to financial success. So, go ahead, be the hero of your family's financial story!

Support Your Employees

If you're a business owner or manager, think about organizing financial information sessions for your employees. Help them understand the ins and outs of company pension plans, insurance coverage, and financial planning. Empowering your team with financial literacy can lead to a more engaged, loyal workforce, and it's a great way to show that you care about their well-being beyond just their work.

Set Boundaries and Focus Your Efforts

While you may want to help everyone, it's important to recognize that not everyone is ready to receive help. Offer your support and guidance, but respect others' autonomy. Focus your energy on those who are eager to learn and take control of their financial lives. You've done your part by making resources available; the choice to use them lies with the individual.

By sharing your knowledge and resources, you're sowing the seeds of financial empowerment and contributing to a brighter future for those around you. Encourage others to seize the opportunity to take control of their financial lives, and celebrate their successes along the way. Together, we can create a community of financially savvy individuals poised for success.

Comprehensive Overview: What We've Covered

Congratulations! You've navigated through the intricate world of financial planning, and now it's time to reflect on what we've learned. This book has been divided into six comprehensive parts, each designed to guide you through the various aspects of managing your finances and securing your future.

PART 1: SETTING THE STAGE FOR SUCCESS

The first part of the book lays the foundation for understanding financial planning, emphasizing its significance in your life. We started by exploring why planning matters and how your financial needs evolve through different life stages. This section also helps you identify the right financial services for your needs, decide whether to manage your finances yourself or seek professional advice, and gain an understanding of Canada's financial institutions. The importance of managing your bank accounts effectively and navigating the credit and debt landscape are also discussed, setting you up with the basics to take control of your financial future.

PART 2: TAXES – TURNING A NECESSITY INTO A STRATEGY

In this section, we dived deep into the Canadian tax system, offering a comprehensive overview of how taxes work and what you need to know when filing your income tax returns. We discussed key tax components for businesses, including the concept of tax integration and whether incorporating your business could save you money. We also introduced the Alternative Minimum Tax (AMT), helping you understand its implications and whether it might affect you.

PART 3: GROWING YOUR FINANCIAL GARDEN

Part 3 is all about building and growing your wealth. It begins with the basics of creating a personal budget and establishing an emergency fund, followed by an exploration of common and not-so-common investment options. This section covers everything from managed investments like mutual funds and ETFs to registered investment accounts like RRSPs and TFSAs. We also discuss risk management, understanding your risk tolerance, and the five keys to successful investing and saving. This part is designed to help you make informed decisions about how to grow and protect your wealth over time.

PART 4: RETIREMENT – THE FINAL FRONTIER

Retirement planning is crucial, and this section simplified the process of determining how much you'll need to retire comfortably. We discussed what to do if you find yourself short on retirement income, and provide a detailed overview of government pensions like CPP and OAS, as well as work-related pensions and other retirement income sources, including group RRSPs and individual pension plans. This part is designed to help you navigate the complexities of retirement planning, ensuring you're prepared for the future.

PART 5: PROTECTING YOUR FORTUNE

In Part 5, we shift focus to protecting the wealth you've worked hard to build. We delve into the essentials of insurance and risk management, covering health and disability insurance, long-term care, and critical illness insurance. The mysteries of life insurance are demystified, and we explored creative ways to use permanent life insurance, such as Immediate Financing Arrangements (IFA) and Infinite Banking. This section also includes a discussion on creditor insurance and the use of trusts as a secret weapon for asset protection. Protecting your wealth is just as important as growing it, and this part provides the tools to do just that.

PART 6: LEAVING A LEGACY

The final section of the book focused on estate planning, ensuring that your legacy is preserved and your loved ones are taken care of after you're gone. We discussed what happens when someone passes away, the steps you can take to prepare, and the intricacies of estate and succession planning for business owners. This part wrapped up with a call to action, encouraging you to take steps today to protect your legacy and support the people you care about.

Together, these six parts provide a comprehensive guide to financial planning, covering everything from managing your money today to planning for tomorrow and protecting your legacy for future generations.

Conclusion: Your Journey Begins Now

Congratulations on completing this journey! Your intellectual curiosity and determination to understand the complexities of managing money are truly commendable. Now, it's time to take action. The path to financial security is not always easy, but with the knowledge you've gained, you're well-equipped to face the challenges ahead. Start with small, manageable steps — set a budget, review your insurance, calculate your net worth — and watch as these actions lead to significant changes.

As you move forward, remember the story of the horse and the donkey. The horse had a clear goal and plan, traveling far to experience the world and live a fulfilling life. The donkey, on the other hand, circled the millstone every day, busy but never moving forward. Don't be the donkey, getting lost in the daily grind with no sense of direction. Be the horse — set your goals, create your financial plan, and experience the richness of life without the burden of financial uncertainty.

Financial empowerment is a lifelong journey. Stay curious, keep learning, and don't hesitate to seek help when needed. By taking control of your finances today, you're not just securing your future — you're setting a positive example for those around you. So go ahead, take that first step, and create the secure financial future you deserve. Thank you for joining me on this journey. Here's to your financial success!